BACKROADS & BYWAYS
OF
TEXAS

BACKROADS & BYWAYS OF TEXAS

Drives, Daytrips & Weekend Excursions

Amy K. Brown

THE COUNTRYMAN PRESS
WOODSTOCK, VERMONT

Interior photographs by the author
Maps by Erin Greb Cartography, © The Countryman Press
Book design by Susan Livingston
Composition by Chelsea Cloeter

Published by The Countryman Press,
P.O. Box 748, Woodstock, VT 05091

Distributed by W. W. Norton & Company, Inc.,
500 Fifth Avenue, New York, NY 10110

Backroads & Byways of Texas, 2nd edition
978-1-58157-146-2

10 9 8 7 6 5 4 3 2

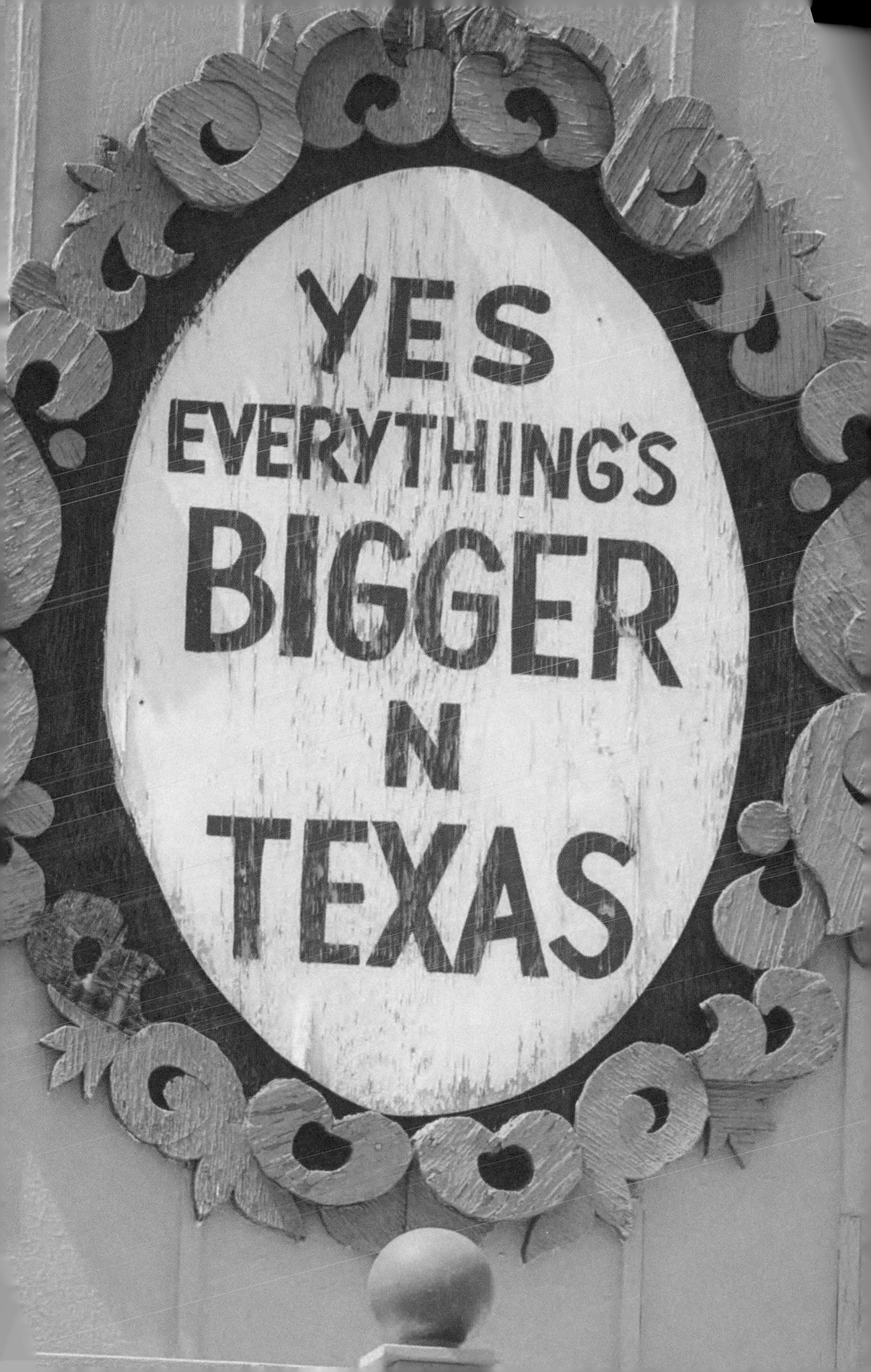
YES
EVERYTHING'S
BIGGER
N
TEXAS

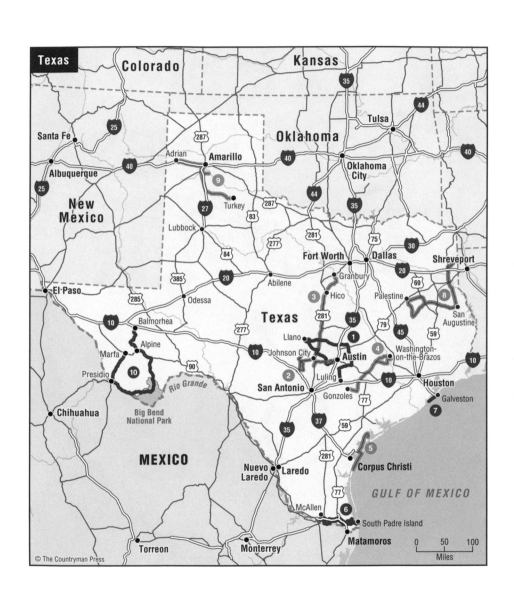

CONTENTS

Texas has a language all its own.

INTRODUCTION

*I have said that Texas is a state of mind, but I think it is more than that.
It is a mystique closely approximating a religion. And this is true to the
extent that people either passionately love Texas or passionately hate it
and, as in other religions, few people dare to inspect it for fear of losing
their bearings in mystery or paradox. But I think there will be little
quarrel with my feeling that Texas is one thing. For all its enormous
range of space, climate, and physical appearance, and for all the internal squabbles, contentions, and strivings, Texas has a tight cohesive-
ness perhaps stronger than any other section of America. Rich, poor,
Panhandle, Gulf, city, country, Texas is the obsession, the proper study
and the passionate possession of all Texans.*

—John Steinbeck, 1962

Texas is the perfect backdrop for adventure. With vast spaces, diverse cultures,
and shoot-from-the-hip sincerity, the Lone Star State is the ultimate road
trip fantasy. To travel Texas is to experience the open road, with the wind in your
hair and convention at your back. Texas has plenty of destinations—exquisite San
Antonio, lively Austin, and fascinating Fort Worth, among many others—but there
is, as a glance at the map makes clear, a whole lot of in-between. The routes outlined in the following pages offer a sampling of this huge state and the essence
of the regions they traverse. For this book I've gone slightly off the beaten path,
highlighting places of natural beauty, cultural heritage, and historical significance,
in the hopes that your trip through Texas, like mine, will become a journey.

Though each of the routes suggested is accessible from at least one major
Texas city, the cities themselves are not generally included. While Texas' cities
are certainly worth visiting, they are also books unto themselves (Countryman's
Explorer's Guide Austin, San Antonio & the Texas Hill Country, A Great Destination,
for example). I may dart into several cities along the way to visit a museum or
historical site of particular interest, but I never tarry long.

Distances in Texas can be deceptive. Driving in the Hill Country, just west of

Austin and San Antonio, it is easy to make stops every 30 minutes or so, while in West Texas you can drive for hours with the distinct feeling that you are getting nowhere fast. To help you keep perspective and better plan your excursion, I have noted the mileage of the segments and the whole of each route. Whether you are planning to drive the coast for the day or take the family camping in Big Bend, this book will be a knowledgeable and helpful companion.

Founded on ambition, guts, and sheer force of will, Texas is the only state in America to enjoy a history of sovereignty, and, in many ways, Texas is as independent, wily, opinionated, self-sufficient, and wide open now as at any time in its past.

Evidence places human habitation in the region as far back as 11,000 years. Until the 16th century, Texas was sparsely inhabited by various groups of Native Americans, who lived as a mix of settled groups and nomadic tribes. The arrival of the Spanish marked the beginning of colonization, and in 1519, Spain claimed Texas as part of its massive holdings in Mexico. However, the country's rule existed primarily on paper and it failed to establish a lasting presence or control over the region.

In 1685, the French attempted to expand the western border of Louisiana by claiming Texas as their own, a stand foiled almost immediately by the Spanish, who in 1690 reclaimed the land they'd lost. This time, serious about expanding its empire, Spain set about establishing *misiones* (missions) to convert Native Americans to Christianity and the ways of Spanish citizenship, and *presidios* (forts) to protect these fledging communities. While the missions did have a huge impact on the lives of Native Americans, Spain was unable to keep its foothold in the new land. When Mexico won independence from Spain in 1821, Texas passed to Mexican rule and into an era of pioneer life, as hopeful immigrants tried their hand at claiming the frontier.

Since the seat of Mexican authority was distant, the new Texans enjoyed a measure of self-rule. When Mexican general Santa Anna set aside the Mexican Constitution in the 1830s, in effect declaring himself king, the seeds of the Texas Revolution were planted. Texas Revolutionaries sparred with Mexican troops in Gonzales, the Alamo in San Antonio, and, finally, in San Jacinto. This final battle, on April 21, 1836, won the state its independence, and the Republic of Texas was born.

Texas' sheer size, wealth of resources, and status as a border state made it

The state's backroads offer adventure.

PESTS

For whatever reason, pests love Texas and thrive in its temperate climate despite efforts to control them. The truth is that many serve an important ecological function and most are harmless, but there are a few pests that should have you watching where you sit, step, or stand.

Fire Ants

The biggest pests in Texas are the fire ants, for which you will frequently see warning signs posted. Fire ants tend to make mounds in sunny, open fields and parks, by the side of the road, and at the base of trees and other objects, such as picnic tables. When their nest is disturbed, they swarm and deliver many simultaneous stings, which are similar to bee stings in look and feel. Usually no medical intervention is required, but as with bee stings, a small percentage of the population may have a severe allergic reaction, in which case emergency medical care is essential. The only prevention is avoidance, so watch where you sit and stand and be especially aware with small children.

Snakes

Snakes are common in Texas, but of the 72 native species and subspecies, only 15 pose any threat to humans. Generally, snakes keep to themselves and do not tend to initiate interactions. If you have the unfortunate experience of being bitten, seek medical attention.

Spiders

Of the 900 species of spiders present in Texas, only two groups pose any threat to humans: the recluse and widow spiders. In many cases, if you are bitten by one of these, you may not notice until the appearance of a suspicious wound coupled with fever, chills, nausea, pain, vomiting, or weakness, among other symptoms. In all cases, swab the wound with alcohol, relieve swelling and pain with ice, and call your doctor or, depending on the severity, visit the emergency room.

attractive as an acquisition. On December 19, 1845, Texas joined the United States of America, passing from a nation to a state. Sixteen years later, the Civil War tore the unstable nation apart and Texas, though advised by Governor Sam Houston to remain neutral or reestablish a Republic, sided with the Southerners. The flag

WEATHER

When it gets hot in Texas, it gets really, really hot. When it gets humid in Texas, it gets really, really humid. Since dehydration and heatstroke are not uncommon conditions, it's important to be aware and prepared. Sunglasses, sunscreen, a light cotton long-sleeved shirt, a wide-brimmed hat, an umbrella, or even a small spray bottle filled with water for misting can help provide protection and relief. Staying hydrated is essential; steering clear of sodas and alcoholic beverages in favor of water, sports drinks, and juices is considered wise.

Storms

Arriving sometimes without warning, summertime thunderstorms can bring torrential rain and flash floods. When flash flood warnings are issued, it is best to exercise caution and avoid creeks, drainage ditches, and low-water road crossings, as signs in these areas will indicate. Tornadoes frequently accompany thunderstorms, so it is best to listen to or watch the news for any words of caution. A tornado or severe-thunderstorm "watch" serves as an alert that conditions are favorable for either event, while a tornado or severe-thunderstorm "warning" means that either event has been detected on radar and danger may be imminent. In this case, it is best to seek cover in a substantial building, away from windows. In cooler weather, ice storms can occur, and since Texas does not maintain a large fleet of sand or salt trucks, the roads can become treacherously slick and hazardous. Texas drivers are inexperienced with slick or icy roads, and during storms accidents tend to be frequent.

Wildfires

According to the Texas Forest Service, approximately 90 percent of wildfires in the state are caused by people. As you travel the backroads of Texas, please check local restrictions on campfires and grilling and be mindful of dry, windy conditions.

of the Confederacy flew over Texas from 1861 to 1865, to be replaced in 1865 by the flag of the United States.

With 268,601 square miles, Texas is ranked behind Alaska as the second largest of the states in the Union. Home to well over 20 million people, it is the

TRAVEL TIPS

Texas can get very rural very quickly. Some points to consider before starting your trip:

• The first thing you will want to do is purchase some good, updated maps, both of the state in general and the specific region you'll be exploring.

• Be sure your vehicle is in good working order. At minimum, check the air in the tires and the fluids, and consider arranging for a tune-up.

• Pack supplies. Be sure to include extra water, both for the engine and for drinking, a flashlight with fresh batteries, a small first aid kit, a blanket, matches, and snacks such as energy bars and dried fruit.

• Fill up with gas frequently. Even if your tank is half full, be sure to top it off if you can rather than risk running out of gas.

• Generally speaking, expect spotty and unreliable cell phone service and plan accordingly. Do not rely on your cell phone to bail you out of an emergency. Call your cell phone provider and check their range of service.

• Be sure to bring sunscreen and, again, plenty of drinking water. The Texas heat is legendary, and dehydration, sunburn, and sunstroke are very real possibilities.

State Park Pass

If you are planning to visit several of the regions outlined in this book, it might be to your advantage to purchase a Texas State Parks Pass, which will give you free entrance to all the state parks in Texas and discounts on camping fees. Visit the Texas Parks and Wildlife Department at www.tpwd.state.tx.us for details.

Internet Resources

Two particularly good Web sites for exploring Texas are www.travel tex.com and www.texasoutside.com.

second most populous state after California, and in Houston can claim the fifth largest city in the country. Much of the population of Texas clusters along I-35, running from Dallas, through Austin and San Antonio, on its way to Mexico. But Texas' urban history, the rise and growth of its cities, is largely a story of the 20th century. The deeper roots of the state's history, peoples, and culture are firmly planted in the rural landscape that is its greatest hallmark.

From the quiet, shaded Pineywoods of East Texas to the mountains, deserts, and stunning sunsets of West Texas, the plains and canyons of the Panhandle to the sandy dunes of the Gulf Coast, the diversity of Texas will astound you. With its vivid wildflowers, poky armadillos, prickly pear cacti, migrating monarch butterflies, and earnest roadrunners, the land is chock-full of the classic icons of the American West. BBQ, sweet tea, and chicken-fried everything speak to the influences of the American South, and savory enchiladas, sizzling fajitas, and nourishing tortilla soup are just some of the Tex-Mex staples that have kept the region's bellies full and souls nourished for centuries.

So, go ahead. Set out on an adventure. Use the routes I've suggested or veer off on your own. Ask the folks you meet where they like to eat, drink, and relax and you will discover something different on the road less traveled. Wherever you roam—no matter how varied the landscape, people, or traditions—rest assured, you are still very much in Texas. The state's treasured natural wonders, historical sites, and cultural treasures are its legacy—gifts from Texans to their fellow Americans. Taken together, they are our "passionate possession," and we're happy to share.

However you spell it, it's good.

1 The Best BBQ in Texas

Getting there: From Austin, take MoPac (Route 1) south to TX 45, turning west, then south onto FM 1826, following it for 8 miles to Driftwood. From Driftwood, follow FM 150 northwest for 5 miles and pick up RR 12. Continue for 10 miles until it dead-ends into Hamilton Pool Road/RR 3238. Turn left and follow signs 6 miles to the park. Leaving the park, take FM 962, US 281, then TX 71 55 miles to Llano.

In Llano, turn right onto TX 16, taking it north through town, then right onto E. Young Street/TX 29, following TX 29 30 miles east to Burnet and an additional 35 miles to Georgetown. From Georgetown, remain on TX 29, heading east until it dead-ends into TX 95 after 15 miles. Turn right, traveling south the remaining 5 miles to Taylor on TX 95. From Taylor, it's a straight shot on TX 95 16 miles south to Elgin and another 18 miles south to Bastrop. Heading back to the west follow TX 21 23 miles until it intersects US 183, and take US 183 10 miles south to Lockhart. Double back north on US 183 and 30 miles later, you'll find yourself back in Austin.

While you can follow this route in either direction, I have chosen to leave Austin and head northwest before arching to the east, and finally south. If you are coming from San Antonio, it's an easy 73-mile drive northeast to Lockhart, where you can begin the route and follow it in reverse. From Llano, you can return to San Antonio, 107 miles to the south, via TX 16 and then I-10/US 87.

Highlights: Folks come to Texas hungry for BBQ, and Central Texas serves it up—hot and juicy—from old-style, family-owned pits. There are countless ways to get it, and everyone has their favorite. From huge mess halls to local gas stations, the BBQ joints in these parts aren't just places to stop in for a bite; they are places to stop in and experience a little history.

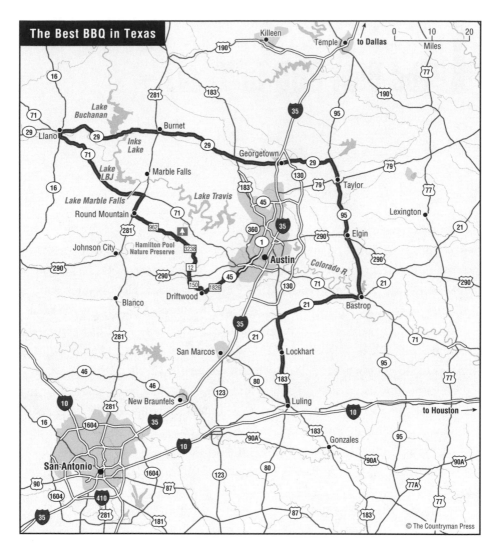

Most classic BBQ spots are no-frills establishments, serving up piping-hot meat with exacting precision, but very little attention gets paid to ambiance. The truth is, eating at well-worn communal tables with little more than butcher paper for a plate, a roll of paper towels by your side, and juice dripping down to your elbows is just the sort of atmosphere folks have come to expect. In Texas, BBQ is the great equalizer; from bikers to bankers, everyone loves good 'cue, as a lunchtime visit to any of the joints below will attest.

While there is plenty of great BBQ in Texas' big cities, fantastic BBQ is worth leaving the city limits behind you. This route visits several small towns—Drift-wood, Llano, Taylor, Elgin, Lockhart, Luling, and Georgetown. Within striking distance from Austin, this is a backroad route hiding in plain sight.

Total distance: 250 miles.

Intersections: Chapters 2, 3, and 4.

There are different ways to approach this route. You can easily take in one or two of the restaurants and recommended sites in a day trip from Austin or San Antonio. Folks from Dallas or Houston will find the route a pleasant week-end getaway. But, however you tackle it, there is always the issue of eating. The only way to find out what you like best is to try it all. So, throw caution, calories, and cholesterol counts to the wind and follow the smoke from the pits. Since great BBQ is admittedly a matter of opinion, I'll introduce you to the classics and let you decide. This route covers six BBQ spots, each a legend in its own right, and several diners, eateries, and even a vineyard; all I can say is if you go, go hungry.

While you may see it spelled "barbeque," "bar-b-que," "barbecue," or "BBQ," in Texas it's all good. The roots of the name have been lost to history, though some believe it may have come from the Spanish version of an indigenous tribe's word, *barbacoa*. One thing is sure, pit cooking is popular in many forms and methods the world over, as this method renders even the toughest cuts of meat moist and juicy. From clambakes to pig roasts, every culture has its version.

In the United States, the style and flavor of BBQ depend on the region. In the Southeast, folks love to drown their pork BBQ in a sweet tomato sauce with a vinegary twang, while the Southwest favors its meat dry-rubbed without any sauce at all. Chicago BBQ is heavy on both the sauce and the pepper. Generally speaking, the farther north you go, the more chicken dominates the menu. But in Texas, it's all about the beef, usually brisket, served straight from the pit. Typically, the meat is dry rubbed, smoked, and served with a side of very optional sauce with various signature concoctions that run the gamut from sweet and smoky to hot and spicy.

A simple Internet search will reveal the depth of opinion and conviction when it comes to Texas BBQ. I don't want to influence your palate unduly, but there are some indisputably great choices, and I present them to you here, un-ranked and uncategorized. As you make your way through Central Texas, mopping up the juices with sliced white bread and paper towel, you can rest assured that you are eating some of the very best BBQ the state has to offer.

No need to leave Austin for some of the best BBQ in Texas. While the city's East Side isn't exactly a backroad, it's a part of town locals gravitate to for experiences like lunch at **Franklin BBQ**. Started as a food truck in 2009, Franklin has outgrown its charming mobile digs, just recently graduating to a brick-and-mortar storefront. 'Cue is served from "11 AM until out of food," which tends to happen quickly. The line forms midmorning and never lets up, and the succulent meats, purple cabbage slaw, and mustardy potato salad are gone in the blink of an eye. No matter how much meat they smoke, the folks at Franklin can't seem to keep up with insatiable consumer demand—they've sold out every day they've been open. Franklin is a laid-back presentation of super serious and mouthwateringly delicious barbeque. Owner Aaron Franklin has been dubbed a "BBQ genius" by *Bon Appétit* magazine. Taste for yourself.

Head south out of Austin on MoPac/Loop 1, passing the Lady Bird Johnson Wildflower Center (p. 38–41); turn west on TX 45, then south on FM 1826 for 8 miles to Driftwood, where **The Salt Lick** has been drawing meat-lovers from far and wide for years. Located on the edge of the Hill Country, The Salt Lick cooks their meat over a blazing hot oak fire in a huge, 40-year-old stone pit, but the secret to the delicious BBQ seems to be in the sauce. The meat is basted in a tomato-less sauce with just a pinch of sugar to help it stay fresh and bright as it caramelizes over the heat for juicy goodness every time. The family-style meal option features big bowls of coleslaw, potato salad, and beans for passing and slices of bread to sop up the juices. You can't beat the Salt Lick's setting. The grounds surrounding the restaurant feel almost ranch-like, with wooden picnic tables nestled under the big oak trees and live music. BYOB and cash-only.

Pulled-pork sandwich at Franklin's in Austin

Take FM 150 north out of Drift-wood, turning right onto RR 12 toward Dripping Springs, then picking up Hamilton Pool Road/RR 3238, passing by **Hamilton Pool Nature Preserve**. A rugged trail leads from the parking lot to the clear natural pool, cool grotto, and 45-foot waterfall. There are no life-guards and you'll need to carry in your own food, water, and other necessities, but this place is a very popular swim-ming spot on hot Texas days. Once the lot is full, parking is first come, first served, and the line can get long. Back on the road, continue north on FM/RR 962, cross over US 281 (see chapter 3), and cruise into Llano on TX 71. The trip from Driftwood to Llano is just over 70 miles.

Llano (pronounced LAY-no) is a former frontier town in the northern reaches of the Texas Hill Country. Lo-cated on the Llano River and TX 71, Llano is a jumping-off point into the Highland Lakes region (see p. 63). This

On the table: sauce, salt, pepper, toothpicks

unassuming slip of a spot also just so happens to be home to one of Texas' culi-nary gems—**Cooper's Old Time Pit Bar-B-Que**, located on W. Young Street, just west of the intersection of TX 16 and TX 29. The first things you'll notice when you pull up to Cooper's are the huge outdoor pits organized under a corrugated metal roof. Step up to place your order and the pit masters will open the heavy metal counterweighted lids wide, inviting you to get a good look inside—the smell of sizzling meat in your nose and tangy mesquite smoke in your eyes—and point to exactly what you'd like. Once you've made your choice, the pit master will ask if you'd like your selection dunked into a huge vat of peppery red sauce before you take it inside for slicing. The dining room at Cooper's has long communal tables and walls adorned with heads of bobcats, deer, and other animals you won't find being slow cooked. Curiously, many of the other BBQ joints in this chapter share this taxidermy theme.

Two historic buildings in Llano deserve special mention, as they have been recently renovated and it is refreshing to see them sparkle again. Square and solid, the **Badu House** is a wonderful classic Italian Renaissance structure built in 1891 as the First National Bank of Llano. It's now a restaurant, sporting an enormous chunk of Llanite, a granite found exclusively in Llano County, atop its formidable bar. Beat the Texas heat with a glass of wine or bottle of beer served in the cool barroom or shady patio of this historic gem. In another happy turn of events, new management at the freshly renovated **Dabbs Hotel** has given that establishment a new lease on life. Plenty of paint, well-chosen furniture, perky flowers, and a good cleaning have made this simple railroad hotel a wonderful place to spend the night. Located on a quiet side street, with a back patio overlooking the river, the hotel is casual and relaxed.

Another great place to cleanse your palate after your first taste of BBQ on this route is **Fall Creek Vineyards,** perched on the north shore of **Lake Buchanan,** part of the chain of Highland Lakes described on p. 63. Its origins go back to 1973, when local ranchers Ed and Susan Auler took a trip to France and quickly noticed the similarities between their Texas landscape and the French wine region. Back home, they took a chance on the location's magical combination of soil, sunny days, and lake breezes and established a vineyard. The oldest and perhaps best known of the Texas vineyards, Fall Creek paved the way for winemaking in the state, and they now have plenty of colleagues throughout the Hill Country (see p. 47). While renowned for their super-premium red wine, Meritus, the vineyard consistently garners praise for all the wines they produce. Try them at their daily wine tastings. To get there, leave Llano, traveling east on TX 29, then north on RR 2241, through Bluffton, to Tow, then south on CR 222; the winery is located 2.2 miles past the Tow post office. To reconnect with the route, retrace your steps to Bluffton and take TX 261 south to rejoin TX 29 and continue eastward, skirting the southern tip of the lake.

The spring-fed Fall Creek, for which Fall Creek Vineyards is named, ambles through that vineyard before cascading into Lake Buchanan in the form of the 90-foot **Fall Creek Waterfalls**. Also of interest on the lake is the **Canyon of the Eagles,** where in the winter and early spring some two dozen majestic American

BLUEBONNETS

Burnet has been designated as the Bluebonnet
Capital of Texas, and you can
print a map of the self-guided
Bluebonnet Trail from the
Chamber of Commerce Web
site, www.burnetchamber.org,
to use for maximum bluebonnet viewing in the springtime.

Texas bluebonnet

bald eagles nest and live. The **Vanish-ing Texas River Cruise**, a beautiful and educational ecologically themed boat cruise, takes in both sights. The cruise leaves from the **Canyon of the Eagles Resort**, on the east side of Lake Buchanan, practically across the lake from Fall Creek Vineyards. The resort is a recreation and retreat center and lodge with fairly basic hotel-room-style accommodations, cabins, a camp-ground, restaurant, and swimming pool spread. Most of the 940 acres of this property is a nature preserve with 14 miles of hiking trails, perfect for nature lovers who enjoy canoeing, kayaking, camping, or star gazing. The resort is a lovely spot from which to explore the lake, making this detour a backroad to tran-quility. From the intersection of TX 29 and RR 2431, drive 3 miles west of Burnet and turn north onto RR 2431, following it 14 miles to the resort entrance.

Farther east, the small college town of **Georgetown** is one of the most sensi-ble and pleasant places on this route to spend the night. Home to Southwestern University, the oldest university in the state, Georgetown also has a particularly lovely downtown, with neatly renovated historic buildings surrounding the town

Louie Mueller Barbeque in Taylor

square, a courthouse at its center, and stately homes from the 1880s. If you'd like to spend the night, Ruth and RC at the **Harper-Chesser Historic Inn** would be happy to host you. The inn was constructed in 1890, is on the National Register of Historic Places, and located directly across from the leafy university campus. The nearby **San Gabriel House B&B** is also lovely. Both establishments have light and airy bedrooms, crisp linens on the beds, and period antiques throughout.

Given that you will eat your fill of BBQ on this route, Georgetown is also a good place to sample something different. The **Monument Café**, located on S. Austin Avenue, has a hit with its recipe for combining comfort foods made from scratch using stellar ingredients—often organic and locally grown—with a 1940s diner atmosphere. Since everything is delicious, just ask folks on their way out the door what their favorite is and order accordingly. Seriously consider saving room for a sliver of their signature chocolate pie. The thick, nutty crust is made from toasted pecans and topped with a chocolate mousse filling and whipped cream—a silky, creamy creation that melts in your mouth.

For something a little more refined, head north on Austin Avenue toward the square, where **Wildfire** serves an imaginative menu featuring southwestern fare cooked over an oak-fired grill. The atmosphere is sophisticated, yet fairly casual, and pairs nicely with dishes such as ostrich medallions drizzled with a cilantro-citrus demi-glacé and agave honey–glazed carrots, oak-grilled Jamaican jerk pork loin with habanero apple chutney, or pepita-encrusted American bison strip loin. The Sunday champagne brunch is especially enjoyable.

If you are in the mood for Tex-Mex food, **Dos Salsas** serves up tacos, enchiladas, tostadas, and tamales stuffed with chicken, beef, brisket, pork, or *carne guisada* (slow-cooked beef tips with gravy). This family-run restaurant on Main Street is a local favorite and, consequently, frequently packed.

If the hot, humid Texas weather is getting to you, then head into **Inner Space Cavern,** where the air is clean, clear, and a constant 72 degrees. The cavern, located underneath bustling I-35, was discovered in 1963 during drilling through 40 feet of solid limestone for highway construction. While there are numerous caves and caverns in the area, this is one of the more accessible ones, with a cable car, paved trails, and an informative tour that lasts just over an hour; just the thing if you've forgotten the difference between stalactite, stalagmite, and spelunker. You'll find the cavern just a minute south of Georgetown at exit 259 on I-35.

Heading out of Georgetown east along E. University Avenue will take you past pretty Southwestern University; the road becomes TX 29, dotted with little homes, pastures, and low water crossings, which dead-ends approximately 16 miles later into TX 95, at which point you will head south, following signs to Taylor.

This small town on the San Gabriel River certainly looks as if it's seen better days, but some local antique shops and an old theater showing first-run movies for $2.50 hold their own. Then there's **Louie Mueller Barbeque.** Folks come from up the street and as far away as Asia to darken the door of Louie Mueller's. This place is the perfect mix of everything you might want in a BBQ joint. The inside is charred to a thick gray-black, and the air is tinged with smoke from the pits behind the counter. There are plenty of well-worn wooden tables, each with its own selection of mismatched wooden chairs.

Step up, take a look at the menu written on butcher paper and taped to the wall, and order. From brisket to spare ribs and homemade jalapeño sausage,

Framed accolades at Louis Mueller Barbeque in Taylor

Mueller's grabs your selection fresh from the pit, loping off a slice for you to taste before carving it up in a flash. While they offer a tangy tomatoey sauce, few people even give it a glance. The meat's just that good.

Salt, pepper, and an oak-fueled fire are all that make up this fantastic 'cue. Yes, and all paintings are made of just canvas and paint. The product depends on the skill of the handlers, and these folks are masters. Their motto seems to be "If it ain't broke, don't fix it," judging from the knives, wear and tear on the cutting block, and simply everything in this place. If Louie Mueller's never changes another thing, they are still well within perfect.

Leaving Taylor, head south again, traveling approximately 16 miles on TX 95 to **Elgin** (pronounced EL-gin). If you like sausage, you will have plenty of chances to eat your fill here; the town is home to three of Texas' best-loved sausage makers, earning it the distinction of the Sausage Capital of Texas.

After entering town, **Southside Market and Barbecue** is the first spot you'll come across, located on US 290, just south of where TX 95 dead-ends into it. The family that originally owned Southside started making sausage in 1882; the current owners took over in 1968, carrying on the very same tradition. This spot started as a meat market, but they added an eating area for people who just couldn't wait to get home before digging in. Whether you choose just a link or take a couple of pounds home to freeze, Southside's sausages are always juicy with just a little bit of a kick.

Loosen your belt and head east on US 290 to **Meyer's Elgin Smokehouse.** The folks here have been making sausage since 1949, using an old family recipe brought to this country from Germany. Until 10 years ago, Meyer's was exclusively a wholesale operation, but sausage lovers demanded more so the company added a dining area. Now you can enjoy sausage, along with port ribs, turkey breast, and, of course, brisket on site. The decor is basic, food comes on butcher paper, and the rolls of paper towels set out on the tables are meant to be used.

The route continues to **Lockhart**, where the triumvirate of **Kreuz Market, Smitty's**, and **Black's** rules the smoking pits that put this town on the map.

SATURDAYS ONLY

Overshoot Taylor and head south on FM 112 until you come to the little town of Lexington, home of Snow's BBQ. If you want to taste the BBQ here, you'll need to hustle—Snow's opens at 8 AM on Saturdays, and they only serve until noon, unless of course they sell out first, which happens a lot. Something this hard to get had better be special, and Snow's is. The brisket is perfectly cooked, a little crisp and salty on the outside and melt-in-your-mouth on the inside, thanks to the efforts of Tootsie Tomanetz, a tiny whirlwind of a woman who's been smoking meats since the late 1960s and is clearly an expert. You might not even end up saucing anything, since the meats are that flavorful on their own. The ribs are outstanding, though the sides aren't particularly notable. Snow's is housed in a bitty shack of a place with an attached covered outdoor eating area. To pick up the route again, travel 20 miles west on FM 696 and 4 miles north on US 290 north to Elgin.

Communal dining tables at Kreuz in Lockhart

The oldest of the Lockhart BBQ joints, **Kreuz** (pronounced KRITES) began as a meat market and grocery in 1900. As was the custom at the time, the market cooked meat as a way of staving off spoilage, and customers often bought pieces hot off the grill for a quick meal. By the 1960s, Kreuz sold BBQ exclusively, serving it on butcher paper, with saltines, bread, pickles, onions, and, uniquely, cheese. In 1999, the business picked up and moved, bringing its 99 years of experience to the brand-new building it inhabits today. While they've expanded the menu somewhat, adding a few newfangled items, thankfully they didn't touch the BBQ, which is just as hot and juicy as it's always been. A trip to Kreuz's usually means spending some time in line. Once inside the front door, you are encouraged to wash your hands at the freestanding sink (consider this a subtle reminder that Kreuz doesn't hand out forks with their BBQ), and then wait to be herded into the cavernous pit room. You place your order, by the pound, at the counter, exit through the double doors, choose your sides, pay, and find yourself a spot to sit down and dig in.

Located just off the town square, these days **Smitty's** minds the pits at what used to be Kreuz. In fact, Smitty's is named for Edgar "Smitty" Schmidt, the founder of Kreuz, whose daughter opened this old-style joint in 1999 after Kreuz moved to its current location. While a disagreement may have fragmented the family, many of their old BBQ traditions survived intact. The menu here is what you'd expect—beef, pork chops, sausage—all served sauceless, on brown paper. Outside, Smitty's looks like little more than a dirty and tattered set of double doors. Once you get inside, you'll realize that it's dirty and tattered all the way to the billowing open fires funneling smoke and heat into the pits. In this case, however, the residue is best described as a patina—that finish that you get through years and years of good use. The dining area is a bit more generic, with tables pushed end to end and florescent lights, but each time the doors swing open and you get a glimpse of the pits, it's like love at first sight all over again.

Black's is altogether different. Located a block or two off the square and in business since 1932, Black's claims to be the "oldest and best major BBQ restaurant continuously owned by the same family." While this may seem like splitting hairs, the point is well taken. Recipes and techniques handed down within the family, not to mention years and years of practice, have produced excellent results, and the proof is in the eating. President Lyndon Johnson once had them cook up a mess of sausage to be sent to the capital. Secret Service and Department of

A packed dining room at Smitty's in Lockhart

Agriculture employees came to oversee preparation, but, to date, Black's trade secrets have remained safe with them.

The ordering experience here is less communal; diners never pass by the pits, but instead go through a cafeteria-style line, sit at four-person tables, and enjoy a view of trophy heads and hunting pictures. The atmosphere doesn't detract from the food, which is, after all, why you are here in the first place. Folks say that the brisket is the best around, smoked over post oak until succulent. Pork, ham, chicken, and sausage are also on the menu, and the thick sauce makes plenty of diners happy. While at most BBQ places the available sides consist of potato salad and onions, Black's offerings are more wide ranging. From green pea salad with ham to hard-boiled eggs, Black's keeps 'em coming back for more…year after year after year.

Several blocks farther south of Smitty's on US 183 (known as S. Colorado Street within the city) you'll find **Chisholm Trail BBQ,** quietly holding its own in the shadow of its more famous colleagues. While out-of-towners tend to gravitate toward one of the aforementioned, locals love this place. Little things like the take-out window rub some aficionados the wrong way, but for others, it's just the quickest way to get great 'cue fast. Younger and less expensive than its cohorts, Chisholm Trail might lack provenance, but it more than makes up for it with its homemade bread, cafeteria-style lunch buffet, and hometown feel. Besides, it's one of the few BBQ joints around where women carve the meat!

BBQ with all the fixin's at Luling City Market in Luling

Back on US 183, follow the signs another 15 miles or so to the small town of **Luling.** In town, the highway becomes Magnolia Street, then veers sharply to the east and continues south to Gonzales (see below). Just a block west of the highway, at 633 E. Davis Street, sits **Luling City Market** ("City Market," for short) surrounded by an aura of mesquite smoke that's been there since it opened in the late 1950s. The place isn't much to look at—by now you've noticed most aren't—but step inside and it's all business. The pit is indoors, at the back of the restaurant, enclosed on all sides, with windows and doors for access. Once in this BBQ antechamber, order up and watch as your meat is handpicked, carved, and passed over the counter. Grab a pickle, some onions, saltines, and maybe some beans, and sidle up to the tables to find yourself a seat. One thing that really sets City Market apart is its sauce. The fact that it has any at all is distinctive, but it is surprisingly tasty, with just enough sweetness and heat to complement the tender and slightly salty meat. Everyone loves the pork ribs, sausages, and, of course, brisket.

The route properly ends here, and I-20 and US 183 are handily located to take you to your destinations, but for those who'd like a little more, travel just a few miles south to **Gonzales,** the spot where the first battle cries of the Texas Revolution were heard. Park yourself in a seat at the **Gonzales Food Market** and get ready for more fantastic BBQ, served by some of the friendliest folks in Texas. (Gonzales Food Market is reviewed and detailed in chapter 4.)

If you finish this route with a heavy heart as well as a full stomach, take comfort in the fact that if you just had some of the best Texas brisket you've ever tasted, you'll never really have to go without. If you live in the area or find yourself passing through, all of these places would love to have you back anytime. And if you live afar, just call up and place an order; most of the places on this route will be happy to ship you whatever you desire. Rest assured, these are the folks who understand the need for great Texas BBQ.

IN THE AREA

Badu House, 601 Bessemer Avenue, Llano, 78643. Call 325-247-1207. Mon. through Wed. 11–2, Thurs. 5–10, Fri. and Sat. 5–11:30, Sun. 11–2. Web site: www.thebaduhouse.com.

Black's, 215 N. Main Street, Lockhart, 78644. Call 512-398-2712. Sun. through Thurs. 10–8, Fri. and Sat. 10–8:30. Web site: www.blacksbbq.com.

Canyon of the Eagles Resort, 16942 RR 2341, Burnet, 78611. Call 512-334-2070. Web site: www.canyonofthe eagles.com.

Chisholm Trail BBQ, 1323 S. Colorado Street/US 183, Lockhart, 78644. Call 512-398-6027. Sun. through Thurs. 8–8, Fri. and Sat. 8–9. Web site: www.chisholmtrailbbq.com.

City Market, 633 E. Davis Street, Luling, 78648. Call 830-875-9019. Mon. through Sat. 7–6.

Cooper's, 604 W. Young Street/TX 71/29, Llano, 78643. Call 325-247-5713. Sun. through Thurs. 11–8, Fri. and Sat. 11–9. Web site: www.coopers bbq.com.

Dabb's Railroad Hotel, 112 E. Burnet Street, Llano, 78643. Call 325-247-2200. Web site: www.dabbsrailroad hotel.com.

Dos Salsas, 1104 S. Main Street, Georgetown, 78626. Call 512-930-2343. Mon. through Sat. 7–10, Sun. 7–6. Web site: www.dossalsas.com.

Elgin Chamber of Commerce, 114 Central Avenue, Elgin, 78621. Call 512-285-4515. Web site: www.elgintx .com.

Fall Creek Winery and Vineyards, 1820 County Road 22, Tow, 78672. Call 325-379-5361. Mon. through Fri. 11–4, Sat. 11–5, Sun. noon–4. Web site: www .fcv.com.

Franklin Barbecue, 900 E. 11th Street, Austin, 78702. Call 512-653-1187. Tues. through Sun. 11–sold out; lunch only. Web site: www.franklin barbecue.com.

Georgetown Visitor Information Center, 101 W. Seventh Street, Georgetown, 78626. Call 512-863-5598. Web site: www.georgetown.org.

Harper-Chesser Historic Inn, 1309 College Street, Georgetown, 78626. Call 512-864-1887. Web site: www .harperchesserinn.com.

Hamilton Pool Nature Preserve, 24300 Hamilton Pool Road, Dripping Springs, 78620. Call 512-264-2740. Daily 9–5:30, subject to water quality; call for daily recorded report. Web site: www.co.travis.tx.us.

Inner Space Cavern, 4200 S. I-35, exit 259, Georgetown, 78626. Call 512-931-2283. Memorial Day through Labor Day daily 9–6; Labor Day through Memorial Day Mon. through Fri. 9–4, Sat. and Sun. 10–5. Fee. Web site: www.myinnerspacecavern.com.

Kreuz Market, 619 N. Colorado Street/US 183, Lockhart 78644. Call 512-398-2361. Mon. through Sat. 10:30–8. Web site: www.kreuzmarket .com.

Lake Buchanan Adventures, at Canyon of the Eagles Resort, 16942 RR 2341, Burnet, 78611. Call 517-756-9911. Web site: www.lakebuchanan adventures.com.

Llano County Chamber of Commerce, The Railyard Depot, 100 Train Station Drive, Llano, 78643. Call 325-247-5354. Web site: www.llano chamber.org.

Lockhart Chamber of Commerce, 631 S. Colorado Street, Lockhart, 78644. Call 512-398-2818. Web site: www.lockhartchamber.com.

Louie Mueller Barbecue, W. Second Street, Taylor, 76574. Call 512-352-6206. Mon. through Fri. 11–6, Sat. 10–6. Web site: www.louiemueller barbeque.com.

Luling Area Chamber of Commerce, 421 E. Davis Street, Luling, 78648. Call 830-875-3214. Web site: www.lulingcc.org.

Meyer's Elgin Smokehouse, 188 Highway 290, Elgin, 78621. Call 512-281-3331. Mon. through Thurs. 10–8, Fri. and Sat. 10–9, Sun. 10–7. Web site: www.meyerselginsausage.com.

Monument Café, 500 S. Austin Avenue, Georgetown, 78627. Call 512-930-9586. Sun. through Thurs. 7–9, Fri. and Sat. 7–10. Web site: www.the monumentcafe.com.

The Salt Lick, 18300 FM 1826, Driftwood, 78619. Call 512-894-3117. Daily 11–10. Web site: www.saltlickbbq.com.

San Gabriel House B&B, 1008 E. University Avenue, Georgetown, 78626. Call 512-930-0070. Web site: www.sangabrielhouse.com.

Smitty's, 208 S. Commerce, Lockhart, 78644. Call 512-398-9344. Mon. through Fri. 7–6, Sat. 7–6:30, Sun. 9–3. Web site: www.smittysmarket.com.

Snow's, 516 Main Street, Lexington, 78947. Call 512-773-4640. Sat. only, 8 AM until it's gone. Web site: www .snowsbbq.com.

Southside Market and Barbeque, 1212 Highway 290, Elgin, 78621. Call 512-281-4650. Mon. through Thurs. 8–8, Fri. and Sat. 8–9, Sun. 9–8. Web site: www.southsidemarket.com.

Taylor Chamber of Commerce, 1519 N. Main Street, Taylor, 76574. Call 512-365-8485. Web site: www .taylorchamber.org.

Vanishing Texas River Cruise, 16942 RR 2341/443 Waterway Lane, Burnet, 78611. Call 1-800-474-8374 or 512-756-6986. Web site: www.vtrc .com.

Wildfire, 812 S. Austin Avenue, Georgetown, 78626. Call 512-869-3473. Mon. through Thurs. 11–9, Fri. and Sat. 11–midnight, Sun. 10–9. Web site: www.wildfiretexas.com.

Hill Country wildflowers

2 Lyndon and Lady Bird's Hill Country

Getting there: The Lyndon Baines Johnson Library and Museum is located on Red River Street in Austin, along the eastern edge of the University of Texas campus. From there, take Red River three blocks south, pick up San Jacinto and follow it south, skirting the Texas State Capitol complex. Turn right on 11th Street and left onto Congress Avenue, using the Ann Richards/Congress Avenue Bridge to cross Lady Bird Lake. From there, turn right into Barton Springs Road, following it to MoPac/Route 1. Take MoPac/Route 1 south to La Crosse Avenue, following signs to the Lady Bird Johnson Wildflower Center, a total of 13 miles from the LBJ Library. Leaving the Wildflower Center, double back to MoPac/Route 1, this time heading west on Slaughter Lane. Follow Slaughter for 2.5 miles, turning left onto US 290 and following it west for 31 miles. US 290 will merge with US 281, so follow the route north to Johnson City. From Johnson City, take US 290 16 miles west to Stonewall and an additional 14 miles west to Fredericksburg. From Fredericksburg, double back on US 290 and take RR 1376 south to Luckenbach.

Highlights: Though several US presidents have hailed from Texas, at his best, President Lyndon Baines Johnson (LBJ) embodied the grand spirit of the state. LBJ's boyhood in rural Texas in the early 1900s planted the seeds of compassion and sense of duty that informed the revolutionary social changes he ushered in during his presidency. Start at the **Lyndon Baines Johnson Library and Museum**, pay a visit and your respects to former first lady Lady Bird Johnson, at her **Wildflower Center** in Austin, and continue west into the Hill Country to see the **Lyndon B. Johnson National Historical Park** and the **LBJ Ranch**. Sample Texas wines and peaches as you make your way to **Fredericksburg**. Enjoy beautiful vistas and abundant wildflowers on the **Willow City Loop, Enchanted Rock**

State Natural Area, and along the backroads between **Comfort**, **Sisterdale**, and **Luckenbach**. Detour: Willow City Loop (see p. 49).

Total distance: Approximately 90 miles

Intersections: Chapters 1 and 3

This part of Texas, so close to the urban centers of Austin and San Antonio, still retains a rural look and feel. Pastures of cows and sheep, ripening vineyards and peach orchards, lazy creeks, and wildflowers along the roadways paint a picture of a bucolic Texas worthy of postcards and calendars. Driving along the backroads of this region makes for a terrific weekend trip. You can certainly do parts of this trip in a day, and three full days would be ideal. The Hill Country is already a popular getaway, so be sure to book accommodations plenty of time ahead and consider an off-season, midweek trip, which is almost always more relaxing.

Starting in Austin, stop in at the well-curated **Lyndon Baines Johnson Library and Museum** on the University of Texas campus for an overview of the life and times of Lyndon Baines Johnson, former Texas state representative and 36th president of the United States. The museum offers changing exhibits on such topics as the Vietnam War, all interesting and all a part of the larger story of the politically charged 1960s, when heady idealism and harsh realities divided the country's citizens.

Leaving the LBJ Library and Museum, swoop down Congress Avenue to **Lady Bird Lake**, the reservoir on the Colorado River which separates downtown Austin from South Austin, and enjoy a stroll. When the Colorado River was dammed in 1960, the resulting lake was named Town Lake. Though it was intended to provide beauty and recreation for Austinites, the lake became overgrown, polluted, and dangerous. After a decade of neglect, Lady Bird stepped in to form the Town Lake Beautification Committee and set about clearing, cleaning, planting, and adding 10 miles of hiking and biking trails along its shores. After her death the city renamed the lake in her honor (a gesture she had resisted during her lifetime), in recognition of her diligent restoration work. Lady Bird Lake is now a hub of outdoor activity in Austin and the site of many cultural, musical, and athletic events.

Head west to Route 1, known within the city limits as MoPac, a reference to the Missouri Pacific Railroad, which runs alongside it, and then south to the **Lady**

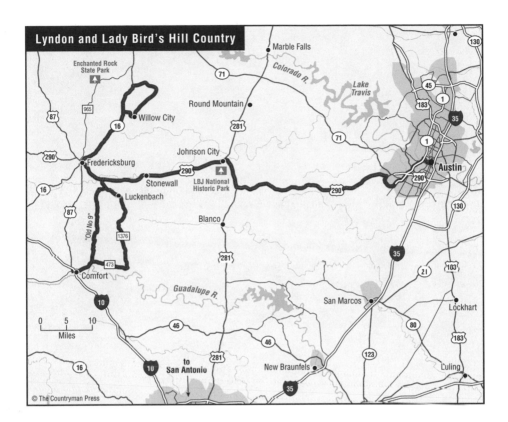

Bird Johnson Wildflower Center. This lovely piece of Central Texas countryside is hemmed in by the ever-expanding Austin suburbs, but the grounds themselves are spacious and private. An environmentalist long before "going green" was popular, Lady Bird Johnson is directly responsible for the many azaleas and dogwood trees dotting the Washington, DC, parks. Back in Texas, in 1982, she transformed her simple idea that "a little beauty can create harmony" into the Wildflower Center, opening it along with her friend, the actress Helen Hayes, on her 70th birthday. The center was designed to protect and preserve North America's native foliage and in doing so has become a foremost authority on the subject, with an encyclopedic Web site that is sure to be of interest to gardeners from every region. When Lady Bird died in 2007 she left a powerful legacy of conservation and environmental custodianship well represented by the Wildflower Center.

While spring and summer are the most vivid seasons at the center, there seems to be a native flower or plant in bloom almost year-round, making it a won-

A President does not shape a new and personal vision of America. He collects it from the scattered hopes of the American past.

Lyndon B. Johnson

President Lyndon Baines Johnson

derful place for nature photography. After a stroll around the grounds, visitors enjoy browsing in **Wild Ideas,** the onsite gift shop, or relaxing over a drink at the **Wildflower Café,** which you'll find tucked into a corner of the hacienda-style main building.

Leaving the Wildflower Center, double back slightly, then turn left at Slaughter and north on US 290, following it to its merger with US 281 in Johnson City, for a total of 40 miles. As you come into Johnson City, US 281 will continue north, following the route laid out in chapter 3, while US 290 will continue to the west, taking you through the rest of this chapter.

Once in **Johnson City,** be sure to stop in at the **Silver K Café** for a bite to eat. Though the Silver K is a relative newcomer—it opened in 2001—its location in an old lumberyard gives it a timeless quality that makes it feel well worn. The café is at once rustic and elegant, capturing the essence of Hill Country style. The delicious breakfast menu of eggs, meats, and pancakes gives way to tasty lunch fare dominated by huge fresh salads and sandwiches. Dinner, served Thursday through Saturday, is fairly formal and more elaborate, while Sunday through Wednesday the focus is on home-style suppers of meatloaf, pot pies, and chicken-fried steaks. The Silver K also has live music most weekends, and diners like to browse the antiques shop on the premises. Located on Main Street/US 290 just four blocks west of US 281.

Just two blocks from the Silver K is the next stop on this route, the **Lyndon B. Johnson National Historical Park.** The visitors center, complete with maps and restrooms, is located beside the parking lot, and from there it is just a short walk to either the **Johnson Settlement,** a log cabin, windmill, and barns dating back to the 1860s and owned by LBJ's grandparents, or **LBJ's boyhood home.** The Johnson family moved to this neat and tidy Folk Victorian in town from a farm in Stonewall in 1912, just before a young LBJ turned five years old. Today the site is owned by the National Park Service and has been restored in mid-1920s style. This restoration was no small feat; it took three years of hard work for historians, architects, carpenters, and stonemasons to give the property the historically accurate look and feel it has today. As you tour the home, take note of the details, particularly the woodstove in the kitchen, which speaks volumes about life in the Hill Country in those days, when the region was still without access to electricity.

Life in the Texas Hill Country in the 1930s was like reliving the 1830s. While much of the rest of the country lived in cities with access to refrigeration, elec-

The Silver K Cafe in Johnson City

tric stoves, ovens, and irons, and indoor plumbing, folks in the Hill Country struggled to meet their most basic needs in the absence of these amenities through backbreaking work and determination. Farms limped along without electricity. Hulking woodstoves were kept burning all year long regardless of the heat. Women, almost exclusively, had to carry water from nearby rivers and streams. Milking was done by candlelight, a dangerous inconvenience in hay-filled barns.

This was the environment in which the young Lyndon Johnson grew up, and he understood all too well its hardships. The work of the people to meet their most basic needs was never ending, and Johnson hated the idea of people suffering needlessly when the innovations that could ease their work were so readily available elsewhere. In fact, he saw this disparity as an injustice. Northeastern electric companies consistently balked at bringing electricity to rural Texas, declaring that folks living on farms and in the country wouldn't be able to pay their utility bills. When he became a congressman, Johnson set out to change things. Thinking that if they couldn't convince the big companies to help, then they had best help themselves, Johnson brought the idea of starting a power cooperative to his neighbors throughout the Hill Country, who, after some initial skepticism, signed on.

In 1935 President Franklin D. Roosevelt unveiled the New Deal, with rural electrification as an integral part of post-Depression economic recovery, and by the 1940s the lights were on in the Texas Hill Country and all across rural America. This simple fact had a social, cultural, and economic impact so profound that it is difficult to grasp today, but as Johnson himself wrote in 1959, "I think of all the things I have ever done, nothing has ever given me as much satisfaction as bringing power to the Hill Country of Texas." So, as you make your way through the countryside outlined in this route, every once in a while let your imagination

SUNDAY HOUSES

Devoutly religious Germans settled on farms and ranches outside Fredericksburg, working the land but determined not to miss church services on the Sabbath. Weather, distance, and road conditions made getting to church difficult, so they built tiny houses on small bits of land in town to use for shopping on Saturday and church on Sunday. Known as Sunday houses, these were wood structures, with steep roofs and a sprinkling of decorative millwork and with little lean-to kitchens tacked on the back and sometimes a staircase to a second floor running along an outside wall. The houses were popular between 1890 and 1910, and small groups of them survive today along West San Antonio Street, near St. Mary's church, on W. Main Street and S. Milam Street.

drift back to a time not so long ago, when the entire region was in the dark. Those numerous utility poles marring the otherwise pristine Hill Country views are the hard-won results of teamwork, diligence, and perseverance.

Leaving Johnson City and heading west on US-290 will take you the 13 miles to **Stonewall,** home of the **LBJ Ranch,** which is operated by the National Park Service. The ranch is a collection of buildings, including the home Johnson was born in, the "Texas White House," and the Johnson Family Cemetery; the Pedernales River, in which Johnson was baptized, flows through the property.

Though Johnson's birthplace was razed in the 1940s, what you will see is a meticulous reconstruction, based on photographs of the original. The reconstructed home has running water, electricity, and other modern amenities that would not have existed at the time, as well as donated antique furniture in much better condition than what Johnson would have seen as a child, but the design of the house, in the regional "dog-trot" style, is just as it would have been. This utilitarian house plan separated the stifling hot kitchen from the rest of the house by a long thin hallway.

The **Texas White House** is so called because Johnson spent so much time here while in office—490 days, a quarter of his presidency. The house became the Johnsons' home after he left office, and Lady Bird lived here until her death in 2007. Both are buried in the **Johnson Family Cemetery** on the property. The ranch, while a national historic site, is also private property; the only way to see it is to take one of the National Park Service's bus tours.

Stonewall is also home to an exquisite bed & breakfast, **Rose Hill Manor,** a Charleston-style home with wide porches and large windows overlooking the Hill Country countryside. The main house has four rooms each with queen-sized beds, sun porches, sitting areas, or access to the veranda and thoughtfully decorated with a restrained use of floral prints. Additionally, the cottages on the property offer rooms as spacious and spotless as those in the main house, though newer, with vaulted ceilings, warm wood floors, and king-sized beds. A full gourmet breakfast is served each morning. For an evening meal, **Austin's,** Rose Hill Manor's onsite restaurant, serves a seasonal and fundamentally French five-course prix fixe menu alongside à la carte dining. An impressive wine list, crisp table linens, candles, and stunning views of the Hill Country make Austin's so special that some folks stay the whole weekend in Stonewall.

Venturing on to Fredericksburg along US 290, you'll come upon **Wildseed**

Farms, a thriving plant nursery surrounded by fields exploding with color in the spring and summer. Wildseed Farms provides both native and nonnative plants and seeds, workshops, tips for growing and identifying native plants, and a "Butterfly Haus" filled with butterflies. While there is a fee to stroll "The Meadows," the distant view is free and you are welcome to meander through the rows and rows of plants for sale, taking photos to your heart's content. A small café serves refreshments, sandwiches, and a selection of Texas wines.

Back on US 290 the road between here and Fredericksburg, several miles to the west, is dotted with wineries (see box, p. 47) offering a nice sampling of Texas wines. Stop in and try a few, or branch off this route entirely and spend the day driving among the Hill Country vineyards outlined on www.texaswinetrail.com.

Fredericksburg is named for Prince Frederick of Prussia. The city was founded in 1846 by John O. Meusebach and a group of 120 German immigrants who came to the area from New Braunfels as participants in the *Adelsverein,* a planned German settlement of Texas, but the region was also home to Native Americans, namely the Comanche, who were not keen on letting in outsiders. In 1847, against all odds, Meusebach and the Native Americans hammered out the

Outhouse at LBJ Ranch

details of an agreement, the Meusebach-Comanche Treaty, establishing peace in their shared valley—a remarkable feat given the times and circumstances—and the town prospered.

These days, Fredericksburg is the hub of tourism in the Hill Country. Located approximately 75 miles from both Austin and San Antonio, Fredericksburg is just close enough to make a comfortable day trip. People come for the food, the boutique shopping, and most of all, the thrill of driving the winding backroads en route. Folks flock here for romantic weekends at the area's dozens of bed & breakfasts, guest houses, and boutique hotels, and it is essential to book a room in advance.

The rooms at **Hoffman Haus** are each unique, but consistently luxurious. Crisp linens, rough-hewn beams, wood floors, understated furniture, and lovely window treatments create an atmosphere that is both rustic and sophisticated. The B&B is not one house, but several buildings arranged on a nicely landscaped piece of property with breakfast delivered straight to your door each morning in a wicker basket. For an extra cozy feel, **Two Wee Cottages** are as adorable as they sound. The charming old-fashioned Granny Hein House and the bright and cheerful My Little House are tucked behind the owner's home on Morse Street, eight blocks north of Main Street. Private hot tubs, hammocks, and homemade baked goods add to the experience. **Magnolia House** is more intimate. The home is full of 1920s charm and is expertly managed by gracious owners, who woo guests with homemade cookies and delicious breakfasts made from locally sourced ingredients. Warm and homey, this B&B is tucked away on a quiet side street several blocks from the center of town and makes a relaxing getaway. **Hangar Hotel**, adjacent to the small Gillespie County Airport on the edge of town, feels a bit more masculine; the furnishings and decor are South Pacific circa 1940s. If you're unable to find a room, try calling the **Main Street Bed and Breakfast Reservation Service** or **Gastehaus Schmidt**, two local reservation services that handle a wide variety of accommodations in the area.

There are plenty of pricey places to eat in Fredericksburg, but in keeping with the back-to-basics nature of this chapter, I've chosen to highlight several casual favorites.

For treats and snacks on E. Main Street, stop in at **Clear River Pecan Company** for ice cream, or **Rustlin' Rob's** to sample some of the dozens of Texas-made jams, jellies, preserves, salsas, and even jalapeño peanut butter. Farther

VINTAGE TEXAS

The Texas Hill Country is also becoming increasingly well known for its wines. The region's limestone outcroppings, rich alluvial soil, and hot, sunny days mimic the more famous wine-growing areas of France, and for the past 40 years vintners in Texas have cultivated, nurtured, and coaxed their vineyards to bear fruit in the Lone Star State. Success has come steadily; there are now close to two dozen vineyards in the Hill Country. All offer tastings; some are complimentary, and others charge a small fee, between $1 and $5. Connoisseurs may want to mine the comprehensive Web site of the Texas Hill Country Wineries (www.texaswinetrail.com) for details about festivals, special events, a list of all member wineries, and the printable Texas Hill Country Wineries Trail Map.

As you travel the route laid out in this chapter, you will be within easy striking distance of the seven wineries that cluster along TX 290 between Johnson City and Fredericksburg. One mile east of Johnson City, Texas Hills Vineyard is on RR 2766, also known as "the road to Pedernales Falls State Park." Becker Vineyards, Grape Creek Vineyards, Torre di Pietra Vineyards, and Woodrose Wineries are all located just south of TX 290 approximately 3 miles west of Stonewall and 9 miles east of Fredericksburg; just follow the signs. Fredericksburg Winery has wines for sale right on Main Street in Fredericksburg, but to sample products from Chisholm Trail Winery, you'll need to head back out of town, travel 9 miles west on TX 290, then 2.4 miles south on Usener Road. Singing Water Vineyards, Bending Branch Winery, Comfort Cellars, and Sister Creek Vineyards are all in or near Comfort (see p. 51).

afield, the Fredericksburg Pie Company on W. Main Street tempts those who dare to stray from the well-trodden path with homemade marvels such as the bourbon orange pecan or the fresh peach pie. They tend to sell out fast, so plan on pie for a morning snack.

For lunch, the Peach Tree Tea Room is a perennial favorite. The fried green tomato BLT and ham and Swiss on raisin bread are two good examples of the dainty southern luncheon fare this casual spot specializes in. It is located on

Adams Street, just south of its intersection with Main, cleaving the thoroughfare into East and West.

Housed in a little bungalow on Adams Street, the **Sunset Grill** is a charmer that manages to be modern and cute at the same time. The dining room is casual, open and bright, with orange walls and fun accents, and the shaded patio is adorable. The smoked salmon Benedict is a creamy, smoky, salty, fluffy wonder atop a toasted English muffin, sprinkled with capers and bits of red onion, then covered with an herb-infused hollandaise—a menu standout. Paninis, burgers, and enormous salads are on the menu for lunch. The Grill stays open for dinner on Friday and Saturday nights.

Gourmet burgers are on offer at **Hondo's**. Hondo, the "clown prince" of Luckenbach (see p. 52), was a local character with a capital *C*. Though he passed away in 1976, his legend, humor, and free-spirited approach to life live on in this part of the Hill Country. The burgers here are tailored to your whims. Made in the shape of a doughnut and grilled over a mesquite fire, they can be customized with irreverent ingredients like goat cheese and poblano peppers.

Some of the best eating around Fredericksburg is actually about 10 miles outside town at a little spot called the **Hill Top Café**. The Hill Top is located atop a truly hilly section of TX 87, 10 miles west of Fredericksburg next to...well, nothing, actually. This little restaurant sits all alone, and if you didn't know to stop, you might drive right on by and miss out on the Cajun-spiced frog legs, pan-seared quail, and *kefalotiri saganaki,* an appetizer of flaming Greek cheese. If the menu sounds a little chaotic, check out the decor. Old signs, posters, license plates, and all sorts of other mementos and memorabilia fill almost every inch of wall space. But don't be fooled. This place serves up food so wonderful you'd be wise to make a reservation. The details, from the homemade bread hot from the oven to the soulful descriptions on the menu ("cornmeal breaded and fried with love") and the nights with live blues, jazz, and boogie-woogie, are all done right. Even if it sat in a valley, the Hill Top would be still the high water mark for food in the Hill Country.

If you are out and about on a beautiful day, consider driving the **Willow City Loop**, a backroad trail well worth a detour. From Fredericksburg, head 13 miles north on TX 16, then right on RR 1323, and left following signs for Willow City and the Willow City Loop. The small country road will loop around for 13 miles, climbing in and out of valleys with plenty of scenic overlooks before rejoining TX 16.

This route is very popular during the height of wildflower season in the spring, but it is a slice of unspoiled Texas all year long. Much of the route is on private land with loose livestock, and while visitors are welcome to drive through and take photos, please be respectful and refrain from hiking or picnicking.

The loop will return you to TX 16, and you can either turn south and head back toward Fredericksburg or north approximately 20 miles along FM 965 to **Enchanted Rock State Natural Area** (see box, p. 53).

Leaving Fredericksburg, take the scenic route—east on US 290 for 3 miles, then south on Old San Antonio Road, aka Old No. 9, traveling for 10.5 miles and following signs to Old Tunnel Wildlife Area until you reach the **Alamo Springs**

Willow City Loop

Café. Known for its outstanding old-fashioned burgers, Alamo Springs is the real deal. Try one of the enormous green chile cheeseburgers served with grilled onions and avocado, or order their most popular burger, a massive patty with cheddar cheese, grilled onions, and mushrooms on a jalapeño cheese bun. The café is located beside the **Old Tunnel Wildlife Management Area**; its caves, from March through October, are home to some 3 million bats, which funnel into the sky and fan out over the Hill Country each night at dusk; an amazing spectacle.

Continue on Old No. 9 to the hamlet of **Comfort**. While it's not much more than a few blocks long, what makes Comfort unique is that almost the entire downtown is on the National Registry of Historic Places. Stop in for a bite at **High's**, on High Street. Serving a mix of comfort foods (chicken pot pie on Fridays) and modern health food (a roasted veggie melt sandwich on Mondays), High's is Comfort's neighborhood café. If the slow place of this little town appeals, spend the night at **Meyer Bed and Breakfast**, a complex of buildings dating from the 1800s to early 1900s, on High Street overlooking Cypress Creek.

Comfort offers a chance to taste Hill Country wines (see box). **Singing Water Vineyards** and **Bending Branch Winery** each have intimate tasting rooms, lovely grounds, and friendly, knowledgeable staff. **Comfort Cellars** has a small tasting room on Front Street. Hop back on the road and head east along rustic RM 473 to **Sisterdale**, home of **Sister Creek Vineyards**. Housed in a restored 1800s-era cotton gin, Sister Creek has earned kudos for their moscato, a sweet and refreshing sparkling white wine.

From Sisterdale, it's a straight shot 16 miles up RR 1376/Sisterdale Road to little **Luckenbach**. If you have heard of Luckenbach, you may think of it as a kind of archetypal small town, but it is really just a cluster of worn wooden buildings nestled in the shade under the sprawling oak trees beside Grape Creek. You'll have no problem finding **The General Store**, the all-purpose store, bar, post office, and hot spot doing business since 1848. The place is old and creaky, with an uneven front porch and holes in the floor made from the boots of thousands of visitors. Want more details? Check out the town's sleek Web site, www.luckenbachtexas.com. Despite its size, Luckenbach has a reputation that has long preceded it. Immortalized in a Waylon Jennings song, "Luckenbach, Texas (Back to the Basics of Love)," the site of Willie Nelson's legendary Fourth of July parties, and host to the annual town "Hug In" in February, Luckenbach is a destination unto itself.

The route ends here, in the rural roots of the Hill Country. Luckenbach's motto, "Everybody is somebody," seems to echo LBJ's sentiments toward his Hill Country neighbors, fellow Texans, and all Americans. A little food for thought as you head back to your city, big or small.

IN THE AREA

Alamo Springs Café, 107 Alamo Road, Fredericksburg, 78624. Call 830-990-8004. Mon. and Wed. through Sun. 10–10. Web site: www.alamo springscafe.com.

Austin's, 2614 Upper Albert Road, Stonewall, 78671, at Rose Hill Manor. Call 1-877-767-3445. Wed. through Sun. 6–close. Web site: www.rose-hill .com.

Austin Visitor Center, 209 E. Sixth Street, Austin, 78701. Call 512-478-0098. Daily 9–5. Web site: www.austin texas.org.

Becker Vineyards, 464 Becker Farms Road, Stonewall, 78671. Call 830-644-2681. Mon. through Thurs. 10–5, Fri. through Sat. 10–6, Sun. 12–6. Web site: www.beckervineyards.com.

Bending Branch Winery, 142 Lindner Branch Trail, Comfort, 78013. Call 830-995-2948. Thurs. through Sat. 11–6, Sun. noon–5. Web site: www.bendingbranchwinery.com.

Chisholm Trail Winery, 2367 Usener Road, Fredericksburg, 78624. Call 1-877-990-2675 or 830-990-2675. Daily noon–6. Web site: www.chisholmtrail winery.com.

Clear River Pecan Company, 138 E. Main Street, Fredericksburg, 78624. Call 830-997-8490. Daily 7:30–7, later during summer. Web site: www.ice creamandfun.com.

ROCK CLIMBING AND BBQ

It is no surprise that the huge pink granite dome of Enchanted Rock State Natural Area is the subject of lore and legend among the Tonkawa Indians. As the tale goes, long ago a Spanish conquistador escaped captivity and eluded capture by hiding near the rock, where he was swallowed and reborn as a Tonkawa, communing with the many spirits thought to inhabit the region around the rock. The rock still casts a spell over the many visitors who come to hike and camp. The park is so popular, especially on weekends, that it often reaches capacity and is forced to close. So, if you come for a hike, you might find yourself out of luck, but you can certainly enjoy good views from several miles away, not to mention the park's parking lot. For guaranteed entrance, and a good workout, pre-schedule a rock-climbing lesson with Mountain Madness Climbing School of Austin and climb Enchanted Rock with the pros.

If you're visiting around mealtime and you get a craving for BBQ, consider driving another 20 miles north, first on FM 965, then north at the merge with TX 16, to sink your teeth into some of the finest mesquite-smoked brisket in Texas at Cooper's (see p. 21) in Llano. You will be leaving this route and picking up the Best BBQ in Texas route featured in chapter 1.

Comfort Cellars, 726 Front Street, Comfort, 78013. Call 830-995-3274. Mon., Thurs., and Fri. 10–5, Sat. 10–6, Sun. noon–5. Web site: www.comfort cellars.com.

Enchanted Rock State Natural Area, 16710 Ranch Road 965, Fredericksburg, 78624. Call 325-247-3903. Web site: www.tpwd.state.tx.us.

Fredericksburg Pie Company, 509 W. Main Street, Fredericksburg, 78624. Call 830-990-6992. Tues.

through Sat. 10–7. Web site: www .fredericksburgtexasshopping.com.

Fredericksburg Winery, 247 W. Main Street, Fredericksburg, 78624. Call 830-990-8747. Mon. through Thurs. 10–5, Fri. and Sat. 10–7:30, Sun. noon–5:30. Web site: www.fbgwinery.com.

Gastehaus Schmidt, 231 W. Main Street, Fredericksburg, 78624. Call 1-866-427-8374. Web site: www.fbg lodging.com.

The General Store, 412 Luckenbach Town Loop, Fredericksburg, 78624.

Call 1-888-311-8990 or 830-997-3224. Daily 9 till close. Web site: www .luckenbachtexas.com.

Grape Creek Vineyards, 10587 E. US 290, Stonewall, 78671. Call 830-644-2710. Mon. through Fri. 11–6, Sat. 10–6, Sun. 11–5. Web site: www.grape creek.com.

Hangar Hotel, 155 Airport Road, Fredericksburg, 78624. Call 830-997-9990. Web site: www.hangarhotel .com.

High's, 726 High Street, Comfort, 78013. Call 830-995-4995. Thurs. through Mon. 8:30–4. Web site: www .highscafeandstore.com.

Hill Top Café, 10661 US 87, Fredericksburg, 78618. Call 830-997-8922. Tues. through Thurs. and Sun. 11–2 and 5–9, Fri. and Sat. 11–2 and 5–10. Web site: www.hilltopcafe.com. Reservations recommended.

Hoffman Haus, 608 E. Creek Street, Fredericksburg, 78624. Call 830-997-6739. Web site: www.hoffmanhaus.com.

Hondo's, 312 W. Main Street, Fredericksburg, 78624. Call 830-997-1633. Wed., Thurs., and Sun. 11–10:30, Fri. and Sat. 11–midnight. Web site: www.hondosonmain.com.

Lady Bird Johnson Wildflower Center, 4801 La Crosse Avenue, Austin, 78739. Call 512-232-0100. Tues. through Sat. 9–5:30, Sun. noon–5:30. Daily in spring 9–5:30. The center's Wildflower Café is open Tues. through Sat. 10–5, Sun. 11–5. Fee. Web site: www.wildflower.org.

Lyndon Baines Johnson Library and Museum, 2313 Red River Street, Austin, 78705. Located one block west of I-35, between MLK and 26th Street. Call 512-721-0200. Daily 9–5. Free. Web site: www.lbjlibrary.org.

Lyndon B. Johnson National Historical Park, 100 Ladybird Lane, Johnson City, 78636. Call 830-868-7128. Visitors center open daily 8–5. Web site: www.nps.gov.

Magnolia House, 101 E. Hackberry Street, Fredericksburg, 78624. Call

FESTIVALS

Oktoberfest (830-997-4810; www.oktoberfestinfbg.com) and the Fredericksburg Food and Wine Festival (830-997-8515; www.fbg foodandwinefest.com) keep visitors busy in October, and the Weihnachten, or Christmas festival and market, helps make December fun. The Easter Fires Pageant commemorates the Meusebach-Comanche Treaty, which brought peace to the region, and the Stonewall Peach Jamboree (www.stonewalltexas.com) in mid-June is a sweet start of summer.

1-800-880-4374. Web site: www .magnolia-house.com.

Main Street Bed and Breakfast Reservation Service, 337 E. Main Street, Fredericksburg, 78624. Call 1-888-559-8555 or 830-997-0153. Web site: www.travelmainstreet.com.

Meyer Bed and Breakfast, 845 High Street, Comfort, 78013. Call 830-959-2304. Web site: www.meyerbedand breakfast.com.

Mountain Madness Climbing School, PO Box 3626, Cedar Park, 78613. Call 512-590-2988. Weekend

PEACHY

Ask anyone in Texas where the best peaches in the state grow and they'll point you in the direction of Gillespie County, specifically the stretch of US 290 between Stonewall and Fredericksburg. Forty percent of the peaches grown in Texas are grown right here, and if your trip coincides with peach season, the opportunities to sample are abundant.

From May through July, peach stands spring up along US 290. If you turn north off US 290 onto Gellerman Lane,

Peaches for sale at a roadside stand

just west of Stonewall (approximately 13 miles east of Fredericksburg), and continue to the intersection with FM 2721, turn west, continue to FM 1631, and go straight until you reach Main Street in Fredericksburg, approximately 35 miles later, you will pass plenty of rural stands with peaches and other Texas produce. For a complete list of area orchards, with opening hours, telephone numbers, and directions, check the Hill Country's Fruit Council's Web site, www.texaspeaches.com. Stonewall hosts the Peach Jamboree during the third week in June, so if you are in town, be sure to swing by.

classes held at Enchanted Rock State Natural Area near Fredericksburg. Fee. Web site: www.mtmadness.com.

Old Tunnel Wildlife Management Area, Office: 102 E. San Antonio, Suite B, Fredericksburg, 78624. Call 866-978-2287. Daily dawn to dusk. Web site: www.tpwd.state.tx.us.

Peach Tree Tea Room, 210 S. Adams Street, Fredericksburg, TX 78624. Call 830-997-9527. Mon. through Fri. 11–2:30, Sat. 11–3, Sun. 11–2. Web site: www.peach-tree.com.

Rose Hill Manor, 2614 Upper Albert Road, Stonewall, 78671. Call 1-877-767-3445 or 830-644-2247. Web site: www.rose-hill.com.

Rustlin' Rob's, 121 E. Main Street, Fredericksburg, 78624. Call 830-990-4750. Mon. through Fri. 10–5:30, Sat. 10–6. Web site: www.rustlinrobs.com.

Silver K Café, 209 E. Main Street, Johnson City, 78636. Call 830-868-2911. Sun. through Fri. 11–9, Sat. 11–3 and 5–9. Web site: www.silverkcafe.com.

Singing Water Vineyards, 316 Mill Dam Road, Comfort, 78013. Call 830-995-2246. Thurs. through Sat. 11–6, Sun. noon–5. Web site: www.singingwatervineyards.com.

Sister Creek Vineyards, 1142 Sisterdale Road, Sisterdale, 78006. Call 830-324-6704. Mon. through Fri. 10–5, Sat. and Sun. 10–6. Web site: www.sistercreekrvineyards.com.

Sunset Grill, 902 S. Adams Street, Fredericksburg, 78624. Call 830-997-5904. Mon. through Sat. 9–3 and Fri. and Sat. 6–9, Sun. 8–2. Web site: www.sunsetgrilltx.com.

Texas Hill Country Visitors Center, US 281, Johnson City, 78636. Call 830-868-5700. Web site: www. hillcountry info.com.

Texas Hill Country Wineries. Call 872-216-9463. Web site: www.texas winetrail.com.

Texas Hills Vineyard, 878 RR 2766, Johnson City, 78636. Call 830-868-2321. Mon. through Thurs. 10–5, Fri. and Sat. 10–6, Sun. noon–5. Web site: www.texashillsvineyard.com.

Torre di Pietra Vineyards, 10915 E. US Hwy 290, Fredericksburg, 78624. Call 830-644-2829. Daily 11–6. Web site: www.texashillcountrywine.com.

Two Wee Cottages, 108 E. Morse Street, Fredericksburg, 78624. Call 1-877-437-7739 or 830-990-8340. Web site: www.2weecottages.com.

Wildseed Farms, 425 Wildflower Hills, Fredericksburg, 78624. Seven miles east of Fredericksburg on US 290. Call 1-800-848-0078. Daily 9:30–5. Web site: www.wildseedfarms.com.

Woodrose Winery, 662 Woodrose Lane, Stonewall, 78671. Call 830-644-2539. Mon. through Fri. 11–6, Sat. 11–7, Sun. noon–6. Web site: www.woodrosewinery.com.

3 Scenic US 281 between San Antonio and Fort Worth

Getting there: This route will take you from San Antonio to Fort Worth or vice versa. From San Antonio, take TX 281 north to Blanco, a distance of approximately 51 miles. Continue north on TX 281 for another 14 miles, passing through Johnson City (see p. 41), then an additional 23 miles to **Marble Falls**. From Marble Falls, travel 13 miles to Burnet (see p. 64), then 68 miles to **Hamilton,** and 21 miles to Hico. At this juncture, you can take TX 6 west for 21 miles to detour to Dublin or continue along the route outlined below by following TX 220 north an additional 22 miles to **Glen Rose**, where it is just an easy 16.5-mile drive northwest along TX 144 to **Granbury.** Fort Worth is only a 41-mile drive north on US 377.

Highlights: From San Antonio, follow your nose to **Blanco,** home of the annual **Blanco Lavender Festival,** and press on to **Johnson City,** home of President Lyndon Baines Johnson, and **Marble Falls,** the jumping-off point into the **Highland Lakes** region. Grab a bite to eat in **Hamilton,** poke around in the charming town of **Hico,** and sip a Dublin Dr. Pepper in **Dublin.** Check out the dinosaur tracks at **Dinosaur Valley State Park** or the endangered animals at **Fossil Rim Wildlife Center,** both in **Glen Rose,** and treat yourself to a night at a bed and breakfast in **Granbury. Detour:** The Highland Lakes (see p. 63).

Total distance: 270 miles

Intersections: Chapters 1 and 2

Driving between San Antonio and Dallas/Fort Worth, many travelers choose I-35. While the highway promises speed, inevitably congestion, fender benders, and breakdowns hold up the show. Those in the know choose US 281, a route that expands and contracts, now a two-lane highway, now small-town Main Street,

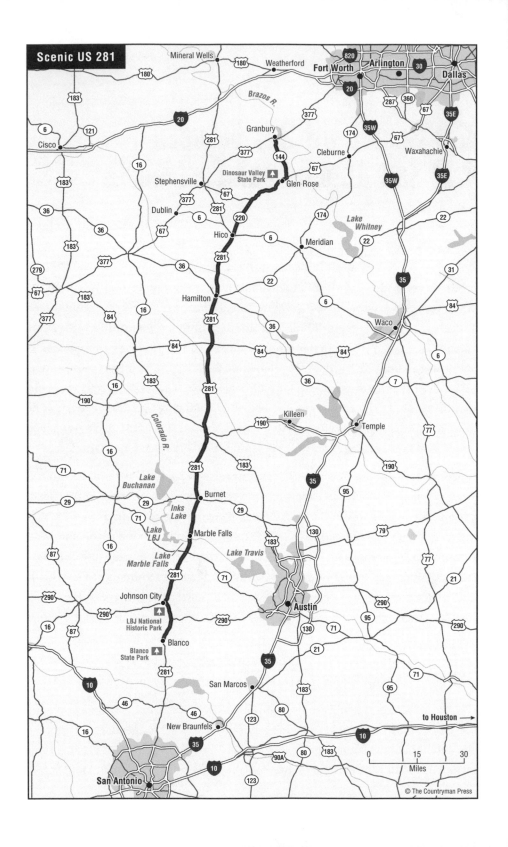

Scenic US 281

as it runs from the US-Mexican border in Texas to the US-Canadian border in North Dakota. The International Peace Garden, straddling the border, marks its northernmost point. US 281 bypasses the sprawl of cities, trading a landscape of big-box stores and chain restaurants for oak trees and pastures. This route offers up a selection of classics—diners, roadside cafés, greasy spoons, bed & breakfasts, and inns—where you can grab a bite or spend the night. Far from the hustle and bustle of the interstate, traveling the Texas backroads is a pleasure.

Leaving San Antonio, it's a breezy 50 miles north on US 281 to **Blanco.** This small ranching and trade town got its start in 1858; it was the county seat until 1890, when the title shifted to nearby Johnson City. Blanco is a typical little Hill Country hamlet, with a courthouse in the middle, shops all around, and hillside surrounding. As US 281 funnels into town, you would be likely to drive right past the **Blanco Bowling Club.** Since they've already got their hands full with locals, the folks here don't feel the need to put on a pretty face to pull potential diners in from the highway. Regulars stop in for a hot cinnamon roll to go with their morning coffee, keeping the seats warm and the Formica tables occupied. The bowling lanes are in constant use, too. Whether you start with a burger, a hot roast beef sandwich, chicken-fried steak, or a Mexican entrée, all meals should end with a piece of one of the Bowling Club's meringue pies. You'll be glad you stopped.

The Hill Country is one of Texas' wine-growing regions (see p. 47), but **Real Ale Brewing Company** in Blanco has also put down some serious roots, offering beer tastings on Fridays from 2 to 5 PM. Fireman's #4 is often cited as a must-try. Beer aficionados might like to take a brewery tour (Fridays 3 and 4 PM) and learn all the details of modern brewing from the folks who are passionate about it. Can't make it to the source? You'll find their beer throughout Texas, or just a short drive away at the **Redbud Café Market and Pub.** This delightful café is located across from the courthouse in the center of town and is owned and operated by local potters Jon and Jan Brieger. In fact, their pottery shop is right next door. The menu is fresh, thoughtful, and healthy. You'll find tasty chicken salad, hot pastrami Reubens on marble rye, pimento cheese sandwiches, homemade soups, quiches, and several delicious vegetarian options including a grilled Portabella mushroom burger and an avocado and vegetable sandwich. The restaurant is open Friday and Saturday evenings, featuring Real Ale on tap, several Hill Country wines, and live music; check the Web site for schedule. After a meal, consider stretching your legs at **Blanco State Park.** With over 100 acres of land on either side of a bend in the Blanco River, Blanco State Park is one of the oldest in the state, known for great trout fishing, shaded campsites, and river tubing—a favorite Central Texas pastime—on warm Texas days. The park is located an easy four blocks south of the Blanco town square on Park Road 23. Inquire at the park store about tube, canoe, and kayak rentals and water safety tips. There are several other state parks within striking distance of US 281, and each offers a close-up look at a piece of the Texas landscape A complete listing and maps can be found online at www.tpwd.state.tx.us.

Before heading out of Blanco, stop at the only street light in town and set your odometer to zero. Drive exactly 3.5 miles north and you will find yourself at **Mc-Call Creek Farms,** located on the east side of the highway. (If you are coming from the north, look for the farm 4 miles south of the US 281/US 290 intersection.) This small farm stand sells locally grown produce, cheeses, and eggs, and locally made jams and preserves. In their own little bakery, McCall Creek Farms makes their signature homemade custard-based ice cream (vanilla, chocolate, and peach) and various other treats. In the fields behind the farm stand you'll find **Hill Country Lavender** (see p. 73), a great place to stop in and get a good whiff of the Hill Country.

Leaving Blanco, proceed another 14 miles on US 281 to **Johnson City,** where you'll have no trouble finding the **Lyndon B. Johnson National Historical Park.** Stop in its informative visitors center and see the **Johnson Settlement,** which features several buildings dating back to the 1860s and **LBJ's boyhood home,** a tidy house that illustrates life in rural Texas in the 1920s. Just a block or two away, the **Silver K Café** is a wonderful spot for a delicious home-cooked meal served in elegant, yet casual, surroundings. (For detailed information on Johnson City and its attractions, see chapter 2.) The **Johnson Ranch,** which includes the "Texas White House," is 13 miles west on US 290 in **Stonewall.** Lodging and dining options in Johnson City, Stonewall, and the surrounding area are discussed in chapter 2. Press on from Johnson City 23 miles northward to **Marble Falls.** Just north of town, on RM 1431, sits what is left of Granite Mountain. Despite its impressive name, the huge dome of pink and red granite was quarried to the ground over time, some of it going directly to Austin, where it was used to construct the Texas Capitol. A plaque across the road from the site tells the tale.

If you pull into town on a weekend and don't notice the **Bluebonnet Café's**

THE HIGHLAND LAKES

Both Marble Falls and Burnet are access points to the region's chain of six lakes, known collectively as the Highland Lakes.

During the early 1800s, the Colorado River was prone to flooding, and resulting logjams made the river impassable, cutting off trade and transportation to and from riverside communities. Finally, in 1935, technology caught up to the problem; the Lower Colorado River Authority (LCRA) constructed a series of six dams along the river to control flooding, creating the Highland Lakes. Here are the lakes listed from north to south.

Lake Buchanan is the largest and northernmost lake, and known as a nesting place of the American bald eagle. Canyon of the Eagles Resort, in Burnet, has a lodge, campgrounds, cabins, and a restaurant, all in the middle of a 1,000-acre park and preserve. The Vanishing Texas River Cruise, also located in Burnet, hosts ecological cruises on the lake, and Lake Buchanan Adventures runs tours and offers boat rentals. At night, stargaze with the Austin Astronomical Society at the Eagle Eye Observatory (www.austinastro.org).

Inks Lake is best known for its location beside the popular Longhorn Cavern State Park. The park features tours of a large river-formed cavern, once a meeting area for Comanche Indians and a hideout for Confederate soldiers.

Lake LBJ has more humans than wildlife and gets crowded on warm, sunny days. Homes line the lake's shores, with the resort development of Horseshoe Bay anchoring its southern edge; boaters crisscross the waters all weekend long. The rich soil surrounding the lake benefits Lost Creek Vineyards, near Sunrise Beach on the northwestern tip. Spicewood Vineyards is a short drive south along TX 71.

Lake Marble Falls feels more like a wide spot in the river than a lake, and its steep rocky shores do little to change the impression. The town is a good place to refuel, get supplies, or enjoy a meal.

Lake Travis is very close to Austin. Crammed with numerous day-trippers and party boats, expect exuberance. Pleasant parks and numerous funky eateries keep things mellow.

Lake Austin is well within the city limits and rife with kayakers, cruises, restaurants, and live music, all with a uniquely Austin vibe.

Online, www.highlandlakes.com, www.lakesandhills.com, www.lcra.org, and www.texasoutside.com spell out the details.

rather small red and white sign, you'll be sure to notice the line of hungry diners snaking out the door and down the porch steps. With a reputation for one of the best honest-to-goodness breakfasts in Texas, the Bluebonnet also keeps customers coming with classic southern comfort foods such as fried okra, catfish, chicken-fried steaks, pot roast, and chicken and dumplings. If you choose nothing else at Bluebonnet, do as the sign on the wall says and "try some pie." From cream to meringue, the Bluebonnet makes plenty of pies each day; your waitresses can recite the long list with impressive efficiency. The Bluebonnet is a perennial Texas favorite, and one that accepts cash only.

Speaking of bluebonnets, the next stop on the route is **Burnet**, 13 miles farther north. The Bluebonnet Capital of Texas, Burnet is host of the **Bluebonnet Festival** (www.bluebonnetfestival.org), complete with a parade, carnival, food, and music, in April. Between April and June, the proliferation of bluebonnets in this region, not to mention other native Texas wildflowers, can be absolutely stunning. Visit the Burnet Chamber of Commerce and ask for a "Scenic Drive and Wildflower Trail Map," or print one at www.burnetchamber.org.

It takes close to an hour and a half to drive the 67 miles north from Burnet to Hamilton, but the time passes quickly as you watch the rugged terrain soften into green hills. Hamilton got its start in the mid-1800s when the first settlers arrived, but the town wasn't incorporated until 1911, after the railroads came through. The town was known for its cotton gins, as well as numerous saloons, which until Prohibition lined an entire side of the town square.

These days, Hamilton is a little less rough around the edges and makes a pleasant place to stop for a bite to eat. Just off the square, **Wenzel Lonestar Meat Company** features the playfully named "Bite My Butt Fridays," featuring barbequed pulled pork sandwiches to welcome the weekend, and deli items all week long.

Take US 281 north out of town. In a few miles—just follow the billboard reminders and directions—you'll find the **Dutchman's Hidden Valley Country Store**. Started as a roadside pecan and produce stand decades ago, this rambling shop now sells hundreds of items ranging from Reuben sandwiches and homemade fudge and candies to bison jerky and handcrafted candles. Dutchman's is a welcome throwback to a time when vacationing families would steer the station wagon into the parking lot and unload for ice cream. During hunting season, Dutchman's will process deer meat for a reasonable fee.

Dutchman's Hidden Valley Country Store in Hamilton

Travel 21 miles farther and you'll find yourself in **Hico**, which you'll notice right away differs from its neighbors. The town is not situated around a courthouse, but laid out as a small boulevard, with grass, benches, and walkways in the center. Originally, the town was a little settlement located a few miles away on Honey Creek, but when the Texas Central Railroad came through the region in 1880, the citizens relocated to be beside the tracks. Just a decade later, a fire destroyed close to half of the town, and a few weeks later a second fire destroyed almost all of what remained. The town rebuilt, this time in stone; the sturdy buildings you see now are from that era.

Hico is a great spot to spend the night, and there are several lodging choices in town. Since each establishment has just a room or two, I've listed several; they are all located in town.

Nothing But Time is a cute-as-a-button 1905 cottage that's been cut in half,

DETOUR TO DUBLIN

What is a "Dublin Dr. Pepper"? While most consumers recognize the Dr. Pepper brand, the addition of "Dublin" may leave you scratching your head.

Dr. Pepper was invented at the Old Corner Drug Store in Waco, Texas, in 1885 by a pharmacist fiddling with soda flavorings. The drug store owner named it Dr. Pepper and sold it at the soda fountain to an enthusiastic public. In 1891, a Texas businessman tried the fizzy concoction, loved it, and set up the first Dr. Pepper bottling plant franchise in the tiny town of Dublin, Texas, 80 miles west of Waco, and serviced the three counties around it. In 1904, Dr. Pepper made its national debut at the St. Louis World's Fair. Though its roots remain in Texas, its countrywide popularity has grown ever since. These days, the Dr. Pepper we know as the national brand is still headquartered in Waco, and there devotees can visit the Dr. Pepper Museum (www.drpeppermuseum.com).

What makes Dublin Dr. Pepper different is its commitment to Imperial Pure Cane Sugar. When the price of sugar rose in the 1970s, other plants replaced the sugar in the original recipe with corn syrup, but the Dublin plant stuck with pure sugar. It's the essence of "dancin' with who brung ya." The sugar gives the drink its distinctive taste; considering that Dr. Pepper itself is already something different in a world dominated by two other sodas, Dublin Dr. Pepper is something really special. So, go ahead, have a taste and be a pepper, too.

moved, and renovated from top to bottom at its current location on Hickory Street. The host is warm and welcoming, the accommodations are clean and comfortable, and white rocking chairs on the front porch feel custom-made for sitting. The **Old Rock House Bed and Breakfast** is a little home on six acres surrounded by centenarian live oak trees. The 1870s home, true to its name, was built of rocks, left exposed in the home's interior, with hardwood floors and other rustic touches.

The **Koffee Kup Family Restaurant** is just past the merger of US 281 and TX 6. The menu here is simple, well priced, and to the point, but it's the extras that make the difference. Homemade doughnuts, fresh-baked bread, and a dozen different kinds of pies piled high with meringues and whipped cream keep locals and out-of-towners stopping in day after day. Downed the last bite of pie, but your sweet tooth is still aching for more? Mosey next door to **Wiseman House Chocolates** for a treat. Located in a lovely Queen Anne Victorian, the shop is fancy and the chocolates are scrumptious. The Snack Pack won't force you to choose between sweet, salty, or creamy; it includes: two peanut butter meltaways, two almond toffee squares, and one pecan caramel cluster.

Hico has a charming, small-town western atmosphere, making it unique to the region. Strolling around town, you'll find Pecan Street to be lined with boutiques and antiques shops selling nostalgia, artwork, and Texana. Take a peek in **Blue Star Trading**, a place that bills itself as a "ranch outfitter," but is much more. From home furnishings to jewelry to artwork by some of Texas' rising stars, along with utilitarian ropes and knives for working horses and hunting, Blue Star sells it all in their lovingly restored 1890s storefront. A block or two off Pecan Street, stop in and browse at **Homestead**, the upscale antiques, furniture, and fixtures shop on Elm Street and leave inspired. Originally doing business in Fredericksburg, the owners of Homestead heeded pleas from folks in the Dallas/Fort Worth area to move their store closer. The Hico store is as sumptuous as the original and just an hour's drive from either city.

Back in the center of town, the small collection at the **Billy the Kid Museum** has a tale to tell. As the story goes, in 1950, as local resident Brushy Bill Roberts lay dying, he professed to be Billy the Kid. Thus Hico was linked

Home furnishings for sale at Homestead in Hico

Dinosaur Valley State Park

to the outlaw legend. Fact or fiction, you decide, but be sure to order a Dublin Dr. Pepper (see p. 66) to sip at the counter while you sit and ponder.

Moving along north, it is a short, 20-minute drive to **Glen Rose**, once a successful mill town, a moonshiner's paradise during Prohibition, and now a spa town for those seeking the healing effects of its mineral-rich waters. These days most visitors come to ogle at the fantastically well-preserved dinosaur tracks in **Dinosaur Valley State Park**. While local fishermen reported seeing the tracks in the Paluxy River bottom as early as 1910, it wasn't until the 1930s that scientific investigations and inquiries earned them worldwide recognition. The park opened in 1972 and has been a popular tourist attraction, perhaps best known for its two huge dinosaur statues just inside the entrance. The Tyrannosaurus and Brontosaurus, both recycled from the Sinclair Oil Company's exhibit at the 1964 World's Fair, stand side by side. Be sure to read all about one sculpture's identity crisis as was revealed along the way: one of the sculptures isn't anatomically correct. From Glen Rose, take FM 205 west to TX 59, following the signs for a total of 5 miles.

Another natural draw near Glen Rose is the **Fossil Rim Wildlife Center**, which has over 60 species of animals, some exotic and many endangered, roaming freely throughout a 2,700-acre spread. A paved 9-mile road winds through the peaceful wooded valley; visitors are encouraged to drive through at a leisurely pace while the giraffes, zebras, ostriches, emus, deer, and antelope roam. Allow at least an hour and a half to complete the circuit. To get to the preserve from Glen Rose, take US 67 to CR 2008 and follow signs; the trip is approximately 5 miles in total. Alternatively, drive past the entrance to the park on CR 2008, continue a

CHICKEN-FRIED ANYTHING

You cannot travel the Texas backroads without coming across more than your fair share of food "chicken-fried." While the term clearly denotes chicken, the subject of the chicken-frying itself is often steak—remember, you're still in Texas. You'll encounter it everywhere, and may wonder just exactly what it is. The lineage of culinary oddities is not always clear, and it can be difficult to pin down details. However, here are two keys to understanding chicken-fried steak: tough meat and Germans.

Tough meat is an age-old, universal problem, and many home cooks have devised ingenious ways to solve it. From stews to BBQ (see pp. 17–35), the cooking is crucial. Time and heat are the key components to juiciness, and while slow cooking often does the trick, so does a fast hot sear. All across the South, cooks fried chicken. Dredging the meat in salt, seasonings, and flour and setting it in a pan of hot grease meant that the meat inside the coating cooked up hot and quick, sealing in juices and steam. Somewhere along the way, perhaps during the Depression, someone figured, "Why not beef?" Whether it was a home cook in the Texas Hill Country or a cowboy cook with his chuck wagon, a steak got a dip in flour, some time in the pan, and was served up with gravy. That, come to think of it, sounds a whole lot like Wiener schnitzel.

In the late 1800s, Germans immigrated to Texas, particularly Central Texas, in record numbers, and brought their recipes with them. Schnitzel is the generic German word for cutlet; Wiener schnitzel is a cutlet, breaded, fried, and served with a squirt of lemon. While in Germany, this technique was usually reserved for veal and sometimes pork, in America beef took precedence. *Rahmschnitzel* is similar, with a cream gravy in place of the lemon.

This brings us to a dining ritual peculiar to Texas. Ordering a meal here means answering a series of questions. Order chicken-fried steak and they'll ask "White or brown?" by which they mean gravy. Order tea and you'll be asked, "Regular or sweet?" Even dessert prompts a question: "Blue Bell on top?" (see p. 83). Confused? Just answer yes, and you'll always be right.

mile or so uphill, take a right at the fork onto CR 2009, and follow signs to the overlook, where you can park for free, shop in the gift shop, pet any sociable animals, grab a bite at the **Overlook Café,** and spend some time enjoying the valley views from the deck.

Back in town, **Hammond's** has been feeding Glen Rose since 1966. If you find it hard to believe the building is that old, it's not. Hammond's has burned to the ground and been rebuilt. Twice. A classic small-town BBQ joint, the restaurant is painted bright red on the outside and filled with old license plates and knick-knacks inside, including a huge sign that welcomes diners with a jovial "Howdy Folks." The brisket, turkey, ribs, and sausage are favorites, and the fact that the sauce is served hot in a little jar on the side makes the meal. Stop in for a piece of pie at the **Pie Peddlers**. The two friends who own this darling shop are recently retired kindergarten teachers who used to teach on weekdays and bake pies on weekends. Trading the patience and creativity needed in the classroom for piecrusts has meant good news for Glen Rose. Pie Peddlers is now open Thursday through Saturday, which means more pie for everyone.

Though the town is small, accommodations run the gamut here in Glen Rose. In the early 1900s, the **Inn on the River** was part of a compound known as Dr. Snyder's Drugless Health Sanitarium; the serenity of the inn still draws those in search of repose. The rooms are snug, decorated with soothing muted colors, ample linens, and delicate antiques. The grounds are spacious, with a pool, large oak trees, and Adirondack chairs scattered about. The onsite restaurant serves an outstanding four-course prix fixe dinner on weekends, with seatings at 6 and 8. If the surroundings haven't helped you relax and reenergize, the meal just might. Next door, **The Glen Hotel,** opened in 1928, still doles out small-town hospitality to all its guests. The entire boutique hotel has just been given a facelift, from the inviting lobby with its deep couches to lightly decorated rooms with renovated bathrooms, and guests seem thrilled with its rejuvenation. Nearby, the **Country Woods Inn** is consistently lauded for being one of the area's most child-friendly establishments, and it's easy to see why. At the Country Woods, you can spend the night in one of 12 cabins or a restored Santa Fe Railroad car, stroll the inn's 40 shaded acres along the Paluxy River, feed the horses, tell stories around a campfire, and eat breakfast in the barn; it's a true backroads experience.

For an experience more like spending the night at a friend's house, try **Bussey's Something Special,** an eclectic and homey spot with two cozy rooms

Downtown Granbury

Nutt House Hotel in Granbury

for rent. Breakfast isn't served, but the rooms are stocked with early-morning essentials such as coffee, cereal, granola bars, and fruit. Be sure to ask Morris about his fossil collection and Susan about her knitting. At the other end of the spectrum, you can pamper yourself at the **Rough Creek Lodge,** 10 miles west of Glen Rose on County Road 2013. There is no roughing it here; the rooms, grounds, spa, and onsite restaurant are all well-appointed and impeccably maintained. Because of its fairly remote location and the fact that it is so self-contained, the lodge is a popular corporate retreat center and weekend getaway for folks from the big city. At Rough Creek, hunting and fishing go hand in hand with aromatherapy and massage and the pseudo-rustic decor—primarily leathers, woods, and rich fabrics.

Another 16 miles north on TX 144 is the historic town of **Granbury.** In 1969, a dam was built across the Brazos River, forming Lake Granbury and the waterfront property that is the town's hallmark. These days, fishing, boating, and golf are popular pastimes for locals and visitors alike, and the town strikes a nice balance between hometown and vacation spot. The town's charm, coupled with its location on the shores of Lake Granbury, just 40 miles southwest of Fort Worth, make Granbury popular for weekend retreats.

In 1866, the Nutt brothers donated a parcel of wild riverfront property to be used for a settlement; one soon sprang up and it became a trading center. Livestock auctions and tons of peanuts, pecans, peaches, grain, and cotton passed through the town and the coming of the railroad boosted development to an unprecedented level. Lining the town square today are several dozen of the solid, two-story limestone buildings built in the 1880s, the height of Granbury's prosperity. The Old Opera House and the red brick train depot, now a museum, are two examples.

The historic **Nutt House Hotel** is a great example of late-19th-century Texas architecture and a good place for folks who like a well-seasoned hotel and a location right on the square. The Nutt House dates back to late 1893, when it was constructed to house overnight guests shopping at the mercantile store owned by the Nutt brothers. The seven suites have been remodeled, with antiques, photographs, and artwork representing the hotel's history; modern touches such as rich colors and cozy European linens give it an updated feel. Downstairs, the **Nutt House Restaurant** offers fine dining amid the historic surroundings. Guests of the hotel get to eat breakfast here; others can have a seat at the table for lunch, dinner, and weekend brunch. The dinner menu consistently features steaks, southern-style sides like mashed potatoes, green beans, and grilled squash, as

LAVENDER

Pull into Blanco at the right time of year and you might detect a hint of lavender in the air. Blanco and the surrounding area are home to over a dozen lavender farms, with new ones opening each year, thanks to the observant eye of lavender pioneer Robb Kendrick. It was Kendrick who, while on a photo shoot in Provence, noticed the similarities between the soil and climate of the South of France and the Texas Hill Country. Lavender blooming season usually stretches from May through July, with the annual Blanco Lavender Festival held in the peak month of May. Visit www.blancolavenderfestival.com for details and to download a map of farm tours held throughout the growing season.

The conditions that favor lavender also favor grapes, a fact that the Beckers noticed when they visited France at about the same time as Mr. Kendrick. They returned home to open Becker Vineyard, one of the now many vineyards in Central Texas; see p. 47 for a partial listing. Print a map from the Texas Hill Country Wine Trail's Web site: www.texaswine trail.com or pick one up on your travels. Driving to and from the many lavender farms and vineyards will take you along some of the most peaceful and scenic backroads in the Hill Country.

well as rich desserts. Across the square, the **Nutshell Eatery & Bakery** is a great place for breakfast, lunch, or brunch. The place is casual, with simple seating and decor, and the hearty no-nonsense pancakes, gooey French toast, and thick sandwiches on homemade bread hit the spot.

Then, of course, there is the lake. Lake Granbury has several nice places to stay surrounding it. A favorite of honeymooners and anniversary celebrators is the **Inn on Lake Granbury**, one of those decadent places that makes special occasions even more special. In many ways the inn feels more like a resort, with two acres of manicured lawn, a flagstone pool, lake views, and wonderfully appointed rooms decorated in soothing, earthy colors with thick window treatments and rugs. Some have fireplaces, others access to outdoor sitting areas, but all are entirely relaxing. Guests rave about the breakfasts. Make reservations well in advance; this one fills up quick. **Baker Street Harbour Waterfront Bed & Breakfast** is another favorite, with fantastic views of the grounds and lake beyond. Shiny wood floors, spotless bathrooms, and quirky room layouts, some with beds tucked under the eaves, give the rooms here a cozy, romantic feel, which may explain why so many guests come to celebrate anniversaries.

The fresh and crispy fish tacos and Saturday-night shrimp boil at **Stumpy's Lakeside Grill** make for good waterside dining in Granbury. Located a few minutes' drive from town, Stumpy's is casual and family-friendly, with a spacious outdoor patio overlooking the boat-filled marina.

The route ends here, where you are poised to follow US 377 to either Dallas (73 miles) or Fort Worth (42 miles). As the population of Central Texas grows, US 281 is somewhat endangered, becoming entangled in highway exchanges in some places and widened for more traffic in others. So drive it while you can, and spend a dollar or two along the way to support all those local spots providing the simple thrills that make the journey worthwhile.

IN THE AREA

Baker Street Harbour Waterfront Bed & Breakfast, 511 S. Baker Street Granbury, 76048. Call 817-579-8811. Web site: www.bakerstharbour.com.

Billy the Kid Museum, 116 N. Pecan Street, Hico, 76457. Call 1-800-361-HICO or 254-796-2523. Daily Mon. through Sat. 11–5, Sun. 1–5. Fee. Web site: www.billythekidmuseum.com.

Blanco Bowling Club, 310 4th Street, Blanco, TX, 78606. Call 830-833-4416. Web site: www.blancobowlingclub .com.

Blanco Chamber of Commerce, 312 Pecan Street, Blanco, 78606. Call 830-833-5101. Web site: www.blanco chamber.com.

Blanco State Park, PO Box 493, Blanco, 78606. Call 830-833-4333. Fee. Web site: www.tpwd.state.tx.us.

Bluebonnet Café, 211 US 281, Marble Falls, TX 78654. Call 830-693-2344. Mon. through Thurs. 6–8, Fri. and Sat. 6–9, Sun. 6–1:45. Web site: www.bluebonnetcafe.net. Cash only.

Blue Star Trading, 112 S. Pecan Street, Hico, 76457. Call 254-796-2828. Mon. through Sat. 9–6, Sun. 1–5. Web site: www.bluestartrading.com.

Burnet Chamber of Commerce, 229 S. Pierce Street, Burnet, 78611. Call 512-756-4297. Web site: www.burnet chamber.org.

Bussey's Something Special, 202 Hereford Street, Glen Rose, 76043. Call 254-897-4843. Web site: www .busseys.net.

Canyon of the Eagles Resort, 16942 RR 2341, Burnet, 78611. Call 512-334-2070. Web site: www.canyonofthe eagles.com.

Country Woods Inn, 420 Grand Avenue # C, Glen Rose, 76043. Call 817-279-3002. Web site: www.country woodsinn.com.

Dinosaur Valley State Park, PO Box 396, Glen Rose, 76043 (about 3 miles west of Glen Rose off FM 205). Call

254-897-4588. Fee. Web site: www .tpwd.state.tx.us.

Dublin Dr. Pepper Bottling Plant and Old Doc's Soda Shop, 105 E. Elm, Dublin, 76446. Call 1-888-398-1024. Daily 10–5. Web site: www .dublindrpepper.com.

Dutchman's Hidden Valley Country Store, 3408 US 281, Hamilton, 76531. Call 254-386-3018. Thurs. through Tues. 9–6. Web site: www.dutchmans -hiddenvalley.com.

Fossil Rim Wildlife Center, 2299 County Road 2008, Glen Rose, 76043. Seasonal hours, generally daily 8:30–5:30. Last car admitted two hours before close. Fee. Overlook Café open daily 9:30–5:30. Call 254-897-2960. Web site: www.fossilrim.com.

The Glen Hotel, 201 S.W. Barnard Street, Glen Rose, 76043. Call 254-898-2068. Web site: www.glenhotel texas.com.

Glen Rose Convention & Visitors Bureau, 1505 N.E. Big Bend Trail, Glen Rose, 76043. Call 1-888-346-6282 or 254-897-3081. Web site: www.glenrosetexas.net.

Granbury Convention & Visitors Bureau, 621 E. Pearl Street, Granbury, 76048. Call 887-936-1201 or 682-936-1200. Web site: www .granburytx.com.

Hammond's, 1106 NE Big Bend Trail, Glen Rose, 76043. Call 254-897-3008. Tues. 11–3 (buffet only), Thurs.

through Sat. 11–8, Sun. and Mon. 11–3. Web site: www.hammondsbbq.com.

Hico Chamber of Commerce, Box 533 or 120 W. First Street, Hico 76457. Call 254-796-4620. Web site: www.hico-tx.com.

Hill Country Lavender, 4524 US 281, Blanco, TX 78606. Call 830-833-2294. Web site: www.hillcountrylavender.com.

Homestead, 100 N. Elm Street, Hico, 76457. Call 254-796-2510. Mon. through Sat. 10–5:30, Sun 1–5. Web site: www.homesteadhico.com.

Inn on Lake Granbury, 205 W. Doyle Street, Granbury, 76048. Call 1-877-573-0046. Web site: www.innonlakegranbury.com.

Inn on the River, 205 SW Barnard Street, Glen Rose 76043. Call 1-800-575-2101 or 254-897-2929. Restaurant serving dinner Fri. and Sat. 6 and 8; reservations required. Web site: www.innontheriver.com.

Koffee Kup Family Restaurant, TX 6 and US 281, Hico, 76457. Call 254-796-4839. Daily 6–9:30. Web site: www.koffeekupfamilyrestaurant.com. Cash only.

Lake Buchanan Adventures, 16942 RR 2341, Burnet, 78611. Call 512-756-9911. Web site: www.lakebuchananadventures.com.

Longhorn Cavern State Park, PO Box 732 or 6211 Park Road 4 South, Burnet, 78611. Call 1-877-441-2283 or 512-756-4680. Web site: www.longhorncaverns.com.

Lost Creek Vineyards, 1129 Ranch Road 2233, Sunrise Beach, 78643. Call 325-388-3753. Web site: www.lostcreekvineyard.com.

Marble Falls/Lake LBJ Chamber of Commerce, 801 US 281, Marble Falls, 78654. Call 830-693-4449. Web site: www.marblefalls.org.

McCall Creek Farms Market, 4524 N. US 281, Blanco, 78606. Call 830-833-0442. Seasonal, call ahead. Web site: www.mccallcreekfarms.com.

Nothing But Time, 306 Hickory Street, Hico, 76457. Call 254-796-4666. Web site: www.hicobandb.com.

Nutshell Eatery & Bakery, 137 E. Pearl Street, Granbury, 76048. Call 817-279-8989. Daily 7–5. Web site: www.nutshelleateryandbakery.com.

Nutt House Hotel, 119 E. Bridge Street, Granbury, 76048. Call 817-279-8688. Web site: www.nutt-hotel.com.

Nutt House Restaurant, 119 E. Bridge Street, Granbury, 76048. Call 817-279-8688. Lunch daily 11–2; dinner Mon. through Thurs. 5–9, Fri. and Sat. 5–10. Web site: www.nutt-hotel.com. Reservations recommended.

Old Rock House Bed and Breakfast, 302 E. Third Street, Hico, 76457. Call 214-538-1201. Web site: www.oldrockhousehico.com.

Pie Peddlers, 102 Walnut Street, Glen Rose, 76043. Call 254-897-9228.

Thurs. through Sat. 10–6, Sun. 11–4. Web site: www.piepeddlers.com.

Real Ale Brewing Company, 231 San Saba Court, Blanco, 78606. Call 830-833-2534. Fri. 2–5. Web site: www.realalebrewing.com.

Redbud Café Market and Pub, 410 4th Street, Blanco, 78606. Call 830-833-0202. Mon. through Thurs. 10:30–3:30, Fri. and Sat. 10:30–9. Web site: www.redbud-cafe.com.

Rough Creek Lodge, 5165 County Road 2013, Glen Rose, 76043. Call 254-488-4753. Web site: www.rough creek.com.

Spicewood Vineyards, 1419 Kromer Lane, Spicewood, 78669. Call 830-693-5328. Web site: www.spicewood vineyards.com.

Stumpy's Lakeside Grill, 2323 S. Morgan, Granbury, 76048. Call 817-279-1000. Tues. through Sat. 11–9, Sun. 11–3. Web site: www.lake granburymarinainc.com.

Vanishing Texas River Cruise, 16942 RR 2341, Burnet, 78611. Call 1-800-4RIVER4 or 512-756-6986. Web site: www.vtrc.com.

Wenzel Lonestar Meat Company, 209 N. Bell Street, Hamilton, 76531. Call 254-386-8242. Mon. through Sat. 8–6, Sun. during deer season. Web site: www.wenzellonestarmeat.com.

Wiseman House Chocolates, 406 S. Grubbs, Hico, 76457. Call 254-796-2565. Mon. through Sat. 10–6m, Sun 1–5. Web site: www.wisemanhouse chocolates.com.

4 Main Street, Texas

Getting there: Brenham is located on US 290, about a 90-minute drive from either Austin or Houston. The lower portion of this route is bound by I-10, the interstate between Houston and San Antonio.

To begin the route, from Brenham, take TX 237 12 miles west to Burton and from there an additional 10 miles to Round Top and 16 miles farther to La Grange. From La Grange, you can take either US 77 south 17 miles to Schulenburg or 22 miles on FM 609 to Flatonia. From Flatonia, it is just another 8 miles south to Moulton on TX 95 and 20 miles west on FM 532 to Gonzales. Backing up, you can also leave Brenham and head 10 miles east on US 290 to Chappell Hill, then north 18 miles on FM 1155 to Washington-on-the-Brazos.

Highlights: Pick up an ice cream cone in **Brenham** or a *kolache* in **La Grange**, two of the largest towns in this verdant region, and stroll the town squares and classic Texas main streets. Tiny **Round Top** has must-try dining and events that draw crowds by the thousands. Start your tour of the painted churches of Texas, lovely reminders of the area's strong German heritage. Restaurants in **Schulenberg, Moulton, Shiner,** and **Gonzales** offer outstanding steaks, beer, and BBQ, respectively. This route also features a trail of Texas history, from the first shots of the Texas Revolution fired in **Gonzales** to the signing of the constitution of the Republic of Texas in **Washington-on-the Brazos.** Detours to the delightful small towns of **Burton, Flatonia,** and **Chappell Hill** round out the trip.

Total distance: Many of the sites on this route are between Brenham and Flatonia, a distance of 60 miles.

Intersections: Chapters 2 and 5.

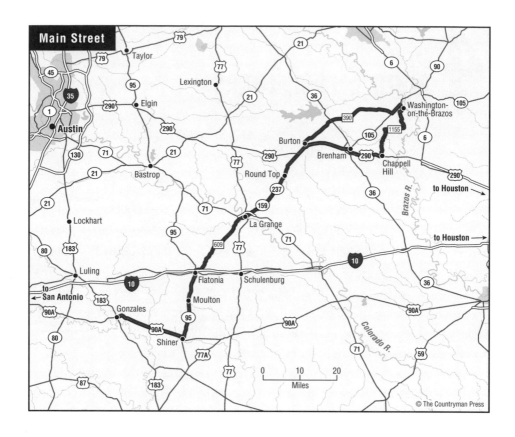

This route traverses the southern tip of what is technically known as the Prairies and Lakes region of Texas, a swath of green that stretches from the Oklahoma border to just south of I-10, where the terrain becomes scrubbier as it makes its way toward the Gulf of Mexico.

Travelers have tended to whiz past this region in the past, but these days they're finding time to stop. Since it is fairly compact, folks come for a day trip from Austin, San Antonio, or even Houston, and many have discovered that it makes a wonderful weekend getaway. Less crowded than the Hill Country— Antiques Fairs and the run of Shakespeare at Winedale in Round Top excepted (see p. 88–89)—the area is also less expensive. Even if you are simply passing through, the ease of the region and the proximity of interesting towns to the high-way—you can be off the beaten track in minutes—make it a terrific spot to stop for a meal. While it's steeped in history and beautiful as can be, with horses and cattle grazing on the gently rolling hills at every bend, when you get right down to it, this route is really all about the food. Sweet *kolaches,* slices of pie, and ice cream. Steaks, BBQ, and burgers. Maybe it's the country air or the lovely setting, but good food just tastes great out here.

Located almost midway between Austin and Houston on US 290, **Brenham** has long been at the center of the action in Washington County. A magnet for immigrants, by the mid-1800s, Brenham was home to African Americans, Germans, Jews, and various European newcomers, and all have left their mark. One enduring tradition is Maifest, a community-wide celebration of German heritage held each year, in mid-May. The town is a well-located home base from which to explore the area; the first order of business is finding a spot to spend the night.

Built in the 1920s and renovated and reopened as a bed & breakfast in 2008, **The Brenham House B&B** greets guests with five cozy, well-appointed rooms and freshly baked treats. The three-course breakfast makes getting out of the warm and comfortable beds more than worth the effort. Ask the affable owners Susan and James about the house's German Lutheran roots; they are also a font of knowledge with respect to the area, and lovely people to boot. Really want to get away from it all? Try the **Murski Homestead B&B**. The expansive countryside property is home to cows, donkeys, horses, and other farm animals; many

Texas denizens

guests choose to spend their stay on the porch swings taking in the view. While the surroundings are decidedly rural, the rooms and breakfasts are sophisticated, with obvious attention to quality and detail. Gracious owners a plus.

Located right in town, the **Ant Street Inn** does have the look and feel of an old-style inn; it's just as cozy as an intimate bed & breakfast. The 14 rooms have different features to recommend them. Try the San Antonio for size, the Mobile for its two queen beds, and the Memphis for the inn's most unusual fixture, a non-working, century-old freight elevator in the center of the room. Another choice, the historic **Fairview Bed and Breakfast**, also has a variety of rooms to choose from. The prairie-style home was built in 1925, and the solid structure is both utilitarian and graceful. Rooms are simply furnished and decorated in soothing colors, some overlooking the pool and the spacious grounds below. The Carriage

House Suite has a small kitchen, and the Pool House Suites are newly constructed, but include old-timey details such as stained glass windows.

Be sure to ask your hosts where they enjoy eating in town, or hit the road again to one of the options in nearby Round Top or Chappell Hill. If you'd like to dine in Brenham for an easy lunch, try **Must Be Heaven**, a local sandwich franchise with several other shops in towns farther afield. Stop in and order a roast beef, peanut butter and jelly, or the regional classic, pimento cheese, among others, to eat in or take on the road. Save room for pie. If you are in the mood for a night out, consider dining at **Ernie's**, an American bistro housed in an old brick

---

BLUE BELL

Order a slice of pie or a piece of Texas sheet cake and you'll be asked if you'd like it with **Blue Bell**. Almost everyone says yes, but if you are new to Texas, then Blue Bell might be new to you. This area of Texas—Washington County—is known throughout the state for its milk production, and as you drive the backroads, you'll notice plenty of cows lazing around the fields, munching their way through the thick green grass. Those cows turn out to be very productive when it comes to milk. As early as 1911, local farmers banded together to start the Brenham Creamery Company to produce butter, and later ice cream, with all the leftover cream from their efficient cows. In 1930, they changed their name to **Blue Bell Creameries**.

The ice cream was a huge hit, and generations of Texans have grown up enjoying scoops of Blue Bell. Although the brand is only sold in 20 percent of the nation's supermarkets, primarily in the South and Southwest, it is one of the top-three best-selling ice creams in the nation. That means that folks down here have strong brand allegiance—plus they eat a lot of ice cream. A Texas treat with southern appeal, Blue Bell has become such an icon that people don't order "ice cream," they just order "Blue Bell."

Blue Bell's headquarters are in Brenham; guided tours of their modern production facility are offered on weekdays. The tours are first-come, first-served, approximately 45 minutes long, and conclude with a scoop of ice cream. Check www.bluebell.com for details.

building in downtown Brenham. The menu features grilled meats, seafoods, and vegetables, all of which pair nicely with the business-casual surroundings. **Volare** is a good bet for Italian. Housed in an old clapboard home from the 1800s, this upscale restaurant has wowed Brenham with classic Italian meals since opening in 1997.

Continue your trip by driving 12 miles west of Brenham on US 290 to diminutive **Burton**. The town, established in 1862, is now best known as the site of the **Burton Cotton Gin and Museum,** which makes it the go-to place for all information on cotton processing. If you visit in mid-April, you may have the pleasure of attending the Cotton Gin Festival, but otherwise folks come just to relax in this sleepy little town; for them the **Knittel Homestead** awaits. The inn's six guest rooms are housed in two historic buildings on the homestead, one a restored farmhouse circa 1914, the other a two-story 1870 Victorian designed to look like a Mississippi riverboat. The rooms are spacious, clean, bright, and individually decorated; some are rather feminine, others a bit more masculine, and some feel just like home. Five of the rooms have queen beds; one attic room has four twins, making it a good choice for friends traveling together. Guests always enjoy the outstanding hot breakfasts served each morning.

If you're visiting on a weekend, have dinner at the **Brazos Belle,** the divine French restaurant in town. From sauces to salad dressings, everything here is made from scratch by Chef Andre and served in an elegant old building that was

---

STOP AND SMELL THE ROSES

Stop and smell the roses at the **Antique Rose Emporium** in Independence, where the collection of fragrant roses, perennials, herbs, and native plants is just astounding. **Ellison's Greenhouses** in Brenham is a Mecca for everyone who loves plants, from the weekend gardener to the horticulturalist. Originally exclusively a wholesaler, Ellison's has opened its doors to let all the green thumbs have a peek at the Easter lilies, hydrangeas, and poinsettias that are their specialty. All the flowers are sure to have your olfactory senses on high alert—the perfect time for a glass of wine! Pull into **Pleasant Hill Winery** for a taste of a Texas vintage.

once the farmers cooperative and general store. The surprise of such a lovely restaurant in such an unexpected place makes the food taste that much better. The Brazos Belle does not accept credit cards, just cash and checks. Simpler fare can be found at the casual **Burton Café.** The café serves hearty German breakfasts, pastries, and schnitzels as well as standard American lunch fare; you might consider making lunch your big meal of the day, since there will be burgers, mashed potatoes, chicken-fried steaks, and pies you'll want to taste without restraint. Dinner served on Fridays and Saturdays.

From Burton, it's a 35-mile drive along scenic FM 390 (see box, p. 89) to the **Washington-on-the-Brazos State Historic Site.** The site, actually several in one, includes the **Star of the Republic Museum, Independence Hall,** and **Barrington Living History Farm.** This serene spot was the site of the signing of the Texas Declaration of Independence in 1836, a pivotal event in the history of the state. The site sits on close to 300 acres of rolling green hills and is a lovely park in its own right. The Star of the Republic Museum and the re-created Independence Hall, where the declaration was signed, are highly interesting. The Barrington Living History Farm, at the home of the last president of the Republic of Texas, brings the era to life through interpreters acting as 19th-century farmers in period dress and using period tools.

After visiting the park, you can either head back to Brenham on TX 105 or zigzag your way south on rural FM 1155, past **Lillian Farms,** a bed & breakfast nestled on 200-plus acres dotted with wildflowers and free-roaming livestock. Pass through the front gate and a long and winding drive will take you to the main house. At first glance, the home seems a historic Victorian atop a hill. With wraparound porches outside and inlaid wooden floors and crown moldings within, it's perfectly appointed. However, the home is relatively new, built to be a B&B. When you look at the home more closely, you'll notice its more modern details such as an elevator, an exercise room, a coffee bar, and a refrigerator stocked with Blue Bell ice cream for guests to share. The rooms are spacious and unfussy, with thoughtful traditional touches. A delicious hot-from-the-kitchen multicourse breakfast is served family-style each morning in the dining room, complete with china, silver, and stemware. Lillian Farms makes a peaceful home base from which to explore the area.

A 10-minute drive south on FM 1155 will deposit you in the little hamlet of **Chappell Hill.** It was once a town growing in both size and importance, but the

THE PAINTED CHURCHES OF TEXAS

In the mid-1800s, Czech and German immigrants moved to Texas in droves, and set about building homes, plowing fields, and establishing churches to guide their communities. As the little towns prospered and they had just a bit of time and money for a few extras, the first priority was to build new churches that more closely matched those they had left behind in Europe.

Today, there are just over twenty of these "painted churches" remaining in Texas, many of them clustered around Schulenburg. Some are made of stone, some of wood, but all would be quite plain inside were it not for the paint. Itinerant artists traveled from church to church, painting; all were clearly highly skilled, but many of their names are lost to history.

The churches are lovely. Each is unique, yet part of the same tradition. The delicate scrollwork and stenciling seem as bright today as they must have been when the churches were painted. In one church the ceiling might be a clear robin's egg blue and in another faux gold leaf. In some cases, columns appear to be marble, but are actually simply painted with a deftness of skill that seems astounding today. These buildings are architecturally straightforward from the outside; the painted interiors make them pop.

There are painted churches in the towns of Schulenburg, Dubina, High Hill, Ammannsville, and Praha, to name a few; you can get a complete list in Schulenburg or most visitors centers. If you happen to drive by one on your route, be sure to stop. Or create a detour using two or three. Just driving along the rolling landscape in between and coming upon a steeple that anchors the country road will give you a sense of the companionship and comfort these immigrants must have given each other as they carved community out of the countryside.

Civil War and a devastating yellow fever epidemic in 1867 left the town with few citizens. These days, tall trees, graceful homes, and well-kept lawns hearken back to a more formal era, giving the town the look and feel of a parlor that has been dusted and cleaned for years while waiting for the lady of the house to return.

If you're here and hungry, have a seat at **Bever's Kitchen;** one of the only dining spots in town, it's fortunately a standout in its own right. Open daily for breakfast and lunch, with extended hours on Friday and Saturday for dinner, Bever's Kitchen is like a friend's house—casual and homey. And the food captures that spirit perfectly. The breakfast menu isn't large, but it includes all the essentials. Eggs, hotcakes, breakfast burritos, oatmeal, and Bever's delicious homemade sourdough bread toast. The offerings expand at lunch, with a daily Plate Special taking center stage and sandwiches, soups, and burgers playing supporting roles. Lunch is when the desserts first appear, so be sure to save room for a piece of cake, pie, or bread pudding. The dinner menu is much the same as the lunch offering, plus fresh Gulf shrimp, fried catfish, and enchiladas. Specials can include anything from King Ranch Casserole to chicken spaghetti to homemade meatloaf. The folks at Bever's are health-conscious, making almost everything from scratch using natural ingredients, and offering a self-serve salad bar, complete with locally made Brianna's gourmet salad dressings.

Doubling back 22 miles west on US 290 to Burton, the route now turns south on TX 237 and heads toward **Round Top,** once a stop on the old La Bahía Road; people have been settling down in Round Top since 1826, first the people of English descent who arrived from the United States, then Germans, who came straight from Europe. As you will see in the architecture of the town's few buildings, the Germans made a lasting impression. The bucolic countryside around the settlement drew artists to the region, and even today, the minute town captures visitors' imaginations.

Round Top has a bevy of B&Bs. Built in the 1800s, the **Round Top Inn** is a collection of guest rooms, cottages, and a little structure dating back to 1882 that was once used as a cigar factory and now stands in as the dining room. The rooms are updated and fresh, but with a distinct historic feel that comes with wood floors, simple antiques, and iron beds. Old oak trees shade the property, which is a short stroll from town. A two-minute drive into the country will lead you to the **Belle of Round Top**, a grand restored Victorian home with generously sized rooms, high ceilings, and tall windows covered with thick drapes. The surrounding meadow is filled with wildflowers, birds, and butterflies, and makes a lovely view from the wicker chairs on the wraparound porch. The Belle is the sort of place folks come to get away from it all and find they never want to leave.

For such a small spot in the road, Round Top has a lot going on. While it is a great place to poke around for antiques year round (check www.roundtop.org for listings), Round Top has made a name for itself with its **Antiques Fairs.** During the first week in October, it draws thousands upon thousands of eager bargain hunters to the enormous **Fall Antiques Fair.** The scene repeats the first full weekend in April, when the **Spring Antiques Fair** rolls out the red carpet. Renowned for the quality and quantity of their antiques, the fairs have been attracting discerning crowds for over 40 years. If you plan a visit at these times, be sure to make lodging reservations well in advance.

People also flock to the region for Shakespeare. **Shakespeare at Winedale** is a program of the University of Texas English Department, first nurtured by a Professor James "Doc" B. Ayres, whose conviction was that the best way to study Shakespeare's plays is to perform them. Doc met Ima Hogg, an extraordinary philanthropist, musician, patron of the arts, governor's daughter, and oil-company heiress, popularly known as the First Lady of Texas, who had just finished a pet project—the restoration and transformation of an old stagecoach inn into the Winedale Historical Center. She then donated the entire 270 acres and its cluster of historic buildings to the University of Texas. Miss Ima, as she was called, suggested to Doc that the old hay barn on the property reminded her of an Elizabethan theater and perhaps he could consider staging some summertime performances there. He agreed and the results were magic; Shakespeare at Winedale has been captivating audiences for almost 40 years now. The program has expanded into a yearlong event, engaging all age groups, from all around the United States. The summer season generally runs mid-July through mid-August, though there can be additional performances bookending those dates; check the Web site

SCENIC DRIVE

A particularly lovely drive in Washington County is FM 390, a scenic route that arcs for close to 40 miles, skirting Brenham 7 miles to the south and connecting Burton (see p. 84) to TX 105, near Washington-on-the-Brazos. Known as **La Bahía Road**, the route existed for centuries as a footpath used by Native Americans, explorers, traders, militia, immigrants, and animals, connecting southeastern Texas and Louisiana. Though El Camino Real (see p. 177) is both longer and better known, La Bahía Road was an important thoroughfare. It ends in Goliad, which was once known as La Bahía (see p. 112). The road is as beautiful as it is historic; traveling it in the spring, surrounded by wildflowers, is a special treat.

(www.shakespeare-winedale.org) for details or drive by and take a look around. From Round Top, turn left onto FM 1457, then left onto FM 2714 into the Winedale Historical Center; the Theatre Barn will be on your right after 1 mile.

As the sign greeting you at the city limits asserts, Round Top is home to only 77 people. On a Friday or a Saturday, you would swear they were all down at **Royers Round Top Café**. In 1987, the Royer family quit Houston for Round Top, purchasing the little café. They learned two things quickly. One, people will drive as far as they need to for fantastic food, and two, pie is always a hit. The café started with burgers and beer, but ended up with pork tenderloin with peach sauce served with wine. The Royers proved for themselves that location, quality, and service with a smile are still what folks are looking for. The café's signature pie, Bud's Chocolate Chip Pie, is the ultimate gooey chocolate chip cookie direct from the oven. Add ice cream and feel the love. The café doesn't accept reservations, but the turnover is brisk. During Antiques Fairs, however, all bets are off. Try your luck in the off hours, perhaps dining earlier than usual, and keep your fingers crossed. Royers doesn't accept credit cards, so be sure to bring cash.

From Round Top, it's a quick 16 miles to La Grange along TX 237 then TX 159. Located at the intersection of TX 71, TX 159, US 77, and TX 609, the city was a former stop along the old La Bahía Road, and it's been a crossroads ever since. It was once even considered as a possible capital for the new Republic of Texas.

In the 1840s and 1850s, large numbers of Germans and Czechs immigrated to the area and left a lasting impression here as elsewhere. One great way to experience a little Czech culture is to sink your teeth into a *kolache,* and one of the best places to do that is at **Weikel's Bakery**, on TX 71 in La Grange. The place is actually a gas station; it won't look promising when you pull up, but open the door and you'll become a believer. The shelves are packed with the slightly sweet Danish-like Czech pastries traditionally filled with prunes, cottage cheese, and poppy seeds. Cream cheese, apricot, and other fruit fillings are also popular.

If you are looking for a full meal, one of the nicest places to eat in town

Kolaches at Weikel's Bakery in La Grange

is **Bistro 108**, just a door or two off the town square. The bistro is intimate and romantic, with cloth napkins and baskets of warm bread, though not the least bit stuffy; you'll feel as comfortable in your jeans and a fresh shirt as you will in your Sunday clothes. The emphasis here is on the food. Entrées such as spinach and roasted rosemary chicken ravioli with a pesto cream sauce are right at home with pork chops and mashed potatoes, and are sure to please either a traditional or adventurous palate. A nice wine list and homemade desserts, including pies brought in from the Hill Country, complete the meal.

Also in La Grange, the Heinrich **Kreische Brewery**, owned by Texas Parks and Wildlife, shares a bluff overlooking the Colorado River with the Kreische family home and **Monument Hill**, where, in 1848, the remains of Texans killed during the War of Independence were interred in a common tomb. A large crowd, which included President Sam Houston, attended the event. In 1849, Heinrich Kreische, a German immigrant and stonemason turned brewer, purchased the

land, eventually building a home and a brewery on the site, and cared for the tomb until his death in 1882. While the brewery was once one of the largest in the state, both it and the tomb declined after Kreische's death. Now a state park, the structures are well cared for today. If you find yourself enjoying the town and want to stay for the night, book a room at **Brendan Manor,** a local bed & breakfast built in the 1840s; antique beds, claw-foot tubs, and lacy doilies give this old inn an old-fashioned touch.

From La Grange, press southward, this time using pretty FM 609 to travel the 22 miles to **Flatonia,** located on US 90 just south of I-10. Once the tiny hamlets of Flatonia and Oso were neighbors separated by a couple of miles, but when the railroad came through, both towns packed up, moved next to the tracks, and merged to become one. Cattle and cotton fueled the economy, and European immigrants came looking for inexpensive land to farm. When I-10 was completed in the 1970s, travel bypassed the town, but today Flatonia is making a new name for itself. Home to just about 1,500 welcoming, outspoken, and community-minded individuals, the little town has a lot of pluck. If you like small, friendly towns, then you'll like Flatonia. Use it as a comfortable, low-key home base for touring the entire region or just stop in for the Czech heritage festival Czhilispiel during the last full weekend in October (www.czhilispielfestival.com).

Lodging in Flatonia is an easy decision; there is only one place in town, and it's wonderful. In describing the **Olle Hotel,** it's best to begin with its gracious and energetic inn-keeper, Kathryn, who is just as lovely as the inn itself. A rooming house and B&B in past incarnations, the Olle is over a century old. Lots of elbow grease, lovely colors, and a few well-chosen antiques later, and the Olle is fresh and spirited again, with modern touches that blend beautifully with its historic charm. Simple, bright, and comfortable rooms, high-speed Internet, and great coffee make it the perfect stay for business travelers. Queen beds, crisp white linens, an open, airy feel, and homemade breakfast treats make it a wonderfully romantic respite. With decor that appeals to everyone, the Olle makes guests always feel comfortable. Kathryn knows everything about the town, so be sure to ask her for recommendations, or just enjoy a small-town tale or two. The Web site gives a very good representation of the hotel, so be sure to click before you go.

Just outside town, **Goose's Roost Ranch** bed & breakfast cottages will get you off the beaten track in a hurry. These lovely cottages on a 236-acre ranch are

A cottage at Goose's Roost in Flatonia

the perfect getaway. Bright and airy, with cozy linens, porches to sit on, and surrounding trees, the two cottages are clean, comfortable, and sophisticated. Animal lovers will enjoy the gaggle of geese and the other birds that thrive on the little pond. While the owner—who is also the owner of the Olle Hotel in Flatonia—lives onsite, the layout of the property ensures privacy for all.

As in most small towns, there aren't many places to eat in Flatonia. **Brenda's** serves up half-pound burgers in its back-to-basics dining room. While the decor is unremarkable, and dark wood and heavy window treatments keep the place dim, the mood is bright and cheerful. The friendly, no-nonsense waitstaff balance good service with plenty of good-natured ribbing, and locals fill the place daily. **Robert's Steakhouse** is 100 percent pure local and a real treat. The specialty here is steak, served with baked potatoes and several choices of vegetables, and the friendly, efficient folks here will cook yours just the way you like it. Alternatively, take TX 95 south to the small town of **Moulton,** home of some of the biggest steaks in Texas. In a bright yellow storefront just beyond the railroad tracks, you'll find **Kloesel's Steakhouse & Bar.** This building was made of the castaway wood from the demolished Moore Hotel, which was the 19th-century hub of social and commercial life in Moulton. The much-loved hotel was razed in the 1940s, but details in Kloesel's such as frosted glass and drawings and photographs of the original hotel pay homage to its legacy. The steakhouse and its bar are a gathering place, with folks coming in for the homemade salad dressings, pies, breads, and steak sauce as much as the steaks. Just up the street at the center of town is the **Ole Moulton Bank;** instead of doling out cash, it now offers live music and libations every night of the week.

The route ends in **Gonzales,** which is where the first shots of the Texas Revolution were fired. In 1835, as tensions mounted between the Anglo settlers in Gonzales and the Mexican government in San Antonio de Béxar, the issue arose of a small cannon in the town. Mexico wanted the cannon, and the settlers were told to relinquish it. Boldly, the Anglos challenged them to "come and take it." Mexican soldiers arriving in Gonzales to retrieve the weapon were met by armed men. The cannon remained in Gonzales. Some of the men who fought to defend it, however, did not: instead they headed north to defend the Alamo. All in all, 32 Gonzales men died at the Alamo. For all the trouble, you may be surprised at the cannon's size (actually an accurate reconstruction). Small, but, it goes without saying, highly symbolic. You can see it at the museum housed in the old town library, where it is surrounded by memorabilia and watched over by a very knowledgeable docent who can give you plenty of history.

Now a peaceful, leafy locale, Gonzales is just like a lot of towns in the region, plenty of old homes and a few businesses scattered around the square. Should you decide to spend the night, the graceful **Belle Oaks Inn** makes a nice choice. Conveniently located in town, the inn is a Louisiana Plantation–style mansion that immediately transports guests to that more gracious time of chandeliers,

Kloesel's Steak House in Moulton

four-poster beds, antique details, and dressed windows. The grounds here are especially lovely, with huge live oak and pecan trees shielding the gardens, seating, and pathways from the strong sun. Modern amenities such as high-speed Internet and a pool add to the comfort and convenience.

If you've just come off the BBQ circuit of Llano, Taylor, Elgin, Lockhart, and Luling (see chapter 1), you'll have reason to compare the **Gonzales Food Market.** Richard, grandson of the founder and the current owner, easily takes the prize for the friendliest BBQ-joint owner in Texas. Jovial and kind, he'll tell you all about the place, let you peek at the sausages smoking in the pit in the back room, and send you on your way with a smile on your face. The townsfolk regularly gather here in this true mom-and-pop spot to bask in both the warmth of friendship and the satisfaction of the well-priced lunch spe-

Smoking sausages at the Gonzales Food Market in Gonzales

cial, which features BBQ and a buffet. The market is an old brick grocery store facing the square, with a meat counter dating back to the 1950s. While the grocery business was brisk, people came from far and wide for the BBQ and slowly a restaurant began to take shape inside the grocery store. Fresh, all-natural, and made with a whole lot of love, the Gonzales Food Market is something special. Leaving Gonzales, you are well-positioned to connect to either the Best BBQ in Texas route or the Texas Coast (see chapter 5), both of which travel along US 183.

While this route may take a little longer than the interstate, the soothing backroad scenery, great food, and restful bed & breakfasts more than compensate. So, next time you make the trip between Austin, San Antonio, or Houston, be sure to schedule in some time to enjoy the space in between.

IN THE AREA

Ant Street Inn, 107 W. Commerce Street, Brenham, 77833. Call 1-800-481-1951. Web site: www.antstreet inn.com.

Antique Rose Emporium, 10,000 Highway 50, Brenham (Independence), 77833. Call 979-836-5548. Mon. through Sat. 9–6, Sun. 11–6. Web site: www.antiqueroseemporium.com.

Belle Oaks Inn, 222 St. Peter, PO Box 57, Gonzales, 78629. Call 830-857-8613. Web site: www.belleoaksinn .com.

Belle of Round Top, 230 Days End Lane, Round Top, 78954. Call 936-521-9300. Web site: www.belleofround top.com.

Bever's Kitchen, 5162 Main Street, Chappell Hill, 77426. Call 979-836-4178. Mon. through Thurs. 11–3, Fri. 11–8, Sat. 11–4. Web site: www.bevers -kitchen.com.

Bistro 108, 108 S. Main Street, La Grange, 78945. Call 979-968-9108. Tues. through Sat. 11–2 and 5–9, Sun. 12–2. Web site: www.bistro108.com. Reservations recommended.

Blue Bell Creameries, 1101 S. Blue Bell Road (Loop 577), Brenham, 77833. Call 1-800-327-8135. Tours Mon through Fri. 8:30–3. Fee. Web site: www.bluebell.com. Reservations sometimes required; call ahead.

Brazos Belle, 600 Main Street, Burton, 77835. Call 979-289-2677. Fri. and Sat. 5:30–8:30, Sun. 11:30–1:30. Extended hours on Antiques Fair weekends. Web site: www.brazos bellerestaurant.com. Cash only.

Brenda's, 1143 E. Old Highway 90, Flatonia, 78941. Call 361-865-3391. Sun. through Thurs. 10–9, Fri. and Sat. 10–9:30.

Brendan Manor, 345 E. Travis Street, La Grange, 78945. Call 979-968-2028. Web site: www.brendanmanor.com.

Brenham Chamber of Commerce/Washington County Convention & Visitors Bureau, 314 S. Austin, Brenham, 77833. Call 979-836-3695. Web site: www.brenham texas.com.

WILDFLOWERS

Bluebonnets, Indian paintbrush, and other wildflowers proliferate along the roadsides and in the pastures of Washington County throughout the spring. To find out just where the best viewing is, you can stop in the Brenham Chamber of Commerce, or check the "Maps" section of their web site, www.brenhamtexas.com, but FM 1155 between Chappell Hill and Washington-on-the-Brazos is always a good bet.

Brenham House B&B, 705 Clinton Street, Brenham, 77833. Call 979-251-9947. Web site: www.thebrenham house.com.

Burton Café, 12513 W. Washington Street, Burton, 77835. Call 979-289-3849. Tues. through Sat. 7–2, Fri. and Sat. 7–2 and 5–9, Sun. 11–2. Web site: www.burtontexas.org/BurtonCafe.

Burton Cotton Gin and Museum, 307 N. Main Street, Burton, 77835. Call 979-289-3378. Winter: Mon., Tues., Thurs., Fri., and Sat. 10–4; Summer: Mon., Tues., Thurs., and Fri. 10–4; Sat. 9–noon. Fee. Web site: www .cottonginmuseum.org.

Chappell Hill Chamber of Commerce, 5145 Main Street, Chappell Hill, 77426. Call 979-337-9910. Web site: www.chappellhilltx.com.

Ellison's Greenhouses, 2107 E. Stone Street, Brenham, 77833. Call 979-836-6011. Mon. through Fri. 8–6, Sat. and Sun. 10–5. Web site: www .ellisonsgreenhouses.com.

Ernie's, 103 S. Baylor Street, Brenham, 77833. Call 979-836-7545. Tues. through Sat. 11:30–2 and 5–9, Sun. 11–2. Web site: www.erniesrestaurant .com.

Fairview Bed and Breakfast, 1804 S. Park Street, Brenham, 77833. Call 1-888-327-8439 or 979-836-1672. Web site: www.fairviewbedandbreakfast .com.

Flatonia Chamber of Commerce, PO Box 610, 208 E. North Main, Fla-

---

CHURCH PICNICS

As you drive around the backroads of this region, be sure to notice any signs announcing church picnics. There are many in these parts that have been annual events for over 100 years. With cake walks, desserts, entertainment, and lots and lots of food, these picnics, open to the public, are a great chance to experience small-town life at its very best.

---

tonia, 78941. Call 361-865-3920. Web site: www.flatoniachamber.com.

Gonzales Chamber of Commerce, 414 Saint Lawrence Street, Gonzales, 78629. Call 830-672-6532. Web site: www.gonzalestexas.com.

Gonzales Food Market, 311 Saint Lawrence Street, Gonzales, 78629. Call 830-672-3156. Daily 8–7.

Goose's Roost Ranch, 815 Scott's School Road, Flatonia, 78941. Call 361-772-8093. Web site: www.gooses roost.com.

Kloesel's Steakhouse & Bar, 101 Moore Street, Moulton, 77975. Call 361-596-7323. Mon. 11–2, Tues. through Sat. 11–10, Sun. 11–9. Web site: www.kloesel.com.

Knittel Homestead, 520 N. Main Street, Burton, 77835. Call 979-289-

---

SHINER

Step into a bar, restaurant, or dance hall in Texas and someone is bound to offer you a Shiner. Spoetzl Brewery, located in Shiner a mere 18 miles south of Flatonia and 18 miles east of Gonzales, has been brewing since 1909, making it the oldest brewery in the state. Its beer and the label on the bottle are Texas icons. From the music scene in Austin to the backroads of rural Texas, it seems just about everyone is kicked back with a Shiner. Stop in for a look, and a taste of history. Check www.shiner.com for tour details.

5102. Web site: knittelhomestead .com.

La Grange Area Chamber of Commerce, 171 S. Main Street, La Grange, 78945. Call 979-968-5756. Web site: www.lagrangetx.org.

Lillian Farms, 12570 FM 1155 East, Washington, 77880. Call 979-421-6332. Web site: www.lillianfarms.com.

Monument Hill and Kreische Brewery State Historic Sites, 414 State Loop 92, La Grange, 78945. Call 979-968-5658. Daily 8–5. Web site: www.tpwd.state.tx.us.

Moulton Chamber of Commerce, 405 S. Lavaca, Moulton, 77975. Call 361-596-7205. Web site: www.moulton texas.com.

Murski Homestead B&B, 1662 Old Independence Road, Brenham, 77833. Call 979-830-1021. Web site: www.murskihomesteadbb.com.

Must Be Heaven, 107 W. Alamo Street, Brenham, 77833. Call 979-830-8536. Mon. through Sat. 8–5, Sun. 11–3. Web site: www.mustbeheaven.com.

Ole Moulton Bank, 101 Main Street, Moulton, 77975. Call 361-596-7499. Mon. through Fri. 3–close, Sat. and Sun. noon–close. Fee. Web site: www .olemoultonbank.com.

Olle Hotel, 218 S. Market Avenue, Flatonia, 78941. Call 361-772-0310. Web site: www.ollehotel.com.

Pleasant Hill Winery, 1441 Salem Road, Brenham 77833. Call 979-830-8463. Sat. 11–6, Sun. noon–5. Web site: www.pleasanthillwinery.com.

Robert's Steakhouse, 1241 N. TX 95, Flatonia, 78941. Call 361-865-3099. Daily 11–10. Web site: www.roberts -steakhouse.com.

Round Top Chamber of Commerce, PO Box 216 or N. Live Oak Street, Round Top, 78954. Call 979-249-4042. Web site: www.roundtop.org.

Round Top Inn, 407 South White Street, Round Top, 78954. Call 979-

249-5294. Web site: www.round-topinn.com.

Royers Round Top Cafe, 105 Main Street, Round Top, 78954. Call 979-249-3611. Wed. 11–2, Thurs. through Sat. 11–9, Sun. 11–3. Web site: www.royersroundtopcafe.com. Cash only.

Schulenburg Chamber of Commerce, 618 N. Main Street, Schulenburg, 78956. Call 979-743-4514. Web site: www.schulenburgchamber.org.

Shakespeare at Winedale, Winedale Historical Center, 3738 FM 2714 Road, Burton, 77835. Call 979-278-3530. For more information, call 512-471-4726. Or write James Loehlin, Director, Shakespeare at Winedale, University of Texas at Austin, 208 W. 21st Street, Stop B5000, Austin, TX 78712. Web site: www.shakespeare-winedale.org.

Spoetzl Brewery, 603 E. Brewery Street, Shiner, 77984. Call 361-594-3383. Mon. through Fri. 9–5; tours weekdays only. Web site: www.shiner.com.

Volare, 102 S. Ross Street, Brenham, 77833. Call 979-836-1514. Tues. through Sat. 11–2 and 5–9, 9:30 on weekends. Web site: www.volareitalianrestaurant.com.

Washington-on-the-Brazos State Historic Site, Washington TX 77880. Call 936-878-2214. Daily 8–dusk; Visitor Center daily 10–5. Free and Fee. Web site: www.tpwd.state.tx.us.

Weikel's Bakery, 2247 W. TX 71, La Grange, 78945. Call 979-968-9413. Mon. through Thurs. 5–9, Fri. through Sun. 5–10. Web site: www.weikels.com.

The rocky shore near Fulton

5 The Texas Coast

Getting there: Take TX 35 from Fulton, through Rockport, and south to Aransas Pass. In Aransas Pass, follow TX 361 southeast to the free 24-hour ferry landing. Take the ferry to Port Aransas and from there it's just a short drive to the Padre Island National Seashore.

Highlights: This route captures the free-spirited Texas Gulf lifestyle. Brush up on your local history in the seaside hamlet of **Rockport**, home to the **Texas Maritime Museum,** or take a tour of the **Fulton Mansion** located in the casual small town of **Fulton.** Get out the binoculars or camera and spend some time birdwatching in the **Aransas National Wildlife Refuge** or one of the other parks and preserves designated by the **Great Texas Coastal Birding Trail.** Take the ferry to the laid-back beach town of Port Aransas and then a short drive to **Padre Island National Seashore. Detours:** Coming from Dallas or Austin, some travelers like to take the less-traveled **TX 183/US 77** to the coast and through Goliad (see box, p. 112), home of **Presidio La Bahia and the Mission Espíritu Santo,** remnants of South Texas' Spanish heritage. The drive south on TX 77 to the Rio Grande Valley, the route outlined in chapter 6, will take you through the legendary **King Ranch.**

Total distance: 25 miles from Fulton to Port Aransas

Intersections: Chapter 6

The Texas shoreline of the Gulf of Mexico is over 600 miles long, with seven barrier islands, including Galveston (see chapter 7), Matagorda, Mustang, and Padre Island (see chapter 6), the longest barrier island in the world, stretched beside it. A utilitarian coast, it supports fishing boats, oil and gas rigs, several

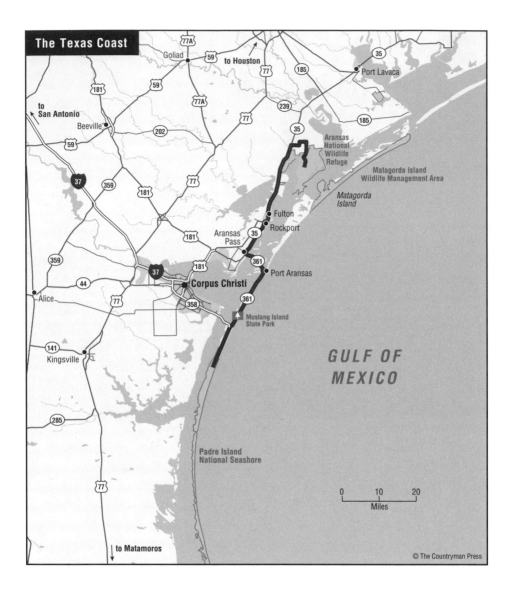

dozen cities, state parks, and recreational beaches. Of course the landscape you see today looks very different than what explorers encountered centuries ago.

As with the rest of Texas, humans have lived in this coastal region for millennia; scientists believe they first arrived 6,000 to 8,000 years ago. Evidence suggests that the nomadic Aransas Indians left the area around A.D. 1200 to 1300; then a century later, the Karankawas moved in. The Karankawas were joined by various other groups of Native Americans who hunted and gathered while on the move along the barrier islands from what is now Galveston to Aransas Pass. Though the Gulf had been sighted previously by several other European explorers, it was Alonso Álvarez de Pineda who put "the hidden sea" on the map in the early 1500s. As the Spanish gained a foothold in the region, native peoples retreated inland or to Mexico. By the 1800s, the Spanish had established a port on Copano Bay with which to serve their settlements in Goliad (see p. 112), Refugio, and San Antonio de Béxar (now known as San Antonio). At the time of the Texas

Snowy egret on the Rockport waterfront

Revolution, in 1836, the Texas coast was sparsely settled, largely wild, and vulnerable to raids by invading Native Americans and Mexicans.

The Civil War brought its ruin to the Texas coast, too, destroying and damaging existing towns. It wasn't until the fighting stopped that the towns of **Rockport** and **Fulton** were founded, in 1867 and 1866, respectively, as centers for processing and shipping cattle. During this boom time, cattle were prized for their hides and tallow; the raw meat was either fed to pigs or thrown into the bay. The advent of refrigeration changed that, but the rise in beef-packing plants in Chicago and Kansas City provided competition. Still, until the 1880s, the Rockport-Fulton area processed over 90 percent of all Texas beef. Commerce faltered when the shipping lines the beef industry relied upon withdrew from the area, leaving the boat-building and fishing businesses to fill the gap. A hurricane flattened Rockport in 1919, but by the 1940s it had rebounded again, this time aided by shrimping and tourism, the industries that sustain the region today.

Though Rockport and Fulton are two distinct towns, they are separated by only 3 miles and are often referred to as **Rockport-Fulton,** a blurring of boundaries that represents their neighborliness. Let's start the journey in relaxed, artsy **Rockport.** The **Hoopes' House Bed & Breakfast** sits at the busy fork in the road where Loop 70 and Business 35 split, just across the street from the water. Painted a pale, weathered yellow, this graceful B&B has been here since the 1890s, and its lovely ambiance has stood the test of time. The main house has four guest rooms, and though you cannot easily see it from the street, there is a four-room addition tacked on back, a refreshing pool, gazebo, and several relaxing benches—an oasis of relaxation that belies the home's hectic location. Inside, period details prevail, updated with high-quality linens. The result is a relaxing and romantic retreat at the shore.

Directly across the street, the **Texas Maritime Museum** is a modest installation right on the Rockport waterfront. Slip inside and have a look at their fine collection of scale model ships, art, and artifacts, and walk out with a new appreciation for hardworking sailors. Next door, the **Rockport Center for the Arts** has several art galleries featuring local, regional, and sometimes farther-flung artists and is the organizational force behind the summertime **Rockport Art Festival** (see p. 121).

Walk out toward the water and you'll quickly come upon **Rockport Beach,** the mile-long sandy beach on Aransas Bay. A well-groomed stretch, with rest-

Chairs in the backyard of the Hoopes' House B&B in Rockport

Bait shop in Rockport

room facilities, picnic cabanas and grills, and a bird-observation deck, the beach is popular for its clear, shallow water and gentle lapping waves. If being so close to the water has piqued your interest in estuaries, island habitats, and marine life, then make a visit to the brand-new **Bay Education Center**, the place to go for all the details of the ecology of South Texas and the Gulf of Mexico. The star of the show is definitely the Science on a Sphere exhibit, which uses multimedia technology to project brilliantly colored images onto a massive globe, illustrating concepts such as weather patterns, the dynamics of hurricanes, and ocean temperatures. Two 45-minute presentations a day have visitors of all ages genuinely enthralled. Make a side trip to the **Texas State Aquarium** in Corpus Christi to find out more about marine life. The aquarium features rescued and rehabilitated animals, many from the Gulf of Mexico, giant sea turtles, and dolphin shows.

Up early and looking for a java jolt? **Rockport Daily Grind** fills the morning food gap nicely; pop in for a cup of coffee and a scone, or try a slice of their savory homemade quiche or a sandwich for lunch. You're in luck for later repasts as well. In the right hands, Texas seafood shines, and **Glow** uses only the freshest fish on the local market for their menu. The restaurant is lovely—slightly upscale, but still very homey—and the food is exceptional. The Rockport Stew consists of locally caught drum, Gulf shrimp, oysters, and crabmeat simmered in a ginger, tomato, lemongrass broth and served with a garlic aioli crostini. Foodies rejoice. Or consider having dinner at **Latitude 28 02 Restaurant and Art Gallery**. Feast your eyes on the menu, then just feast. Choices include the zippy Latitude Oyster appetizer of fresh oysters with a margarita and jalapeño sorbet, and the rich and creamy oysters Rockefeller with spinach Florentine and Hollandaise sauce. The catch of the day comes broiled with crab meat and asparagus, or steamed in a brown paper bag with white wine, or encrusted in a garlic butter crust, among other preparations. Latitude 28 02 is only open for dinner, when, predictably, reservations are strongly encouraged.

Leaving Rockport, heading to Fulton along Aransas Bay, S. Austin Street will become N. Austin Street. Follow the fork in the road slightly to the east, and N. Austin Street funnels into Broadway, which in turn becomes S. Fulton Beach Road, then N. Fulton Beach Road, before finally merging into TX 35 at the northern tip of the peninsula.

From Rockport, it's just a quick trip north on N. Fulton Beach Road to the

---

ISLAND TIME

The little towns along the coast rely heavily on the ebb and flow of seasonal tourism. As you make your way from one to the next, consider resetting your internal clock to "island time" and prepare to be flexible. Service may be a little slower and hours of operation a little relaxed, especially off-season. The very same establishment can be empty one day and swamped with customers the next; it just depends on the day. Make like a local and go with the flow.

Fulton Mansion in Fulton

Fulton Mansion, which is set back from the road, grand and dignified. One can only imagine what the neighbors thought in 1874 when the Fulton family started building this overstated French Second Empire home by the sea, complete with newfangled amenities such as plumbing, heat, and gas lights. Easterner George Fulton came to Matagorda Bay as a fighter in the Texas Revolution and stayed to marry Harriet, a woman who inherited thousands of acres of Texas land from her father, the secretary of the treasury of the Republic of Texas. The Fultons founded the Coleman-Fulton Pasture Company, becoming cattle barons in the midst of a cattle boom, and the mansion stands as a testament to both their wealth and ingenuity. The home, now under management of the Texas Parks and Wildlife Department, is impressive from the roadside, and the guided tours really show off all its interior details.

Just up the street, **The Lighthouse Inn** is a popular place to spend the night. The inn offers typical rooms and larger suites, the latter with kitchens; those overlooking the bay tend to be the guests' favorites. Decorated in gold, sage green, and crimson red, the rooms feel updated and pleasant. The outdoor pool is a plus, and the rocking chairs on the porches overlooking the harbor and the lighted fishing pier are a big draw. The towering white lighthouse in front makes the inn easy to spot.

Across the street, **The Boiling Pot** restaurant steams up pots of Cajun-style seafood—shrimp, crab legs, and crawfish with sausage, corn, and potatoes—every night, dumping it straight onto the butcher-paper-covered tables for guests to dig into with their bare hands. The place is almost always crowded and stays open till the food's gone. Since you cannot make reservations, be sure to get there early. Start the morning with beignets, café au lait, and eggs Benedict with fried shrimp, served alongside fantastic views of the Gulf courtesy of **Cheryl's.** Many return for a relaxed dinner, enjoying dishes such as shrimp in a lime cream sauce over orzo or coconut curried shrimp. The eclectic decor pairs well with the eclectic menu. **Moondog Seaside Eatery** is a very casual seaside spot at which to while away the afternoon nursing a beer and snacking on fish tacos.

Jump on TX 35 and take it a bit north to the **Pelican Bay Resort,** a throwback to the family-style camps of yesteryear. Individual, closely spaced cottages are painted in tropical pastels, their tiny front porches shaded by dozens of leafy oak trees. Each cottage has a fully equipped kitchen; sitting areas with foldout couches make them perfect for extended families or groups of friends traveling together. The resort has an outdoor pool and a lighted fishing pier so there are plenty of opportunities for swimming or fishing.

Oak trees are common here, and there's a famous one nearby. The **Big Tree of Lamar,** located approximately 10 miles north of Rockport, is more than 35 feet in diameter and 44 feet tall, with branches spreading 89 feet across, supported by cables and iron braces. Estimated to be over 1,000 years old, the tree is thought to have been a council meeting place for the Carancahua Indians. The Big Tree has seen a lot in its time. It's survived dozens of hurricanes, floods, wildfires, droughts, and even the Civil War. To reach it, take I-35 north from Rockport, crossing the Copano Causeway; you will see signs approximately half a mile over the bridge on the right, directing you through the oaks on Park Road 13. Nearby, **Goose Island State Park** is a peaceful place for camping.

Even farther north on TX 35, you'll find the **Aransas National Wildlife Refuge,** established in 1937 to protect the habitat of the endangered whooping

THE MISSIONS OF GOLIAD

Goliad dates back to 1749, making it one of the oldest Spanish colonial settlements in Texas. Home to the Nuestra Señora del Espíritu Santo de Zúñiga Mission (**Mission Espíritu Santo**) and its protective fort, **Nuestra Señora de Loreto de La Bahía del Espíritu Santo Presidio** (**Presidio La Bahía**), the town makes for an interesting historical detour en route to the Texas coast.

Mission Espíritu Santo, located in the **Goliad State Park and Historic Site,** is a reconstruction of a Franciscan mission—the original was decimated by a hurricane in 1886—that was home to one of the most expansive ranching operations in its day. Across the river, the Presidio La Bahía figured prominently in the Texas Revolution. Colonel Fannin and his men were executed here by the infamous Santa Ana; the nearby **Fannin Memorial Monument** marks the burial spot of the war heroes. Beside the presidio, the **Zaragoza Birthplace State Historic Site** is the reconstructed birthplace of Mexican general Ignacio Zaragoza, who defeated the French at the Battle of Puebla on May 5, 1862. Cinco de Mayo (May 5) celebrates the victory with festivities throughout Texas and Mexico.

The massive trunk of the Big Tree of Lamar in Lamar

crane and now managed by the US Fish and Wildlife Service. The refuge takes in a large swath of land on the Blackjack Peninsula (named for the prevalent blackjack oak trees) north of Lamar and northwest of Matagorda Island. The refuge's many sand dunes, tidal marshes, small ponds, and vegetation make it attractive to almost 400 separate species of birds, among them the large flocks of magnificent whooping cranes that swoop in around November and stay through March. From Rockport-Fulton, take TX 35 to FM 774, turn right and follow to FM 2040, turn right again and proceed to the entrance.

While you can hike the trails, watch from the observation tower, or cruise the paved tour road, one of the best places to see the cranes is on a boat. **Rockport Birding and Kayak Adventures** routinely takes passengers from Rockport to the refuge aboard the *Skimmer* and is particularly known for its Whooping Crane Tours. (In Port Aransas, stop in at Fisherman's Wharf for more information on fishing trips and boat tours to both the Aransas National Wildlife Refuge and St. José's Island; see p. 115.) The truly dedicated might be able to catch a glimpse of the cranes from the fishing pier at Goose Island State Park in Lamar.

Back in Rockport and heading south, it is a 17.5-mile drive to **Port Aransas,** including the ferry trip over the Port Aransas Causeway. This trip can take anywhere from one hour to two, depending on the time of day, week, and year. From Rockport, take TX 35 south to TX 361, following signs to the ferry.

Port Aransas, or "Port A" as it is known, anchors the northern end of Mustang Island, so named for the wild horses found running free here in the 1800s. While

Laughing gulls hitch a ride on the ferry to Port Aransas.

PORT ARANSAS ON THE WEB

Like many of the towns featured in this book, Port Aransas has an informative Web site (www.portaransas.org) that can come in quite handy as you plan your trip. The sections on birds and nature will be of particular interest to nature enthusiasts, who will find detailed directions to the town's somewhat hard-to-find birding sites and nature preserves. The fishing and boating sections outline fishing regulations and permits, provide photographs to help with fish identification, and spell out details of the Seagrass Law, which places depth restrictions on outboard motors.

it is now a fishing community and consummate beach town, Port Aransas got its start when Englishman Robert Mercer used it as a grazing station for sheep and cattle. In time a small community grew, acquiring the name Port Aransas in 1910. Today, commercial fishing boats lumber in and out of the port, a reminder of the local economy's dependence on the Gulf waters.

The biggest draw here is the beach. Port A is laden with shops hawking swimsuits and sunscreen to retirees, college students on spring break, and families down for a week at the shore.

A pelican stretches its wings.

Just to set the record straight before you go, at the beaches here, like at all beaches in Texas, you won't find soft, white sand; instead it's dark gray and hard-packed with plenty of washed-up kelp, shells, and shark teeth. They are perfect for long walks and sand-castle building, and the relatively low waves are fun for novice boogie boarders.

Nearby the ferry, **Fisherman's Wharf** offers fishing trips, and boat tours to Aransas National Wildlife Refuge and St. José Island, known around here as simply "St. Jo." The island, 28 miles long and less than 2 miles wide, is located just north of Port Aransas. Privately owned, but open to the public for gentle recreational use, St. Jo is a great place to fish, bird-watch, or roam the beach. There are no facilities or shelters on the island, and the only access is by boat, making it a wind-swept paradise for those who want to commune with nature.

While today most of the lodging in Port Aransas consists of condominium rentals, the **Tarpon Inn,** on E. Cotter Avenue across from Fisherman's Wharf, has been renting out rooms since 1886. The Tarpon has recently had a much-needed facelift, but considering that this simple, two-story wooden inn is continuously exposed to the harsh elements, it must be hard just to keep a coat of paint on it. Come for the relaxed, coastal ambiance, not the luxury.

For a memorable gourmet meal, from Cotter Avenue, head southwest on Alister Street to Beach Avenue, where you will find the **Venetian Hot Plate,** one of the more enjoyable restaurants on the island. The menu features Italian dishes skillfully made by the restaurant's Italian owners, including wonderful fresh pastas, some with vegetables and some with seafood, and homemade lasagnas. Keep

Lunch at the Venetian Hot Plate in Port Aransas

your eye on the specials board, where you'll find the chef's daily creation and some of the most expertly cooked seafood around. While you can probably squeeze in for lunch, reservations at dinner are essential.

Port Aransas is a good spot to eat your fill of seafood; there are a number of places that will bake, sear, grill, or fry the catch of the day—theirs or yours. The very casual **Beach and Station Street Grill** doesn't look like much from the street, but one bite of the jumbo lump crab cakes with homemade sauce and you might just be smitten. The Grouper Pontchartrain, frequently the daily special, is a favorite. The restaurant is well-worn from lots of business and the outdoor patio is pleasant. Tucked into the coastal development known as Cinnamon Shores, **Lisabella's Bistro** is known for its fresh fish and inventive menu, with Latin, Mediterranean, and Asian influences, Lisabella's wows diners with items such as lobster enchiladas, grilled salmon topped with mango habanero, and beef tenderloin with a roasted

Rocking chairs on the porch of the Tarpon Inn

GREAT TEXAS COASTAL BIRDING TRAIL

Amazingly, three-fourths of all American birds are represented in the diverse avian habitats of Texas. While some are year-round residents, others are migratory. Texas, the center of the Central Flyway between Canada and Central and South America, hosts an abundance of migratory birds in the spring and fall of each year. Though many migratory birds were hunted to near extinction by European settlers in the 19th century, laws are now on the books to protect them, as most of these birds are insect eaters and play a crucial role in keeping regional insect populations in check. Now seen as both beautiful and useful, the birds fascinate enthusiasts who flock to the coast to observe the phenomenon of migration up close.

In October, birds share the Central Flyway with the monarch butterfly, Texas' State Insect. Monarchs are unique among butterflies in their ability to migrate instead of hibernate; those that make the trip through Texas tend to originate in the upper Midwest, funneling through the state on their way to Mexico. Plan your trip just right and you may be treated to the sight of millions of orange and black butterflies flitting and floating along on the breezes, with miles to go, but taking the trip one day at a time.

Given that Texas is one of the top birding destinations in the world, it made sense to map out the best viewing locations to help birders know where to go.

tomato, garlic, and feta salsa. The dining room is more chic than most in Port Aransas, making Lisabella's a terrific choice for a special night out. Casual food is plentiful at **Café Phoenix**, which has made a name for itself with generous portions of creative food. The Thunderbird sandwich—grilled chicken breast, roasted poblano peppers, caramelized onions, manchego cheese, and a dollop of chipotle aioli—is the most popular. The menu is small, with a Mediterranean influence, and the consensus so far is that it's all delicious. **Coffee Waves** coffeehouse offers an alternative to the seafood-shack vibe. Coffee, couches, grilled panini sandwiches, and gelato make this a good place to take a break from the

Texas Parks and Wildlife established the Great Texas Coastal Birding Trail to guide bird-watchers as well as protect these valuable natural resources.

The trail is divided into three regions. The Upper Coast covers the area from the Louisiana border to the region west of Houston. The Central Coast takes in Matagorda Bay, the area surrounding Victoria and Corpus Christi, and south past Kingsville. The Lower Coast picks up here, encompassing the south Texas towns of Brownsville, Harlingen, and McAllen, and South Padre Island. (The Rio Grande Valley area is also served by the World Birding Center, described in chapter 6, p. 132.) The Great Texas Coastal Birding Trail exemplifies continuing efforts in the Lone Star State to highlight native wildlife, foliage, and ecosystems. These efforts have spurred economic development, preserved habitats, and created recreational opportunities. They provide an education now that one hopes will lead to conservation later.

Brown and white signs featuring a bird flying over the coast at sunset mark the Great Texas Coastal Birding Trail. Maps are available online at www.tpwd .state.tx.us/huntwild/wildlife/wildlife-trails/coastal. As you migrate along the trail, you'll notice that some of the designated sites along it are in rural areas, and others are hidden in the bustle of cities; some are on the thoroughfares and others are on the backroads. In all cases, if you pause and really look, you'll see something special—a bird, a butterfly, perhaps a plant or insect— that you definitely wouldn't have noticed from the highway.

sun, sand, and surf. The fact that they are open daily from 5 AM to midnight guarantees their popularity.

While there are miles of public beach to enjoy in Port Aransas itself, a short drive south will take you even closer to nature. Heading out of town now on Padre Island Drive/TX 361, you'll find Mustang Island State Park approximately 13 miles south of Port Aransas. Located right on the beach and away from the crowds, the park is a popular spot for camping. The policy is first come, first served. Be sure to call in advance to make sure there aren't any closures due to high tides or other weather conditions.

Continue on Padre Island Drive/TX 361 to the end of this route, **Padre Island National Seashore.** The park, dedicated in 1968 by Lady Bird Johnson, is the longest seashore in the National Parks System and a magnet for nature lovers. What makes this stretch of beach special is the lack of development around it. There's nothing here but a visitors center with an observation deck, snack bar, and showers. Intact dunes, migratory birds, and miles of beach to comb make this park a must. There is not necessarily very much to do or see—wildlife, waves, and the sunsets over the Gulf excepted—and the folks here wouldn't have it any other way.

IN THE AREA

Aransas National Wildlife Refuge, PO Box 100, Austwell, 77950. Located on FM 2040. Call 361-286-3559. Daily sunrise to sunset; visitor center daily 8:30–4:30. Web site: www.fws.gov /southwest/refuges/texas/aransas.

Bay Education Center, 622 E. Market Street, Rockport, TX 78382. Call 361-749-6832. Tues. through Sat. 1–4. Free. Web site: www.utmsi.utexas.edu.

Beach and Station Street Grill, 235 Beach Avenue, Rockport, 78382. Call 361- 749-2303. Wed. through Sat.; hours are seasonal. Web site: www .beachandstationstreetgrill.com.

The Boiling Pot, 201 S. Fulton Beach Road, Rockport, 78382. Call 361-729-6972. Mon. through Thurs. 4–9:30, Fri. through Sun. noon–9:30. Web site: www.the-boiling-pot.com.

Café Phoenix, 229 Beach Avenue, Port Aransas, 78373. Call 361-749-9277. Daily 5 through midnight. Web site: www.coffeewaves.com.

Cheryl's, 212 S. Fulton Beach Road, Rockport, 78382. Call 361-790-9626. Hours subject to change but normally Tues. (optional) 5–9, Wed. through Sat. 5–9; call to confirm. Web site: www.cherylsbythebay.com.

Coffee Waves, 1007 TX 361,Port Aransas, 78373. Call 361-749-0825. Daily 5 through midnight. Web site: www.coffeewaves.com.

Fisherman's Wharf, 900 Tarpon Street, Port Aransas, 78373. Call 1-800-605-5448. Web site: www.wharf cat.com and www.texaswhoopers.com.

Fulton Mansion, 317 Fulton Beach Road, Fulton 78358. Call 361-729-0386. Tues. through Sat. 10–3, Sun. 1–3. Fee. Web site: www.visitfulton mansion.com.

Glow, 1815 Broadway Street, Rockport, 78382. Call 361-727-2644. Serving dinner seven nights a week, 5–9. Web site: www.glowrockport.com.

Goliad State Park & Historic Site, 108 Park Road 6, Goliad, 77963. Call

FESTIVALS

The Rockport-Fulton area hosts Oyster Fest (www.fultontexas.org) in March; the Rockport Art Festival (www.rockport-fulton.org), a juried fine arts fair, on the first weekend in July; and Seafair (www.rock portseafair.com), an October celebration, complete with a carnival, parade, and gumbo cook-off, that reels in over 20,000 visitors.

In Port Aransas, SandFest (www.texassandfest.com) in April is the largest master sand-castle competition in the United States, with participants coming from all over the world to line the beach with amazingly detailed sand sculptures. Catch a big one at the Deep Sea Roundup (www.paboatmen.org) in July, one of the coast's largest and oldest fishing contests.

361-645-3405. Web site: www.tpwd .state.tx.us.

Goose Island State Park, 202 S. Palmetto Street, Rockport, 78382. Call 361-729-2858. Web site: www.tpwd .state.tx.us.

Great Texas Coastal Birding Trail. Web site: www.tpwd.state.tx.us/hunt wild/wildlife/wildlife-trails/coastal.

Hoopes' House Bed & Breakfast, 417 N. Broadway, Rockport, 78382. Call 1-800-924-1008 or 361-729-8424, ext. 300. Web site: www.hoopeshouse .com.

Latitude 28 02 Restaurant and Art Gallery, 105 N. Austin Street, Rockport, 78382. Call 361-727-9009. Tues. through Sun. 5–last table. Web site: www.latituderockport.com. Reservations recommended.

The Lighthouse Inn, 200 S. Fulton Beach Road, Rockport, 78382. Call 1-866-790-8439. Web site: www.light housetexas.com.

Lisabella's Bistro, 5009 TX 361, , Port Aransas, 78373. Call 361-749-4222. Lunch Tues. through Sat. lunch 11–2; Dinner Tues. through Sat. 5–8:30. Web site: www.lisabellasbistro .com.

Matagorda Island State Park. Call: 979-323-9553. Web site: www.tpwd .state.tx.us.

Moondog Seaside Eatery, 100 Casterline Drive, Fulton, 78358. Call 361-729-6868. Thurs. through Tues. 11–9.

Mustang Island State Park, 17047 TX 361, Port Aransas 78373. Call 361-749-5246. Web site: www.tpwd.state .tx.us.

MATAGORDA ISLAND STATE PARK

While the huge green island to the north marked Matagorda Island State Park might catch your eye if you're scanning the map, this state park and wildlife refuge is accessible only by private or chartered boat through its northernmost point of entry, Port O'Connor. While there are campsites for the adventurous, you'll need to bring all your own supplies, including drinking water, and there are no motorized vehicles allowed on the island. Your efforts will be rewarded with pristine nature, utter seclusion, and silence, except for the sounds of the wind and the waves. Visit www.tpwd.state.tx.us for details.

Padre Island National Seashore, 20420 Park Road 22, Corpus Christi, 78418. Call 361-949-8068. Fee. Web site: www.nps.gov.

Pelican Bay Resort, 4206 N. I-35 at Pelican Bay Lane, Rockport, 78382. Call 361-729-7177. Web site: www.pelicanbayresort.com.

Port Aransas Chamber of Commerce Tourist & Convention Bureau, 403 W. Cotter, Port Aransas, 78373. Call 1-800-45-COAST or 361-749-5919. Web site: www.portaransas.org.

Rockport, 78382. Call 1-877-892-4737. Web site: www.rockportadventures.com.

Rockport Birding and Kayak Adventures, 216 N. Fulton Beach Road, Fulton, 78382. Call 361-727-0643. Web site: www.whoopingcranetours.com.

Rockport Center for the Arts, 902 Navigation Circle, Rockport, 78382. Call 361-729-5519. Tues. through Sat. 10–4, Sun. 1–4. Web site: www.rockportartcenter.com.

Rockport Daily Grind, 302 S. Austin Street, Rockport, 78382. Call 361-790-8745. Tues. through Sat. 7–3. Web site: www.rockportdailygrind.com.

Rockport-Fulton Chamber of Commerce, 319 Broadway, Rockport, 78382. Call 1-800-242-0071 or 361-729-6445. Web site: www.rockport-fulton.org.

Tarpon Inn, 200 E. Cotter Avenue, Port Aransas, 78373. Call 361-749-5555. Web site: www.thetarponinn.com.

Texas Maritime Museum, 1202 Navigation Circle, Rockport, 78382. Call 866-729-2469. Tues. through Sat. 10–4, Sun. 1–4. Fee. Web site: www.texasmaritimemuseum.org.

Texas State Aquarium, 2710 North Shoreline Boulevard, Corpus Christi, 78402. Call 361-881-1200. Daily 9–5, an hour later in spring and summer. Fee. Web site: www.texasstate aquarium.org.

Venetian Hot Plate, 232 Beach Avenue, Port Aransas, 78373. Call 361-749-7617. Summer Tues. through Sat. lunch 11:30–1:30; dinner 5–10. Winter Tues. through Sat. lunch 11:30–1:30; dinner Tues. through Thurs. 5–9, Fri. through Sun. 5–10. Web site: www .venetianhotplate.com. Reservations recommended.

The Alamo Inn in Alamo

6 The Rio Grande Valley

Getting there: To reach the region from San Antonio, it is approximately 140 miles south to McAllen on I-37 and US 281. From Corpus Christi it is approximately 160 miles to Brownsville on US 77, passing through King Ranch (see Box) en route.

From McAllen, travel 12 miles north on US 281 to Edinburg or 8 miles east on Business 83 to Alamo. Directly south of Alamo, approximately 7 miles on FM 907, is the Santa Ana National Wildlife Refuge. Retrace your steps north and continue along Business 83 to Weslaco, then hop on US 83, taking it east to McAllen, then south to TX 100, and finally to Los Fresnos for a total of 37 miles. From Los Fresnos, continue along TX 100 23 miles to South Padre Island. Details for touring the sites in the World Birding Center are found on pp. 132 and 133.

Highlights: Folks who grew up here say that you used to be able to smell the sweet scent of orange blossoms wafting in on the breezes. Needless to say, times have since changed. The Rio Grande Valley, or simply "the valley" to most Texans, abuts the Rio Grande and neighboring Mexico, and has been drawing people and wildlife for centuries. This route begins at the **Museum of South Texas History**—winding its way through the region's many parks and preserves that have been set aside for the millions of migratory birds in the area, including the popular **Santa Ana National Wildlife Refuge** and those designated as part of the network of the World Birding Center—and ends on the shores of **South Padre Island**. You'll spend much of the route on Business 83, considered a slow and scenic byway and not to be confused with the longer and busier US 83, with detours south to sights along the border.

Total distance: 80 miles from McAllen to South Padre Island

Intersections: Chapter 5

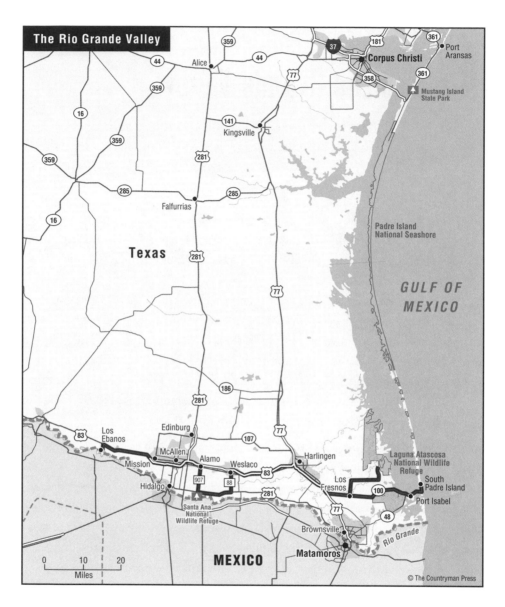

The Rio Grande Valley is relatively small, approximately 40 miles by 140 miles. It is diverse, growing, fascinating, and vulnerable. I recommend taking at least five days to see it, more if you are a serious birder or nature lover. This corner of Texas has a culture all its own, so leave plenty of time for chatting with locals. You can either pick one place to stay for the duration of your tour, and make day trips, or move every other night or so just to experience a new perspective. I have laid out a basic route that includes the essentials of a sojourn into the valley, suggesting detours to help you customize or extend your trip, according to your schedule or interests.

The history of this region is complex, and most likely unknown to the first-time visitor, which is why the **Museum of South Texas History** in Edinburg is the perfect place to start any journey into the Rio Grande Valley. The museum began in 1967 as a county museum housed in the 1910 Hidalgo County jail. A massive $5.5 million expansion yielded the present building in 2003. An impressive space, the museum has plenty of catching details, from the grand lobby with its fantastic iron and stonework to the well-presented interpretative exhibits tracing regional history from prehistoric days to the 20th century. With even more improvements and additions already in the works, this museum is on the rise, and set to join the ranks of other extremely well-done regional museums such as the Panhandle-Plains Historical Museum in Canyon (see p. 195). Walking through, visitors will grow to appreciate the borderland heritage of South Texas and northeastern Mexico, and the old and enduring relationship between the two countries. In fact, many of the exhibits overlook national boundaries, treating the region as a unified whole, highlighting its shared ecology, geology, and prehistory, and speaking to the shared cultural influences of both native peoples and European colonization. Be sure to spend some time in this pleasant and informative museum. You'll leave with a much better idea of the depth of this region's history, history not readily apparent on its 21st-century surface.

The next stop is **McAllen,** 12 miles to the south. The land that McAllen currently occupies was once the Santa Anita Ranch, established in 1797 and known for raising cattle, sheep, goats,

Entrance to the Museum of South Texas History in Edinburg

and horses. Eventually, through marriage and inheritance, it became the McAllen Ranch. To give you an idea of the size of the enterprise, consider the fact that McAllen, a city of over 100,000, now sits within the former boundaries of the McAllen Ranch. As with many other regions of Texas, the arrival of the railroad in the 1900s ushered in new patterns of commerce and transportation. Here, the effect of the railroads was compounded by the establishment of large-scale irrigation, a combination that set the stage for changes that would alter the way of life in South Texas forever.

South Texas was put to work growing many of the nation's staples. Cotton, corn, alfalfa, citrus fruit, grapes, and figs grew fast in the hot Texas sun; by 1920, McAllen was booming. Over time, this transformation from a ranching to a farming economy heightened cultural tensions as Hispanics, who historically had exercised a certain amount of self-determination, were overpowered by largely Anglo business interests. To this day, the region continues to grow, stretching the limits of its ecology, cultures, and borders.

The busy, modern city of McAllen is home to one of the lodging options on this route, the Colonial-style **Renaissance Casa de Palmas Hotel**. While the hotel is part of the Marriott chain, like all of their Renaissance establishments it retains much of its original charm. Painted brick, exposed beams, and a lush courtyard with a gurgling fountain complete the Old South Texas ambiance. The Casa de Palmas is a good bet for visitors who like such practicalities as a convenient urban location paired with such amenities as a swimming pool.

The **Patio on Guerra** is pricey enough to be on the "special occasion" list, but the combination of food and ambiance really does make it a standout. Located in the 17th Street Arts and Entertainment District, the building features exposed brick, well-worn wooden doors, wrought ironwork, and

BZZZ

South Texas is subtropical, which means that the sun is hot, the air is humid, and mosquitoes are abundant. Before venturing out into the region's various parks and nature preserves, be sure to bring along some extra sunscreen, insect repellent, and water. Despite the heat, consider wearing closed footwear (not sandals or flip-flops) and long pants for protection.

KING RANCH

King Ranch is legendary. One of the world's largest ranches, it spreads over 825,000 acres of pure South Texas between Corpus Christi and Brownsville. Founded by Captain Richard King and Mifflin Kenedy, former steamboat owners, in 1853 the ranch encompassed a rugged region known as the Wild Horse Desert, with the cool Santa Gertrudis Creek running through it. When Captain King started stocking the ranch with cattle, as the story goes, he traveled to the tiny northern Mexican town of Cruillas in the state of Tamaulipas to purchase herds that were advertised for sale. Upon his arrival, King was so taken with the townspeople, who were suffering a persistent drought and selling their livestock as a last resort, that he offered jobs on his ranch to anyone who might like to follow him back north to Texas. The promise of food, shelter, and work was too much to resist and much of the town's already skilled cattle workers took him up on the offer. They became known as Los Kineños—King's people. Expert horsemen and cattlemen, Los Kineños soon became legends themselves, a revered and essential part of the ranch's success.

a lovely cobbled patio dotted with palms. The restaurant is known for its succulent steaks, serving some of the best in the valley. **Alhambra** has a high-energy lounge vibe that pairs well with the creative menu, vibrant ambiance, and live salsa and merengue. A good place for drinks and tapas-style noshes—try the chorizo lollipops, crab cakes with avocado mousse, and stuffed dates wrapped in bacon. The expansive outdoor courtyard feels romantic. Serious tamale lovers won't mind the effort it takes to seek out **Delia's**, a no-frills Rio Grande Valley institution, located along a nondescript stretch of south 23rd Street. Folks say the ones with jalapeño and cream cheese are genius.

Another option is the **Alamo Inn** in the little town of **Alamo**, just 8 miles east of McAllen along Business 83/TX 347. Gracious owner Keith very much embodies the spirit of the valley and is someone any birder would love to meet. A native Australian who in the 1960s spent a year as an exchange student in a Progreso-area high school, Keith returned in the 1990s to marry his high school sweetheart and settle down in South Texas. A walking encyclopedia of birding knowledge and an all-around nice guy, Keith shares handy maps with guests, patiently gives directions, and is happy to make recommendations of nearby restaurants.

Originally built as an office building, the inn was remodeled as apartments in the 1940s; consequently all of the rooms are actually roomy suites, containing a bedroom (sometimes two), bathroom, and living room. The charming period tile work remains in the bath, and the high ceilings, wooden floors, and comfortable furniture create an open, airy feel. Breakfast is served each morning. Should you need birding books or insect repellent, Keith has them for sale in his bird-centric boutique. Alamo's small-town personality combined with the innkeeper's per-

LA VIRGEN DE SAN JUAN DE LOS LAGOS

Leaving McAllen and heading southeast on Business 83 you will soon pass the town of San Juan, home of the shrine of La Virgen de San Juan de los Lagos. Built in 1954, the shrine quickly became a popular destination for tourists and pilgrims until the building was destroyed by a small wayward airplane in 1970. The crash turned out to be intentional; the person responsible radioed 20 minutes before the strike that all Methodist and Catholic churches in the region should be evacuated. These malicious motives weren't enough to destroy the statue of the virgin, which was pulled from the wreckage unscathed. Though the crash caused $1.5 million in damages, the community of San Juan rallied, raising funds to rebuild the shrine, which was rededicated in 1980. If you are passing by, it is worth pausing for a look—not only at the statue of the virgin and the grounds of the shrine, but at the diverse crowds that come in droves daily to pay their respects.

sonal, yet unobtrusive manner make the Alamo Inn a terrific experience.

More Texas hospitality awaits at **El Dorado**. This Mexican restaurant located just across the street from the Alamo Inn is a local favorite and buzzes with diners from breakfast through dinner. The menu is inexpensive—a plate of traditional *migas,* eggs scrambled with strips of corn tortilla, will set you back only $3.50—and the food and atmosphere are both family-friendly. Comfortable and casual, El Dorado serves seafood fresh from the Gulf, Mexican staples such as enchiladas and slow-cooked *carne guisada* (beef tips in gravy), and American burgers, more than enough to keep the locals happy and coming back.

MAMA'S COOKIN'

While you'd think that great Mexican food would be easy to find on the border, the fact is, pickings are a bit slim. Everywhere I went, I asked folks where their favorite place to eat was, and the answers fell into one of two categories, either "my mother's house" or "my grandmother's house." As this tight-knit, family-centered culture knows, the best meals in the world are almost always prepared at home.

In many ways, the Rio Grande Valley is a region of contrasts. The location of some of the nation's richest farmland, it is also home to the nation's poorest county. The region has an astounding amount of diversity, from ecosystems to cultures, but the diverse parts don't necessarily coexist in harmony. The natural environment in South Texas is as endangered as the species that rely on it for life. In Texas, 97 percent of the land is privately owned, and so its fate is directly linked to the ethics and interests of its owners. With so much development in the region, economic interests tend to be put before any other. But, by that very token, tourism is becoming a larger part of the South Texas economy, and **ecotourism** and **birding** top the list.

More and more, people are coming to South Texas to see the birds. There are 11 separate and distinct biotic communities in the Lower Rio Grande Valley. From temperate to tropical, desert to forest, saltwater to freshwater, the variety of landscape and the wildlife it supports is truly remarkable. Whether birds are migrating between North and South America or wintering in Texas, you can count on seeing hundreds of species right here in the valley. Migratory travel tends to be

THE WORLD BIRDING CENTER

The World Birding Center is a network of parks and preserves in the Rio Grande Valley dedicated entirely to birding and the preservation of the native habitat of South Texas. Illustrating the truism that "birds of a feather flock together," the center represents the extraordinary vision, cooperation, and shared interests of various valley organizations that have pooled resources and expertise to give visitors the best opportunity to see the Rio Grande Valley for the ecological treasure that it is.

A series of nine sites, strung along 120 miles of the Rio Grande from Roma to South Padre, the center is an intense concentration of birding opportunities. It's a paradise for birders and hikers, nature lovers, and photographers alike who also enjoy the parks and preserves year-round. All visitors can appreciate the beauty of the native South Texas landscape, especially after driving through the growing sprawl of the McAllen/Harlingen/Brownsville metro area. The center ultimately hopes to preserve 10,000 acres of native habitat, with paths and bird-watching stations for the public.

The headquarters of the center is the Bentsen–Rio Grande Valley State Park in Mission. What makes this spot particularly distinctive are its many "valley specialties," birds so unique they are found only in the park, and "Mexican vagrants," birds that occasionally cross over from northern Mexico to visit the region. It is no accident that this area along the Rio Grande is so attractive to birds. The river has a natural cycle of trickling and flooding, and this ebb and flow of water has made the earth on its banks very rich and fertile, able to support the cedar elm, sugar hackberry, Rio Grande ash, Texas ebony, and anaqua trees the birds favor. In the 1950s, Falcon Dam was constructed across the Rio Grande, restricting and controlling its flow for purposes of irrigation, water storage, and flood management. What was good for people wasn't especially good for the ecosystem, and the birds' habitat suffered. These days, the center, like the Santa Ana National Wildlife Refuge (see p. 134), simulates the original conditions of the river, re-creating the natural habitat of the birds, who can't resist returning.

from mid-March to May and again from September to December, though there is an enormous variety on view all year long, including rare species unlikely to be seen elsewhere.

While McAllen and its environs do constitute a metropolitan area, as far as the birds are concerned it's just a place to fly over on their way to a respite. Several wildlife refuges are within easy reach of the city, and birders flock here as frequently as the birds themselves.

A mini-backroads route, the **World Birding Center** is fascinating to the serious bird-watcher. Approximate directions are: From McAllen, it is about 8 miles west on US 83 to Mission and an additional 48 miles to Roma. Within more immediate proximity to McAllen, it is 13 miles north on US 281 to Edinburg or 9 miles south on TX 336. Heading east, it is 18 miles to Weslaco and an additional 20 miles to Harlingen, all driven on US 83. You can then continue on US 83/US 77 27 miles south to Brownsville and then an additional 28 miles east along the Brownsville/Port Isabel Highway before ending on South Padre Island. The sites included in the World Birding Center are organized here from west to east:

Roma Bluffs is a small preserve in Roma that sits on what was, in the days when the Rio Grande was allowed to run its natural course, a steamboat port. Wooded and right beside the river, this unique habitat is home to birds so specialized they are not seen even a few miles farther downstream.

The **Edinburg Scenic Wetlands** is located in the city of Edinburg, just north of McAllen, and has pathways and observation platforms spread out over 40 acres.

Back in McAllen, the **Quinta Mazatlan** ("country estate," in Spanish) is a lovely 1930s Spanish Revival adobe hacienda built in what was then a rapidly developing McAllen. Today the facility, used as an events and conference center, is surrounded by the city, but its grounds are a study in conservation. Lush native foliage and more formal gardens are an oasis for birds and visitors, both of whom come seeking peace and quiet. One visit and you'll want to go home and start planting.

The **Estero Llano Grande State Park** is made up of 200 acres of wetlands in Weslaco. Abundant water in late summer makes this park a magnet for migrating waterfowl.

In Hidalgo, the **Old Hidalgo Pumphouse,** a leftover reminder of the area's agricultural history, is now a museum. The museum's grounds, along with the neighboring 600 acres of US Fish and Wildlife land, are home to dozens of kinds

Waterfowl enjoying a perch beside a resacas

of birds, especially hummingbirds. The land is being restored, with native grasses and trees, in the hopes that the preserve's popularity will grow.

The **Harlingen Arroyo Colorado** has peaceful wooded paths amid a tangle of highways in Harlingen.

The **Resaca de la Palma State Park** is the largest piece of land in the World Birding Center. This park, located in Brownsville, features the region's characteristic *resacas*, the shallow ponds that remain when a swollen river retreats, and the wildlife they support.

Finally, the **South Padre Island Birding and Nature Center** is a wonderful spot of natural land on an island bursting at the seams with development.

Approximately 7 miles directly south of Alamo, on FM 907, is the **Santa Ana National Wildlife Refuge,** considered one of the top 10 birding destinations in the country. The 2,000-acre refuge runs along the banks of the Rio Grande in an area where the subtropics, Gulf Coast, Great Plains, and Chihuahuan desert merge. Surrounded by cities and fields, this pocket of subtropical forest is an oasis for 400 different types of birds, not to mention half the nation's butterfly species. When the Rio Grande flowed in its natural state, flooding across the delta formed distinctive lakes, called *resacas,* which supported both plants and animals. Dams have altered this pattern, threatening the river ecosystem, but the Santa Ana Wildlife Refuge has taken steps to re-create the normal flooding cycle of the river to sustain the region's native foliage, trees, birds, animals, and insects.

Visiting Santa Ana is not only a chance to spot birds and other wildlife, but to see the land of South Texas as nature intended it. The refuge has 12 miles of hiking trails, a portion of which is wheelchair and stroller accessible. There is an ad-

THE BORDER

The Texas-Mexico border has a culture all its own. Far from displaying the rich cultural heritage of Mexico's interior, the border towns can seem crass markets desperate for dollar-spenders from north of the border. Factories just over the border, maquiladoras, supply US companies with products at what many consider great environmental and social cost. Many Americans, harboring no great curiosity about Mexican culture, come to border towns to buy trinkets, name-brand knockoffs, and cheap medications, venturing just a few hundred feet into the country before returning stateside.

Should you decide to make a trip into Mexico, the most manageable town in the region is Progreso. Be prepared for a dramatic culture shift; while south Texas may not be prosperous, the Mexican side of the Rio Grande is downright poor. While haggling over prices might be the way business is transacted here, be sure to be respectful. Be especially mindful of your surroundings and personal safety, and careful to abide by the country's laws. As with any culture, a smile goes a long way.

You can drive to the border, park your car in an unsecured though relatively safe lot for $1.50 and simply walk across. Most car insurers' policies do not extend into Mexico, so confirm the extent of your policy. It will cost you 25 cents to walk the bridge to Mexico and 30 cents to walk back, and you will need to provide proper identification, ideally a passport, for each individual crossing.

COLONIAS

Though McAllen is a modern city, it is bordered, as are most of the cities and towns in South Texas, by colonias. These unregulated settlements are the homes of immigrants from both Mexico and Central America, both legal and illegal, who are employed as agricultural workers but are unable to pay for proper housing in the United States. In Texas many of the colonias are tiny plots of former farmland that cotton farmers sold to workers for very little money after the cotton market collapsed in the 1960s. While the land was unregulated with minimum building requirements, a plus for workers looking to build their own modest homes, there were also little or no public utilities. Though promises were made about future services, the utilities rarely followed; many have lived in these colonias without running water or sewers for decades. Not surprisingly, these conditions have been the breeding ground for illness; dysentery, hepatitis, tuberculosis, and skin rashes can be common. This complex problem serves to illustrate the political and social complexities of life on a border, especially a border between two countries at such different stages of development.

ditional 7-mile tour road, which you can drive at your own convenience, and an interpretive tram leaves the visitors center three times a day to make an hour-and-a-half circuit of the property.

Continue southeast on US 281, turning north on FM 88, which becomes S. Texas Boulevard. Head north to S. Texas Boulevard, the entrance to **Frontera Audubon Preserve and Visitor's Center** in **Weslaco**. The center is located just four blocks south of downtown, but, as a stroll on its wooded trails will show, might as well be miles away. The preserve contains many citrus trees, reminders of its former role as an orchard. Several man-made waterways and plenty of native vegetation draw wildlife like a magnet. The paths are flat, easy to navigate, and while they aren't entirely paved, in dry weather the dirt is packed hard enough to make stroller and wheelchair use a possibility. The center has undergone many changes over the years, with more to come. As you approach the center, you'll find an older home gracing the front of the property (drive around to the left to find parking in the back). An outstanding example of local architecture and rife with charm and detail, the home had fallen into disrepair by the time it was donated to the center. The dream is to see this gem restored and used for social functions and events. Also in Weslaco, the **Valley Nature Center** is a modest community-center-style building tucked into a shaded public park. A good resource for nature lovers, the center can offer helpful suggestions and tips.

From Weslaco, take the larger US 83 20 miles east to Harlingen, and follow US 83/US 77 south 18 miles to TX 100 and cruise into the small town of Los Fresnos. Here you'll find the **Inn at Chachalaca Bend**, one of the most relaxing and luxurious places to stay in the valley. The place is so lovely they are booked every weekend for weddings and private functions every weekend a year in advance. However, there is usually room at the inn Monday through Thursdays, making it the perfect midweek respite. The gated property is on the edge of Los Fresnos

Aloe vera plant growing on a bluff overlooking the Gulf of Mexico

Lush grounds of the Inn at Chachalaca Bend

and thick with native foliage and spectacular trees teeming with buzzing, cawing, and chirping wildlife. Stone paths wind their way throughout and the porches, balconies, and waterside seating are inviting. Each room has a king-size bed, Jacuzzi, and outdoor access for relaxing. Complimentary refreshments are available in the comfortable common room throughout the day, and the morning buffet breakfast of fresh fruit, eggs, and pancakes is superb. Once you arrive at the Inn at Chachalaca Bend, you may not want to leave. It isn't a place to spend the night so much as it is a retreat, and just the sort for travelers who like solitude.

Many people find Los Fresnos to be a good jumping-off point into either the **Laguna Atascosa National Wildlife Refuge** or **South Padre Island**, as it is equidistant to both. The Laguna Atascosa National Wildlife Refuge is the largest surviving swatch of natural habitat in the Rio Grande Valley. The 45,000-acre refuge is located on the mainland, protected from the Gulf of Mexico by South Padre Island. The refuge has many *resacas* that become low-level ponds and tidal mud flats (*atascosa* means "muddy" in Spanish). In addition to hundreds of species of birds, the refuge is also home to the endangered ocelot and other mammals, and native brush has been planted in former agricultural fields in an attempt to regain habitat for this wildlife. To get there from Los Fresnos, take Paredes Line Road north, then east on San Jose Ranch Road to the refuge.

Going south, South Padre Island is a breezy half-hour drive from Los Fresnos, just 23 miles along TX 100. South Padre is Texas' vacation hot spot. From "spring breaks" to summer vacations, thousands upon thousands of tourists descend on South Padre for sun, sand, and surf. TX 100 takes you from Port Isabel, on the mainland, to the southern tip of South Padre, where it is a short drive north along Padre Drive to the start of the **Laguna Madre Nature Trail**, the southern anchor of the World Birding Center. Located beside the convention center and whaling wall no. 53, the Laguna Madre Nature trail is the antidote to the high-rise condos, hotels, and restaurants that weigh down the island. The 1,500-foot boardwalk allows visitors to gingerly cross 4 acres of wetlands for an up-close look at the many birds, butterflies, and other wildlife that live in the natural dunes of the Laguna Madre.

Since South Padre Island is the first strip of land birds encounter on their migration north across the Gulf, many stop to rest and refuel, gracing the region with their presence. The island's diverse habitat of dunes, salt marshes, and intertidal flats attracts a huge variety. Spring rains attract warblers, orioles, and

Boats docked near South Padre Island at sunset

thrushes to the thick native foliage, and the wetlands host the endangered brown pelican and peregrine falcon. For photographers, it's ideal.

While you may have had your eye in the sky looking for birds, when you're this close to the Gulf, it's a great time to take a look in the water. On South Padre, there are several organizations dedicated to the survival of marine creatures. **Sea Turtle, Inc.**, began in 1977, when the "Turtle Lady of South Padre Island," the spirited Ila Loetscher, championed the cause of the at-risk Kemp's Ridley sea turtle. Together with the US Fish and Wildlife Service, Sea Turtle scouts local beaches for nests; they maintain a facility for rescued and recovering turtles. The public is welcome to attend the "Meet the Turtles" demonstrations, led by volunteers, which focus on education, conservation, and interesting turtle tips and facts. Sea Turtle, Inc., is a home-grown, seaside learning experience with a big heart. Another local organization with an admirable mission is the **South Padre Island Dolphin Research and Sea Life Nature Center.** Visitors can spend some time in the low-tech, high-interest Sea Life Nature Center checking out all the photos and display about the different dolphins the center has been researching. Get out on the water with **Breakaway Cruises** and see the dolphins up close in their natural habitat of the Gulf.

Pay a visit to the spectacular Rio Grande Valley and make an investment in the future of Texas. Spend some time—and money—supporting some of the great organizations that are contributing to the survival of this complex and fragile region and working to preserve it for generations to come.

IN THE AREA

Alamo Chamber of Commerce, 130 S. Eighth Street, Alamo, 78516. Call 956-787-2117. Web site: www.alamo chamber.com.

Alamo Inn, 801-B Main Street, Alamo, 78516. Call 956-782-9912. Web site: www.alamoinnsuites.com.

Alhambra, 519 S. 17th Street, McAllen, 78501. Call 956-772-4252. Tues. through Wed. 5–10, Thurs. through Sat. 5–midnight; lounge stays open later. Web site: www.alhambra on17th.com.

Bentsen–Rio Grande Valley State Park, 2800 S. Bentsen Palm Drive (FM 2062) Mission, TX 78572. Located several miles southwest of Mission, at the end of FM 2062, and can

be reached from several marked exits off Loop 373 and/or US 83. Fee. Call 956-584-9156. Web site: www.the worldbirdingcenter.com.

Breakaway Cruises, 1 Padre Boulevard, South Padre Island, 78597. Call 956-761-2212. Fee. Web site: www .breakawaycruises.com.

Delia's, 4800 S. 23rd Street, McAllen, 78503. Call 956-630-3502. Mon. through Sat. 6–8, Sun. 7–6. Web site: www.deliastamales.com.

El Dorado, 755 Main Street, Alamo, 78516. Call 956-787-8822.

Frontera Audubon Preserve and Visitor's Center, 1101 S. Texas Boulevard, Weslaco, 78596. Call 956-968-3275. Fee. Web site: www.frontera audubon.org.

Inn at Chachalaca Bend, 20 Chachalaca Bend Drive, Los Fresnos, 78566. Call 1-888-612-6800 or 956-233-1180. Web site: www.chachalaca.com.

King Ranch Visitor Center, 2205 TX 141 W., PO Box 1090, Kingsville, 78364. Call 361-592-8055. Web site: www.king-ranch.com.

Laguna Atascosa National Wildlife Refuge, 22817 Ocelot Road, Los Fresnos, 78566. Call 956-748-3607. Daily 10–4; call for summer hours. Fee. Web site: www.fws.gov/refuges.

Laguna Madre Nature Trail, 7355 Padre Boulevard, South Padre Island, 78597. Call 956-761-3005. Daily 9–5. Web site: www.worldbirdingcenter.org.

McAllen Chamber of Commerce, 1200 Ash Avenue, McAllen, 78501. Call 956-682-2871. Web site: www.mcallenchamber.com.

Museum of South Texas History, 200 North Closner Boulevard, Edinburg, 78541. Call 956-383-6911. Tues. through Sat. 10–5, Sun. 1–5. Fee. Web site: www.mosthistory.org.

The Patio on Guerra, 116 S. 17th Street, McAllen, 78501. Call 956-661-9100. Mon. through Wed. 5–11, Thurs. through Sun. 5–midnight. Web site: www.patioonguerra.com.

Quinta Mazatlan, 600 Sunset Avenue, McAllen, 78503. Call 956-681-3370. Tues. through Sat. 8–5, Thurs. until dark. Fee. Web site: www.quintamazatlan.com.

Renaissance Casa de Palmas Hotel, 101 N. Main Street, McAllen, 78501. Call 956-631-1101. Web site: www.renaissancehotels.com.

Santa Ana National Wildlife Refuge, FM 907, off US 281, Alamo, 78516. Call 956-784-7500. Web site: www.fws.gov/refuges.

Sea Turtle, Inc., 6617 Padre Boulevard, South Padre Island, 78597. Call 956-761-4511. Tues. through Sun. 10–4. Fee. Web site: www.seaturtleinc.com.

FESTIVALS

Experience South Texas hospitality; visit during a festival. Mission kicks off the festivities in January with the Texas Citrus Fiesta (www.texascitrusfiesta.net), followed in March by SpringFest in McAllen, and the wildly popular BorderFest (www.myborderfest.org) in Hidalgo. The Texas Tropics Nature Festival (www.mcallen.org) in April and the Fourth of July Fajita Cookoff in July are both in McAllen. And Harlingen hosts the Rio Grande Valley Birding Festival (www.rgvbf.org) in November.

LOS EBANOS FERRY

On the Rio Grande, 18 miles northwest of Mission is the little border town of Los Ebanos, the site of the last international ferry crossing on the border. This fact is made all the more remarkable by the ferry's source of power: several men pulling a rope. This little boat hauls people, cars, and any number of other items across this shallow 25-foot span of the Rio Grande each day as they've done without fail for years. There's been talk of building a bridge, but no one seems in a rush to get it done. After all, this hands-on method has worked for over two generations with enormous efficiency, punctuality, and friendliness. Due to its size, the ferry can only transport several dozen cars a day, and it stops running in bad weather. On a good day, however, the crossing takes about eight minutes, and the charge is a reasonable 50 cents per person or $2.50 per automobile. A quick, easy, and low-cost—not to mention low-tech—alternative to driving the half hour to the nearest bridge in nearby Rio Grande City.

There isn't much to the town of Los Ebanos except a little collection of homes and a border patrol outpost hugging the river. On the Mexican side of the crossing you'll be greeted by an open field, a taxi willing to take you the mile and a half south to Diaz Ordaz, and a shaved ice truck. While there's nothing scenic about it, Los Ebanos serves to illustrate that while the Rio Grande may be an international border to some, to others it is still just the local river that needs crossing.

South Padre Island Chamber of Commerce, 600 Padre Boulevard, #B, South Padre Island, 78597. Call 956-761-4412. Web site: www.spichamber.com.

South Padre Island Dolphin Research and Sea Life Nature Center, Lighthouse Square, 110 N. Garcia, Port Isabel, 78578. Call 956-299-1957.

Mon. through Sat. 10–4, Sun. 11–4. Fee. Web site: www.spinaturecenter.com.

Valley Nature Center, 301 S. Border Avenue, Weslaco, 78599. Call 956-969-2475. Web site: www.valleynaturecenter.org.

World Birding Center. Web site: www.theworldbirdingcenter.com.

Fishing from a rock jetty

7 Galveston Island

Getting there: From Houston, take I-45 50 miles south to Galveston.

Highlights: From the historic old business district, the **Strand**, to the architectural charm of the lovely homes on the tree-lined blocks of the **East End**, to the sun and sand along the **Seawall**, Galveston offers multilayered insights into Texas history. Nature lovers will enjoy a trip to **Moody Gardens**, and bird-watchers will relish the opportunities to comb the beach, particularly at **Galveston Island State Park.**

Total distance: Galveston Island is 27 miles long and less than 3 miles wide at its widest point. The city of Galveston anchors the northern end of the island. This entire chapter is devoted to the island, much of it within the city itself.

G raceful and gritty, storied and stately, Galveston Island is a backroad to another time. Its own history is as old as any in Texas. One of the sandy barrier islands strung across the length of Texas, Galveston first appears in the historical record as home to the Karankawa Indians. It is thought to be the site of the 1528 shipwreck of explorer Alvar Núñez Cabeza de Vaca, the first European to set foot on Texas soil. In 1785, José de Evia, an explorer mapping the Texas coast, named these waters Galveston Bay, after Bernardo de Gálvez, the viceroy of Mexico. The name was soon shortened to Galveston and applied to the island. The first European inhabitants began living here in 1816 when Louis Michel Aury, an opportunistic privateer, established a port and began running ships to Mexico to aid in the Mexican Revolution. In 1817, Jean Lafitte grabbed control of the island and used it for smuggling and pirate activities until 1820, when the United States government ran him off the island.

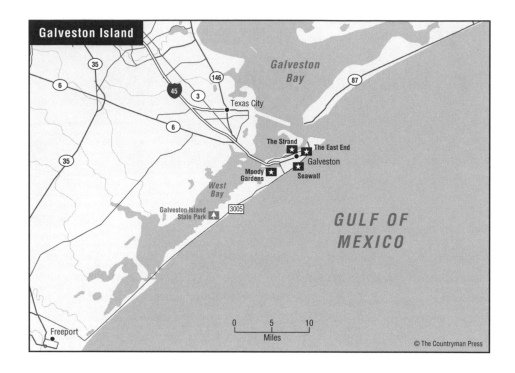

Under the Texas flag, Galveston got organized. A group of investors purchased over 4,500 acres of harborside land, laid out a grid, and started building a city. Its port grew by leaps and bounds, shipping cotton, monitoring oceangoing traffic and the steamers moving along the coast, and welcoming immigrants. A new bridge brought the railroad, linking the island to the mainland, to Houston and East Texas.

Then came the Civil War, spelling disaster for Galveston, as for much of the south. The city struggled under Union troops' occupation. After the war, beginning in 1867, an outbreak of yellow fever killed 20 people a day for years. Despite this rough spell, Galveston quickly regained its prominence. The largest city in Texas by 1870, it would be the first to have electricity, telephones, newspapers, and even baseball games. The Galveston you see today, with its layered and intricate architecture, arts, and cultural organizations, is very much a legacy of this period. At the twilight of the 19th century, genteel Galveston was thriving, paving the way to the 20th century. Then disaster struck. In 1900, the Great Storm (see box) hit Galveston head-on, taking thousands of lives and crippling its infrastructure.

No matter how wounded the city was, it still had the waterfront; in just a few years, Galveston had remade itself as a seaside resort. Grand hotels such as the Galvez (see box) opened; the Balinese Room (see box, p. 158) and numerous other nightclubs kept visitors and locals entertained through the 1950s. Big names in showbiz—Frank Sinatra, Bob Hope, Jack Benny—all came to perform. Gambling was commonplace: roulette, blackjack, craps tables, and slot machines fed the frenzy. In addition, Galveston became known for drinking, carousing, and prostitution. While this debauchery was frowned on by some, it was embraced by others who saw the rogue city as "the free state of Galveston." Illegality was rampant until 1957, when Attorney General Will Wilson rode in with a pack of Texas Rangers to restore the city's dignity.

These days, Galveston is still a popular destination. Visitors come to stroll its three distinct neighborhoods—the Seawall, the Strand, and the East End—and the leafy blocks in between. Each of Galveston's districts offers great places to

The beach beside the Seawall

THE GREAT STORM

On September 8, 1900, a hurricane roared into Galveston, killing 6,000 people within the city limits and between 4,000 and 6,000 others nearby. Winds of 135 miles an hour, rain, and sea surges meant flooding and the near destruction of the city. The storm is often referred to as the Galveston Hurricane of 1900 or the Great Galveston Hurricane, but locals call it simply the Great Storm or the 1900 Storm.

In many ways the disaster was unavoidable, but it was not without warning. Throughout the 1800s, the citizens of Galveston watched nearby towns succumb to powerful and unpredictable hurricanes. Though there was talk of building a seawall to protect the island, Galveston had handily survived all previous storms; people believed their luck would continue into the future. Instead of building a seawall, the city went right on building, expanding the municipality, increasing its vulnerability.

While the United States Weather Bureau had reports of hurricane conditions in the Gulf, in those days their skill at predicting a storm's path was rudimentary, as was their ability to communicate with residents. In the hours preceding the storm, though a hurricane warning had been issued, the weather was still pleasant and residents didn't grasp its urgency.

Conditions quickly changed. Soon rising winds and water cut off all roads, bridges, evacuation routes, and telegraph communication; as darkness fell, the city began to crumble. When the 15-foot storm surge washed over the city, it mowed down over 3,600 homes; those that survived often have a plaque reading "1900 Storm" on display. Daybreak revealed cloudless skies and mass devastation.

spend the night; each is atmospheric with plenty of individual detail, each a little piece of the city's history.

Wyndham Historic Hotels has done a lovely job with three hotels that are consistently recommended by fellow travelers. The **Hotel Galvez,** which opened in 1911, has always been known as the Queen of the Gulf for its seaside location.

Without telegraph service, residents sent several messengers to the mainland to get help and waited for a ship to come. It took several days for aid to arrive. Rescues were attempted, the dead moved, and damage assessed. In the final count, it was found that 20 percent of the island's population had lost their lives. The Great Storm remains the deadliest natural disaster in American history.

In order to prevent such devastation in the future, Galveston reconsidered the idea of a seawall; by 1902 construction was under way. The 17-foot-tall, 7-mile-long Seawall was completed eight years later. It protects the city to this day.

Coupled with the Seawall, there were efforts to raise the city itself above the danger of the sea. Workers moved massive amounts of sand to the island, placing it underneath buildings and filling in low-lying areas. Over time, thousands of buildings were elevated in this manner, a feat so remarkable that the entire project has been dubbed a National Historic Civil Engineering Landmark by the American Society of Civil Engineers.

In 2008, Hurricane Ike—classified as a high Category 2 hurricane—roared ashore following much the same route as the Great Storm and cresting the seawall. While the compromised wall provided some protection, many homes and businesses and much of the city's infrastructure were damaged or destroyed. Strongly worded evacuation warnings encouraged residents to leave the island in advance of the storm, minimizing injury and loss of life. When all was said and done, while Ike dealt the island a blow, thanks to lessons learned in the Great Storm it wasn't fatal.

The future fate of Galveston Island, though all possible precautions have been taken, is ultimately Mother Nature's decision.

The hotel is very elegant and makes quite a first impression. A grand entrance with rich fabrics, lush Victorian-era elements, and striking architectural detail make the hotel a standout. By modern standards, the rooms may seem small, but they are cozy and charming, and there are plenty of common spaces in which to stretch out and relax. The pool is private, nestled in below sidewalk level and sur-

Sculpture on Pier 21

rounded by trees and foliage; it's particularly enjoyable in the evening, when the entire area is softly lit and the warm Gulf breezes blow by.

In the historic Strand District, and therefore not within walking distance to the ocean, the **Tremont House** is another renovated beauty. Once a warehouse, this hotel has an urban, European feel, with a four-story atrium lobby complete with airy birdcage-style elevators, and full-grown palm trees. Period furnishings, high ceilings, wood floors, and marble bathrooms give the rooms an understated elegance; details like towel warmers provide luxury, while the rooftop deck is all fun.

Nearby, the **Harbor House** is altogether different. Located in another renovated warehouse at Pier 21, behind the Strand and along Galveston Bay, the Harbor House is more casual and more nautical in its details. The rooms feel large, with tall ceilings and

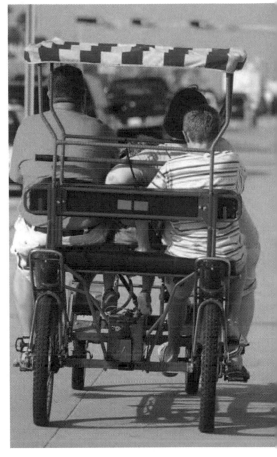

Riding a surrey bike along the Seawall

windows, exposed beams, and plenty of light. The decor and bathrooms are updated, and the price includes a morning coffee bar and fresh-baked locally made muffins. Regardless of which Wyndham you stay in, you are welcome to use the pool at the Galvez free of charge. Each of these hotels has different policies regarding parking and breakfast options, so be sure to inquire when you make your reservations.

For a more personal stay, **The Garden Inn,** a survivor of the Great Storm, is an architectural gem tucked into a neighborhood of gorgeous homes. It's just a few minutes' walk to the Strand and the East End, and only a slightly longer walk to the Seawall. While the house is certainly old, it feels clean and fresh, with

Star Drug Store on the Strand

cheerful wall colors and a mixture of heirlooms and antiques. There are three rooms in the house. The Rose Room has its own private balcony with views of the gardens. The Oleander Room features a king bed and a distinctive, though nonworking, fireplace. And the Magnolia Suite is actually two rooms with a Jack-and-Jill bath, perfect for up to four people traveling together. The rooms don't have phones or televisions, but the inn does have a pool, seats scattered throughout the gardens, and lots of historic charm to compensate.

Eating out is a pleasure in Galveston; if you visit the places listed below, you are sure to leave happy.

The Strand is home to a variety of eateries, from cafés to sandwich shops to date-night restaurants. Many diners just enjoy a leisurely walk up and down, checking out the options. One of the favorites is the **Saltwater Grill**, which features imaginative cuisine, served in an upscale yet casual setting on Post Office Street. The menu has steaks, salads, and seafood, some with an Asian flare; diners rave about the almond-coconut-entrusted shrimp served with peanut sauce. From grilled snapper to gumbo loaded with shrimp, the food is all excellent—a little pricey—and service is consistently top-notch. Folks like to go to **Rudy and Paco** for birthdays, anniversaries, and special occasions. The mixture of romantic, old world ambiance and the flavors of Latin American cuisine make events feel extra festive. The baked Gulf red snapper with sautéed lump crab meat, pico de gallo, and avocado slices is a favorite. Be sure to leave room for one of their decadent desserts. Reservations recommended and no shorts allowed. Nearby, **The Gumbo Bar** proves that New Orleans–style seafood fits right in all along the Gulf Coast. The soft shell crab po'boys have a Tabasco-laced mayo that gives 'em a little kick, and the Mumbo Gumbo includes shrimp, crab, oyster, chicken, sausage, and, in case you forgot you are in Texas, prime rib. The restaurant has a buzzing, bistro vibe, with a smallish, cozy dining room and shaded seating on the sidewalk patio.

If you are looking for a treat, stop by **La King's Confectionery** for some homemade ice cream, peanut brittle, or fudge. La King's dates back to the 1920s; they've been doing business on the Strand since the 1970s. Another easy choice is **Star Drug Store**. The store traces its roots back to 1886, but the current building you see, a brick replica of the original wooden structure, was built in 1909. Though the store has changed hands several times since, the milkshakes still taste just the way they should. Stop in at lunchtime for the nice selection of burgers, sandwiches, and salads served at the horseshoe-shaped soda fountain.

Many of Galveston's more off-beat and down-home eateries cluster in an area known as the East End, particularly along 14th Street. If you don't plan wisely around their operating hours, you just might miss dinner at the **Mosquito Café**, though lunch or breakfast is always a safe bet. Best described as "understated upscale," the Mosquito Café uses such ingredients as goat cheese, homemade fruit chutney, oven-roasted tomatoes, basil herb mayonnaise, and tamari sesame vinaigrette to enliven burgers, roasted chicken, grilled portabello mushrooms, and yellowfin tuna. The super-fresh meals run the gamut from Mediterranean to Asian, with lots of solid American standbys too. Before you order, be sure to take a peek at the daily specials on the chalkboard. Farther down the block you'll find the **Sunflower Bakery and Café**, where cinnamon rolls and a wonderfully moist blueberry coffee cake are the stars of the morning. The Texas Gulf crab cakes topped with poached eggs and hollandaise sauce are a brunch hit, and the over-

GALVESTON ON THE WEB

Galveston Island has an excellent Web site for visitors (www.galveston.com). Not only can you check every detail of your trip, but you can also create itineraries to print before you go. Seasonal, cultural, and special events information is constantly updated, making this site an invaluable resource.

Architectural beauty in the East End

stuffed sandwiches made with homemade bread are perfect to take along for picnicking at the beach. The dessert case will undoubtedly catch your eye, as it's difficult to walk by such an enormous concentration of chocolate and whipped cream and not notice.

This close to the ocean, you'll want to sample some seafood. Folks come from all over the city, and beyond, to the Seawall for a meal at **Gaido's**. Universally praised for both service and food, Gaido's has been making a name for itself since it opened in 1911. The consensus is that the grilled shrimp and the shrimp bisque are wonderful, as is the snapper, cooked any way you like it. This is not a seaside clam shack, it's old-school dining, complete with fresh bread on the table and a dessert cart at the end. Not only does Gaido's shuck their own oysters and peel shrimp by hand, but they make all their own sauces and salad dressings as well. This dedication to real food, along with white table cloths and an efficient wait-staff, has people coming back year after year. Dining is first come, first served, so go early.

Since Gaido's can be pricey as well as packed, diners looking for value stop in next door at **Casey's Seaside Café,** one of the best bargains on the Seawall. A more causal, family-friendly version of its neighbor, Casey's is owned by the same family and serves up huge portions of grilled Gulf shrimp, fried Galveston Bay oysters, and delicious daily specials that sell out quickly. If "huge" is too big for you, half-size meals are available.

The Spot is also laid back, with a distinctive beach-town ambiance. Burgers, some seafood, and plenty of fried appetizers are all available, as are drinks in the Tiki Bar, but mostly people come for the view. When it comes to watching the waves, the Spot really is the spot. The folks behind it have become mini-moguls of shoreside dining. They also own **The Drip**, a coffee bar with a wraparound deck, the festive **Rum Shack,** and funky **Squeeze**, featuring 'ritas and tequilas. Each has a similar menu and fantastic Gulf views.

For another great vantage point, visit **Murdoch's Bathhouse,** just down the street on the beach side. You can purchase all sorts of souvenirs here, from T-shirts to seashells, but the best things about this store are the dozen or so white rocking chairs on the deck out back, offered free to customers for their enjoyment. Murdoch's has been doing business here for over 100 years, but not always in the same building. The original bathhouse was destroyed by the 1900 Storm (see p. 148) and rebuilt, only to be battered by the storms of 1909 and 1915. Hur-

Galveston Island pier

ricane Carla washed Murdoch's out to sea in 1961 and it was rebuilt again, this time on piers. In 2008, Mother Nature struck yet again and Hurricane Ike took Murdoch's out to sea. Amazingly, the beloved souvenir shop was rebuilt in 2009 and has carried on selling seashells by the seashore ever since.

Leaving the Gulf shore, head across the island to the **Strand,** one of Galveston's oldest neighborhoods. Located along Avenue B, between 20th and 25th Streets, the area was known for handling the commerce that floated in and out of Galveston Harbor; it was nicknamed the Wall Street of the Southwest. Part of the original settlement of the city in the 1830s, the district was occupied by Confederate troops during the Civil War. It thrived throughout the 19th century with merchants, bankers, attorneys, and seamen sharing the bustling streets. The Great Storm damaged many of the buildings; restoration efforts have saved those you see today. That the area is so atmospheric is as much a testament to the tremendous community revitalization efforts as to 19th-century architecture. At the annual Mardi Gras celebration and a holiday-season production of "Dickens on the Strand," the district is especially vibrant.

Despite the loss of buildings in the 1900 Storm, Galveston still represents one of the largest concentrations of Victorian architecture in the United States. A stroll down Broadway will take you past some of the highlights, all managed by the **Galveston Historical Foundation.**

At 2328 Broadway sits **Ashton Villa,** built in 1859 by one of the richest men in Texas at the time, James Brown. The brick Italianate mansion is an antebellum masterpiece—an architectural treasure. Though the home represents the apex of design for its time, it was almost demolished in 1970 due to lack of interest and money. The **Galveston Historical Foundation** was formed to save it, and has since gone on to save other local buildings; it now offers tours of each. At number 1402 Broadway, **Bishop's Palace** is a fantastic study in Victorian turrets, stained glass, carvings, and sculpture. The stone building was designed by local architect Nicholas Clayton and built by Colonel Walter Gresham, a lawyer, in 1888. Grand, yet delicate, rife with detail, the building proudly occupies a spot on the American Institute of Architects' list of the 100 most important buildings in America. Farther along, at number 2618, **Moody Mansion** was the home of one of

Shells for sale at Murdoch's

THE BALINESE ROOM

The Balinese Room, built on a pier at 21st Street and Seawall Boulevard across from the Hotel Galvez, was a local institution with a very colorful past.

When the Balinese Room opened in 1929, the club immediately attracted big names. Bob Hope, Frank Sinatra, and George Burns all worked the club, while Howard Hughes and other celebrities rubbed elbows with Texas oil barons in the audience. In 1932, the establishment became a Chinese restaurant; after WWII, the Balinese Room.

Advertisements of the day encouraged folks to "Come Down and Play on Galveston Island." By "play," of course, they meant gamble. High rollers rolled in, attracting the Mob like bees to honey, and the whole operation flourished in spite of its illegality. Corruption ruled, and payoffs and favors were traded regularly. According to the record, when the sheriff of Galveston was asked in front of the Texas Legislature why he had not put a stop to the gambling at the Balinese Room, he stated that since he wasn't a member of the private club, he'd never been in. It was answers like this that got the attention of the attorney general, who rode into town with the Texas Rangers in 1956 to put an end to the shenanigans. The Balinese Room did not go down easily. Each time the Rangers raided the nightclub, the band would play "The Eyes of Texas"; it was a signal to warn employees and patrons farther down the 600-foot pier that the law had arrived and they had better hide the evidence. Eventually, the Rangers adopted a siege strategy. They simply sat in the club all day long, making it the last place in the world anyone would want to "come and play."

The club was finally shut down in 1957, and it sat vacant for years. It was purchased in 2001 and brought back to life—minus the gambling—by a respectable local attorney. Things were pretty quiet for a while as the Balinese Room slipped into a respectable retirement as a quiet place folks would come for a drink or two. Hurricane Ike destroyed the club in 2008, and a piece of Galveston's colorful history was reclaimed by the sea.

Galveston's most powerful families, and one home that the hurricanes just don't seem to miss. As the story goes, W. L. Moody purchased the home less than a week after it was damaged in the 1900 hurricane. He raised his family in its 28,000 square feet, parceled out into 32 lavishly decorated rooms. The home was also hit by hurricane Alicia in 1983, but has since been restored. Visitors can tour these properties individually or purchase a ticket to see all three of the "Broadway Beauties."

Make time to catch two short films—*The Great Storm* and *The Pirate Island of Jean Lafitte*—shown at the **Pier 21 Theater**. Each under a half hour, the films will give you a great overview of the formative events in Galveston's history. Hop next door to the **Texas Seaport Museum**, also on Pier 21, home to the tall ship *Elissa*. This three-masted beauty was constructed in Scotland in 1877 and moved to Galveston in 1982. The *Elissa* spent the intervening 90 years roaming the seas, her rigging trimmed again and again as she was bought and sold. She finally ended up as a smuggling ship in the Greek Isles. There she caught the eye of a curator for the National Maritime Historical Society in Britain, who appreciated her as one of the last surviving square-riggers in the world. He purchased her and solicited requests from cities who would like to own her.

San Francisco and Vancouver both made bids for the ship, but in the end she came to Galveston. Years of renovation brought her back to her original splendor. The *Elissa* now stays docked in Galveston, though she did travel north in 1986 to join other famous ships in New York Harbor as part of the Statue of Liberty's 100th birthday celebration. A throwback to the romance of sailing the open sea, the *Elissa* is a thrill for young and old.

If you've had enough of the shore, then hop aboard the *Seagull II* at the Texas Seaport Museum and take a tour of the harbor and shipyard. The red and white engine-powered catamaran, operated by the Galveston Historical Foundation, was built for comfort, with restrooms, a roof for protection from sun and rain, and plenty of views from all angles. The captain narrates the tour, pointing out tidbits of the history, ecology, and marine biology of the fourth-largest seaport in America.

Baywatch Dolphin Tours tools around the channel offering fun and educational tours with plenty of dolphin action. Tour guides are knowledgeable, presenting marine facts and answering questions with ease, and the dolphins seem to show up on schedule. Dolphins also perform for riders of the free **Galveston–Port Bolivar Ferry**, which can feel like a high seas adventure with them swim-

BURIED TREASURE

Jean Laffite, the French pirate, was an accomplished mariner; his exploits on the sea were legendary. One story goes so far as to claim he rode a massive storm surge up and over Galveston Island, guiding his ship to the safety of the inner coastal harbor. The most enduring of the tales about Lafitte involve buried treasure.

Since the pirate was known to have plundered many ships in his time spent trolling the Gulf—none American, he insisted—he was thought to possess a trove of treasures. Lafitte took his secret with him to the grave. His death was never documented, and speculation as to the whereabouts of his booty abounds to this day. Some believe that the man and his loot went down with his ship, *The Pride*. Others suspect it is buried in the marshes, swamps, and bayous of the Louisiana coast. The most common assumption is that it is buried on Galveston Island. So when you are out making sand castles on the beach, be sure to dig deep. You just might get lucky.

ming alongside. Back on land, there are two more points of interest in the Strand neighborhood. **The Grand 1894 Opera House** showcases the grand style that Victorian Galveston was famous for. Built in 1894, the opera house has been restored several times, once after the Great Storm and again in the 1970s and '80s. It has been declared "The Official Opera House of Texas," and hosts a wide variety of performances. Along different lines, the **Railroad Museum**, housed in an art deco former train depot, tells the story of the railroads in Texas, so important to the state's history. It has one of the largest collections of railroad memorabilia in the country, as well as three steam and three diesel engines.

With the historical portion of the visit under your belt, consider a trip to **Moody Gardens**. The organization that runs this educational attraction began as a therapeutic horseback-riding program for people with various disabilities and neurological issues. It has grown into a multifaceted facility that draws two million visitors a year. Moody Gardens' grounds are organized under three glass pyramids, each with a theme. The hot, humid, and lush **Rainforest Pyramid** has reptiles, lots of green foliage, and Technicolor-like birds. The **Discovery Pyramid** is best described as a science museum. You enter the **Aquarium** through an

Sailboat entering Galveston Harbor

GALVESTON ON FOOT

One of the most enjoyable things to do in Galveston is just wander around on foot. Considering that you have most likely paid for parking, get your money's worth; leave your car in the lot and walk the seawall, the shady neighborhoods, or the piers. Rent a bicycle or hop on and off the trolley (see box, "Getting Around Galveston") as you make your way from neighborhood to neighborhood.

One particularly nice urban neighborhood to stroll is the historic East End. Bound by Broadway to the south, 10th Street to the east, Mechanic Avenue to the north, and 19th Street to the west, the entire district is a National Historic Landmark.

The amount of architectural detail concentrated in this area is impressive. From stained glass and turrets to wrought iron fences and side porches with swings, there are many different styles represented and something interesting to look at around every corner. Some of the homes are grand mansions and some modest cottages, but they co-exist easily, just as they have, through good times and bad, for over a century.

The East End Historical District Association has a downloadable walking tour. Visit www.eastendhistoricdistrict.org.

aboveground pyramid, but quickly move underground, past enormous tanks of tropical fish, sharks, penguins, and other aquatic animals. Moody Gardens allows guests to customize their visit by purchasing individual tickets to the different pyramids. The Aquarium is always on everyone's list. Wet and wild family fun awaits next door at Schlitterbahn, a popular Texas-based water park with three locations throughout the state, consistently voted "best water park in America."

For a less-crowded, natural setting, leave Galveston and drive southwest along the Seawall. As development thins, the road becomes FM 3005; and approximately 12 miles from the city, you'll come to Galveston Island State Park, which extends from the Gulf to the bay. This park has seen a lot of use, but people looking for that quintessential low-cost, family-style beachside experience will find it quite serviceable. There is camping right on the beach, but many just come to enjoy a walk on the sand and the unobstructed views. The bayside is best for bird-watching.

IN THE AREA

1859 Ashton Villa, 2328 Broadway, Galveston, 77550. Call 409-762-3933. Web site: www.galvestonhistory.org.

Baywatch Dolphin Tours, 2101 Harborside Drive, Galveston, 77550. Call 832-859-4557. Daily 10–5. Fee. Web site: www.baywatchdolphintours.com.

Bishop's Palace, 1402 Broadway, Galveston, 77550. Call 409-762-2475. Wed. through Mon. 11–6. Fee. Web site: www.galvestonhistory.org.

Casey's Seaside Café, 3828 Seawall Boulevard, Galveston, 77550. Call 409-762-9625. Sun. through Thurs. 11–9, Fri. and Sat. 11–10; closes later in summer and earlier in winter. Web site: www.gaidos.com.

Gaido's, 3800 Seawall Boulevard, Galveston, 77550. Call 409-762-9625. Sun. through Thurs. 11:45–9, Fri. and Sat. 11:45–10. Web site: www.gaidos .com.

Galveston Historical Foundation, 1861 Custom House, 502 20th Street, Galveston 77550. Call 409-765-7834. Mon. through Fri. 8:30–5. Web site: www.galvestonhistory.org.

Galveston Island State Park, 14901 FM 3005, Galveston, 77554. Call 409-737-1222. Dawn to dusk. Fee. Web site: www.tpwd.state.tx.us.

Galveston Island Trolley, pickup at 25th & Seawall Boulevard, Galveston, 77550. Call 409-797-3900. Fee. Web site: www.islandtransit.net.

Galveston Island Visitors Centers, 2027 61st Street (main) and 2215 Strand (satellite), Galveston, 77551. Call 1-888-425-4753. Web site: www .galveston.com.

Galveston–Port Bolivar Ferry, 502 Ferry Road, Galveston, 77550. Call

---

THE GREAT TEXAS COASTAL BIRDING TRAIL

Organized by the Texas Parks and Wildlife Department, the Great Texas Coastal Birding Trail comprises several recommended sites for bird-watching up and down the Texas coast. The trail is divided into three segments. Galveston Island, falling into the region known as the Upper Texas Coast, has birding sites both in the city and along the shores of its state park. Some sites are all-season, and others are active during migrations, but all are lovely little natural spots. The route is marked with roadside signs featuring a white bird, sunset, and coastline on a brown background. You can print or purchase a map at www.tpwd .state.tx.us.

GETTING AROUND GALVESTON

Horse-drawn carriages circulate the Strand and the East End, giving elegant tours of the historic neighborhoods; try Island Carriages or Seahorse Carriages. On the seawall, the Island Bicycle Company, among others, rents bicycles and multi-seat surrey bikes for exploring the island at a leisurely pace. They also let fishing poles, boogie boards, binoculars, and everything you'll need to recreate on the beach. The Trolley used to be a great way to see Galveston, but it was damaged during Hurricane Ike in 2008. Designed to resemble the trolleys that lumbered around the city between the late 1800s and the late 1930s, the Galveston Island Trolley circulates between the Strand Landmark Historic District, Pier 21, the seawall, and the University of Texas Medical Branch. Check www.galveston.com for news of its reinstatement.

361-749-2850. Daily. Free. Web site: www.txdot.gov.

The Garden Inn, 1601 Ball (Avenue H), Galveston, 77550. Call 409-770-0592. Web site: www.galveston.com /gardeninn.

The Grand 1894 Opera House, 2020 Postoffice Street, Galveston, 77550. Call 1-800-821-1894 or 409-765-1894. See Web site for schedule. Web site: www.thegrand.com.

The Gumbo Bar, 2105 Postoffice Street, Galveston, 77550. Call 409-744-8626. Mon. through Thurs. 11–10, Fri. and Sat. 11–midnight. Web site: www.galvestonrestaurantgroup.com.

Harbor House, Pier 21, Galveston, 77550. Call 1-800-874-3721 or 409-763-3321. Web site: www.harborhouse pier21.com.

Hotel Galvez, 2024 Seawall Boulevard, Galveston, 77550. Call 1-877-999-3223 or 409-765-7721. Web site: www.wyndham.com.

Island Bicycle Company, 1808 Seawall Boulevard, Galveston, 77550. Call 409-762-2453. Web site: www .islandbicyclecompany.com.

Island Carriages, 2528 Postoffice Street, Galveston, 77550. Call 800-979-9201 or 409-765-6951 for hours and reservations. Cash only.

La King's Confectionery, 2323 Strand, Galveston, 77550. Call 409-762-6100. Sun. through Fri. 10–6, Sat. 10–9. Web site: www.lakings confectionery.com.

Moody Gardens, One Hope Boulevard, Galveston, 77554. Call 1-800-582-4673. Daily 10–6 or 8. Fee. Web site: www.moodygardens.com.

Moody Mansion Museum, 2618 Broadway, Galveston, 77550. Call: 409-762-7668. Daily 11–3. Fee. Web site: www.moodymansion.org.

Mosquito Café, 628 14th Street, Galveston, 77550. Call 409-763-1010. Tues. through Fri. 11–9, Sat. 8–9, Sun. 8–3. Web site: www.mosquitocafe.com.

Murdoch's Bathhouse, 2215 Seawall Boulevard, Galveston, 77550. Call 409-762-7478. Sun. through Thurs. 9:30–6, Fri. and Sat. 9:30–8, later in seasonal weather. Web site: www .galveston.com/murdochsbathhouse.

Pier 21 Theater, Pier 21 at Harborside Drive, Galveston, 77550. Call 409-763-8808. Sun. through Thurs. 11–6, Fri. and Sat. 11–8. Fee. Web site: www.galvestonhistory.org.

Railroad Museum, 2602 Santa Fe Place, Galveston, 77550. Call: 409-765-5700. Daily 10–5. Fee. Web site: www.galvestonrrmuseum.com.

Rudy and Paco, 2028 Post Office Street, Galveston, 77550. Call 409-762-3696. Mon. through Fri. 11–2 and 5–9, Thurs. until 9:30 and Fri. until 10, Sat. 5–10:30. Web site: www.rudyand paco.com.

Saltwater Grill, 2017 Postoffice Street, Galveston, 77550. Call 409-762-3474. Lunch Mon. through Fri. 11–2. Dinner Mon. through Thurs. 5–10, Fri. and Sat. 5–11, Sun. 5–9. Web site: www. saltwatergrill.com. Reservations strongly recommended.

Schlitterbahn, 2026 Lockheed Road, Galveston, 77554. Call 409-770-9283. Call or check online for seasonal schedule. Fee. Web site: www.schlitter bahn.com.

Seagull II, Texas Seaport Museum, Pier 21 (Harborside Drive at 21st Street), Galveston, 77550. Call 409-763-1877. Daily 11:30, 1, 2:30, 4. Fee. Web site: www.galvestonhistory.org.

Seahorse & Classic Carriage Companies, departing from downtown Galveston, Galveston, 77550. Call 409-925-3312. Cash only.

The Spot Restaurant and Tiki Bar, 3204 Seawall Boulevard, Galveston, 77550. Call 409-621-5237. Daily 11–10. Web site: www.islandfamous.com, which also covers **The Drip, Rum Shack,** and **Squeeze.**

Star Drug Store, 510 23rd Street, Galveston, 77550. Call 409-766-7719. Kitchen daily 9–3, soda fountain 9–4. Web site: www.galvestonstardrug.com.

Sunflower Bakery & Café, 512 14th Street, Galveston, 77550. Call 409-763-5500. Mon. through Fri. 8–7, Sat. 8–9, Sun. 8–3. Web site: www.thesun flowerbakeryandcafe.com.

Texas Seaport Museum, Pier 21, Galveston, 77550. Call 409-763-1877. Daily 10–5. Fee. Web site: www .galvestonhistory.org.

Tremont House, 2300 Ship's Mechanic Row, Galveston, 77550. Call 1-800-996-3426 or 409-763-0300. Web site: www.wyndham.com.

The Texas State Railroad

8 The Pineywoods

Getting there: From Dallas, take I-20 east to Marshall and TX 59 north to Jefferson for a total of 170 miles. From Jefferson, it is approximately 19 miles east to Uncertain along FM 134 and FM 2198. Double back to TX 59 and take it 34 miles south to Carthage and an additional 49 miles south to San Augustine. From San Augustine, take TX 21 west to Nacogdoches, where you can take either TX 21 or TX 7 west approximately 60 miles to Crockett.

Highlights: Follow TX 59 from the former port town of **Jefferson** to **Nacogdoches**, a small college town tucked in among the pine trees. Nacogdoches, **San Augustine**, and **Crockett** were all once points along the historic **El Camino Real**, the legendary trade route that passed through the region on its way from Louisiana to San Antonio, and are still pleasant places to stop today. Nature lovers will enjoy the stillness and solitude of both **Caddo Lake** and the **Davy Crockett National Forest**. Overall, the route captures the unhurried pace of the road less traveled.

Total distance: 150 miles from Jefferson to Crockett, via San Augustine.

This route leads through the towns that the steamboats and the railroads built, towns that first linked commercial Texas to the rest of the new, post–Civil War United States. In time, however, major interstate highways and airports passed the region by, depressing its economy and leaving it a bit stuck in the past. This corner of the state has shouldered on, however, and now, as it turns out, is reviving its economy by trading on its past. Country lanes, flowering dogwood trees, and old-time eateries are just what frazzled city folks crave.

The pace in East Texas is decidedly slower. The towns feel a bit dated in decor,

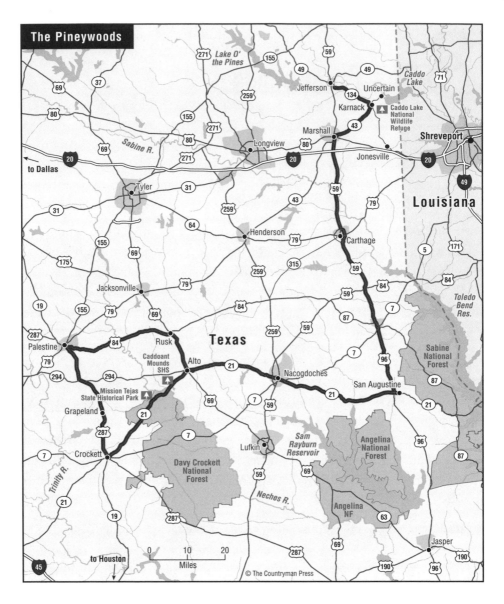

but the region's old-fashioned friendliness is heartwarming. And, thankfully, hospitality never went out of style here; there's butter in the pie crusts, homemade rolls on the table, and the hot coffee's always on. This route is best traveled with an eye toward detail. Slow down and you'll hear folks greeting each other by name or catch a glimpse of the light glistening off the dew of the still-damp forest floor.

Though **Jefferson** is approximately two and a half hours east of Dallas, it is only 40 minutes from Shreveport, just over the Louisiana border, so it isn't surprising that this little pocket of Texas feels a bit like the Old South. Over the years, Jefferson has shrunk from a bustling port to the little East Texas town you see today, known mostly now for its history, concentration of detailed Victorian architecture, and old-fashioned small-town atmosphere.

Built on a bluff overlooking the Red River, Jefferson was perfectly positioned to become a port. In the 1840s, Jefferson was shipping cotton and produce to Shreveport and New Orleans, and quickly establishing itself as a wealthy city. In fact, by 1870, only the Gulf port of Galveston was doing more commerce than Jefferson.

In 1873, two unfortunate events conspired to end the era of prosperity for Jefferson. First, a naturally occurring dam, called the Red River Raft, was removed, lowering the water levels in Caddo Lake and the surrounding waterways, making riverboat passage difficult and, at times, impossible. Second, a newly completed railroad line bypassed Jefferson on its way to Marshall, diverting trade away from the port city. While a second rail route completed the following year did pass through the town, Marshall and Dallas had gotten a head start and quickly

MARSHALL

Marshall was once a power player in East Texas, though its prominence has clearly waned. Come and visit Marshall Pottery, a local business that has been making pottery since 1895. The dirt in East Texas is rich in white clay, which, when combined with water, is perfect for pottery. At the precise moment in history that pottery jugs, jars, and crocks were being displaced by metal containers, Prohibition began. According to Marshall Pottery's owners, the money they made from selling jugs for moonshine saw the business through the tough times. In the 1940s, the discovery of a different sort of clay led the company to produce simple red clay flowerpots; today, Marshall Pottery remains America's number one producer of the ubiquitous garden containers. It is the hand-turned pots, though, and the gift shop where they are sold that people come to see.

surpassed Jefferson in importance. As the water level sank and the dominance of the railroads rose, Jefferson became just a charming East Texas town filled with history and ghosts of the past (see box, p. 174).

As you may have noticed by now, most towns in Texas are laid out around a town square with a courthouse in the center. Jefferson is different. The town is organized in a neat grid pattern along Big Cypress Creek, with an addition tacked

DIAMOND BESSIE

In the late 1870s, Jefferson became the unwitting location of one of the region's more gruesome and sensational murders. In January 1877, Bessie Moore, a New York girl and sometime prostitute, pulled into town with Abraham Rothschild, son of a wealthy jeweler. Just a few days later her body was found in the woods.

Diamond Bessie, so known for the many diamonds she'd been given as gifts from admirers, was certainly living a rough life with Rothschild, and their relationship was tumultuous, but no one predicted that murder would be the result. One day the couple, who were staying at the Brooks House in Jefferson, went out for a picnic, but several hours later only Mr. Rothschild returned, wearing some of Bessie's diamonds. Several weeks later, a woman collecting firewood stumbled upon the remnants of a picnic and a body. Since Bessie died from a bullet shot, the case was declared a homicide and Mr. Rothschild was charged with the crime.

The prominence of Mr. Rothschild's family pushed the story into the headlines, and they quickly secured 10 high-powered attorneys to defend him. Since the Jefferson jury was considered tainted by all the publicity, the case was moved to Marshall, where he was convicted and then sprung on appeal. The case was retried in Jefferson, where the defense was so overpowering that Rothschild was acquitted.

While the case was sensational, involving a handsome and wealthy man and a woman known to live by her wits, the shocking outcome of the trials shook many folks' faith in the justice system. Now, while Rothschild's notoriety has come and gone, Diamond Bessie is something of a cult figure. Tourists visit her grave and the city performs a play telling the tale each year during the annual Pilgrimage Festival.

Horse-drawn carriage in front of the Jefferson Hotel in Jefferson

on to the east at a jaunty 45-degree angle. Tall shade trees shelter the homes and hang over the streets, covering all with a dappled light. Squint your eyes and you can practically see the horse and buggies and hear the whistle of the steamboats pulling into the docks.

Want to delve a little deeper into local history? Stop by the **Jefferson Historical Society Museum** and get a clearer picture of what living here was like years ago. The museum, housed in a stately brick building built in the late 1800s, has four floors of collections on display ranging from Caddo Indian artifacts and early Texas quilts to Civil War–era items and Victorian china. When it comes to lodging, while most of East Texas might be lacking, Jefferson has a surplus. Known as the Bed and Breakfast Capital of Texas, Jefferson has so many choices that it can be hard to sort through them all. On one end of the spectrum are the historic hotels; the best examples of these are the **Jefferson Hotel** and its neigh-

Excelsior House in Jefferson

bor just up the street, the **Excelsior House.** Both are steeped in lore. A peek into the lobby of each gives you a pretty good idea of what to expect throughout. The Jefferson and Excelsior are perfect for guests who love the low-lit and slightly musty ambiance of living history. The older rooms will feel small to some and cozy to others, the bathrooms either charming or worn; it all depends on how you look at it and what you enjoy. The Jefferson, though, is thought to be haunted, and guests report hearing voices, capturing unexpected images on their cameras, and getting the heebie-jeebies all night long. It's a must for folks who like to vacation with the spirits.

Head down S. Alley Street and behold the promise of a porch. It's like an invitation to drop everything, have a seat, and just watch the world go by. If numbers of porches corresponds to degrees of relaxation, suffice it to say that the **Claiborne House** will be tranquil. The home was built in 1872 by Captain Claiborne; it's a modified Greek Revival gem that's neat as a pin, painted a crisp white with black trim and surrounded by greenery. Communal breakfasts are served in the dining room, and guests tend to be a friendly bunch, chatting as they eat. Food takes center stage at the **Old Mulberry Inn Bed & Breakfast,** where the three-course breakfast has been elevated to an art form, served on china with silver and stemware. The inn's signature artichoke quiche and fresh-from-the-oven cinnamon buns will linger in your memory long after you've gone home to breakfast cereal. The rooms are crisp, clean, and painted in soothing, contemporary colors. Polished wood floors, immaculate linens, and modern bathrooms make this inn an unfussy counterpart to some of its more extensively decorated peers.

Built in the 1920s, the **Delta Street Inn** is a lovely example of prairie-style architecture, with generously sized, sun-filled rooms, each with tall windows and beautiful wood floors, and a wide front porch overlooking the peaceful property. The gracious owners have stylishly updated the home, while preserving its his-

toric look and feel, making it a sought-after place to spend the night. The **Carriage House B&B** exudes a welcoming feeling that has guests returning again and again. A white picket fence greets visitors and homemade quilts adorn the beds at this charming and cheerful B&B.

For a memorable dinner, locals and out-of-towners enjoy **Lamache's Italian Restaurant,** located in the Jefferson Hotel. Despite, or perhaps because of, its persistent spiciness, the chicken diavolo is very popular, as are the lasagnas, shrimp carbonara, and other classic Italian specialties. Another wonderful meal can be had at the **Stillwater Inn,** an 1890s Victorian home. Fine dining prevails; the grilled duck with either blackberry or rosemary red wine sauce comes highly recommended, as do the rack of lamb and pecan-encrusted fresh trout.

Old Mulberry Inn Bed & Breakfast, Jefferson

Stop in the **Hamburger Store** for a more casual meal. From jalapeño chili cheddar burgers to chicken-fried steaks, the Hamburger Store churns out a steady stream of comfort foods behind its weathered exterior. Be sure to leave room for the pies. From chocolate pecan to strawberry to chocolate cream and lemon, topped with a dome of meringue, these pies are tasty. Very popular, the Hamburger Store is frequently crowded, so stop in midafternoon for a late lunch, an early dinner, or just a piece of pie. Another casual option is **The Bakery,** on the same block as the Excelsior House, where you'll have plenty of treats to choose from along with lunch staples such as soups and sandwiches made with freshly baked breads.

Afternoon or weekend evenings are a good time to pop in to the **Jefferson General Store** on E. Austin Street. This old-fashioned soda fountain, in business since the 1870s, is great for a milkshake, Coke float, or a five-cent cup of coffee. The Store makes its own pralines fresh every day, as well as jellies and hot sauces. They sell retro toys, knickknacks, and all sorts of things you didn't know you wanted. Have a look around and take home a little bit of Texas.

JEFFERSON GHOST WALK

Jefferson bills itself as the most haunted city in Texas. If you want to find out for yourself just how haunted it is, consider taking the **Jefferson Ghost Walk.** The walk begins in front of the Jefferson Historical Society, at night, naturally, and will take you wandering the streets of Jefferson, lamp in hand and your wits about you, to hear of the various oddities, sightings, and unexplained phenomena that the city has embraced with pride and pragmatism.

Over the years, the stories have added up. The Jefferson Hotel has countless ghost stories to tell. The way they figure it, if you hear it directly from them, then the creaky floors, dancing shadows, and other logic-defying peculiarities might seem a bit less intrusive. Room 19 is said to be one of the more "visited" rooms, so if you enjoy a good haunting, be sure to request it. You don't have to be a believer to enjoy Jefferson; just come with an open mind and consider yourself warned!

Stop by the chamber of commerce for detailed information or visit www.jeffersonghostwalk.com.

Leaving Jefferson, it is a 14-mile ride to **Caddo Lake.** Surprisingly, Caddo Lake is the only natural freshwater lake in Texas. The lake was formed by a naturally occurring logjam so thick that it was known as the Great Raft of the Red River. In 1874, the dam was broken apart to make way for riverboats, but so much water drained away, only a swamp remained, defeating the purpose. A man-made dam was constructed to replace the old logs, and the lake has filled again.

Its unique history makes Caddo Lake much different than any other lake in Texas. It has a very distinct primeval quality and is even a bit surreal. A thick forest of bald cypress trees, draped with Spanish moss, grows throughout the lake. The aquatic growth is so dense that 42 miles of channels, or "boat roads," have been created just to make navigation possible. Its age means it is a mature lake, with an astounding diversity of species and ecosystems. Alligators, turtles, frogs, and snakes all live in the lake, and raccoons, minks, and beavers are popular on its shore. Anglers come to Caddo Lake for the 71 species of fish including bass, crappie, blue gills, and catfish.

Spanish moss in the trees beside Caddo Lake

One of the best ways to see the lake is to visit **Caddo Lake State Park.** Dense and shady forest trails are popular for hiking, and you can stroll to the end of the observation deck jutting out into Saw Mill Pond. Almost immediately, you'll be struck by the sound of squawking birds, buzzing insects, and squirrels jumping among the trees. The place is just teeming with life and growth. While the lake is pretty year-round, blooming dogwoods during the last part of March and the first part of April make it something really special. Overnight guests love the little log **cabins** in Caddo Lake State Park; built by the Civilian Conservation Corps in the 1930s, they are still popular for their simple, rustic charm. Enjoy a tour aboard the *Graceful Ghost,* a reproduction 1890s steam paddlewheeler, which makes the rounds of Caddo Lake in spring, summer, and fall.

From Jefferson, it's an easy 52-odd miles along US 59 to **Carthage,** home of the **Texas Country Music Hall of Fame and the Tex Ritter Museum**—a must stop for country-music lovers who will appreciate the chance to snap their photo with the statue of Tex out front. From Carthage, it's about another 49 miles south on US 59 to sleepy little **San Augustine,** the start of the Texas portion of **El Camino Real**, the 18th-century route that ran between the Spanish missions. While *camino real* is a rather generic term, also used to describe routes in California and New Mexico, El Camino Real in Texas is also known as the King's Highway, or the much more descriptive San Antonio–Nacogdoches Road. It makes the most sense to think of El Camino Real not as one road, but as a series of interconnected trails, almost like a braid, that fell in and out of use depending on their purpose, travelers, and weather. While many of these trails already existed as footpaths used by Native Americans, the missions established by the Spanish

---

A TEXAS CHRISTMAS

The Victorian charm of Jefferson is the perfect backdrop for Christmas, and every year the town pulls all the lights, ribbons, wreaths, garlands, and ornaments out of storage and decks the halls. Residents wear period clothing and a horse-drawn carriage makes its way through the streets. Throughout the month of December, there are candlelight tours of various historic homes. The only thing missing is the snow. For Candlelight Tour information call 903-665-3692 or visit their Web site at www.historicjeffersonfoundation.com.

Downtown San Augustine

increased their traffic. The route was used for trade, protection, cattle drives, and immigration, delivering products, goods, animals, and people to the interior of Texas, a role it filled for centuries. Many Texas roads and highways lie over the footpaths carved by the El Camino Real. Rising public awareness and interest in these historic trails have spawned renewed efforts to preserve them. Visit www .elcaminorealdelostejas.org and www.elcaminorealtx.com to learn more.

The **Mission Dolores Visitor Center** welcomes the curious who would like more information about the historic route. Located on the site of the Mission Nuestra Senora de los Ais, established in 1717 but no longer in existence, the new visitor center evokes the mission's spirit with interesting exhibits and an informative film depicting the lives and times of the Spanish missionaries and the Ais Indians who once lived here, and the relationship between them.

Mention you need a sip of something cold and the friendly folks in San Augustine will send you right down to the **San Augustine Drug Company** with instructions to order the signature drink, the Grapefruit Highball. After establishing the drug store in 1904, the adventurous owner began experimenting with mixing drinks. By 1928, everyone in the region was swooning for the Grapefruit Highball, a nonalcoholic mix of grapefruit and orange juice, sugar, and a secret ingredient. Though the drug store burned to the ground, the soda fountain was rebuilt in 1988, thanks in large part to locals' dedication to the highball. Stop in and taste a little bit of history; be sure to tell them it is your first time—they'll serve you the drink in a frosty glass cowboy boot, on the house.

Ask anyone in San Augustine where the best place to grab lunch is and they'll tell you **Mary Kay's.** Located just north of the intersection of Highway 21 and 96, Mary Kay's is a simple building with a distinctive black awning surrounded by a parking lot jammed with cars. While the burgers and sandwiches are great, the daily lunch buffet can't be beat for both value and taste. You'll get your choice of classic comfort foods, cold sweet tea, and a dessert such as lemon icebox pie, for around $8. Comfort food at a comfortable price.

Press on, traveling TX 21 west to **Nacogdoches,** that small East Texas town with the lived-in feel of a place that's been around awhile, but with the youth of the college town that it is. Folks here say it's the oldest town in Texas, and the fact is it's been here an awfully long time. Nacogdoches (pronounced nack-a-DOE-chiz) is often confused with Natchitoches (pronounced NACK-a-tish), the Louisiana town to its east. According to Caddo legend, an elderly Caddo chief sent

DETOUR TO JONESVILLE

Pulling into sleepy little Jonesville, you might drive right past T. C. Lindsey & Co. if you weren't sure what to look for. The big white clapboard building has a squeaky screen door and several long wooden benches out front, but it's what's inside that has people pulling over to park. The old general store is so old and so chock-full of curios of a by-gone era that Disney has used it as a setting in several movies. The place has been in continuous operation since 1847, and is a wonder to behold and a treat to poke around in.

T. C. Lindsey & Co., FM 124 where it intersects I-20, just 2 miles shy of Louisiana.

his grown twin sons, Nacogdoches and Natchitoches, in two different directions to settle and prosper. Nacogdoches was sent three days' journey toward the set-ting sun, and Natchitoches was sent to travel three days toward the rising sun. The men became leaders of their own communities, but remained in contact, the road between them friendly, safe, and well traveled. Nacogdoches was a Caddo settle-ment until 1716, when the Spanish established a mission and staked their claim in East Texas. By the later quarter of the century, the French were a formidable challenge and the settlers in the area picked up and moved to San Antonio, far from the arm of France. But, in 1779, some settlers moved back to the region and asked the government of Mexico, whose flag was flying over Texas at the time, to declare them a pueblo. Despite politics and changing influences, the town re-mained in close contact with its twin, Natchitoches, and together they compose the eastern section of the historic El Camino Real.

Of the few places to stay in Nacogdoches, the one with the most character is the **Hotel Fredonia and Conference Center**. Decades ago, in an effort to wel-come more visitors to their city, 75 citizens of the town decided to pool resources and build a hotel to be owned by the community. By the end of 1952, the little town of 13,000 had raised a half a million dollars, and won over many naysayers. In fact, over a thousand residents bought stock in the fledgling project. Work started in 1954 and the doors were opened in 1955 to a crowd of 6,000 optimistic well-wishers. The hotel has since had its ups and downs, several different owners, and a facelift or two, but it remains what it was in the beginning, "the city's living room." The hotel is very well located, just blocks from the center of town. It is clearly an older establishment, and the rooms are small and modest, with slightly worn rugs and dated decor, but frequent conventions and college events keep it abuzz with activity. Visitors like to chat in the common rooms, have a drink by the pool, or step into the restaurant for a steak; the hotel staff is very eager to please. The Hotel Fredonia is a nice place for folks who are laid back about particulars and enjoy a bit of community spirit.

Though the choices are somewhat limited, eating is easy in Nacogdoches. For lunch, a nice choice is **Shelley's Bakery Café.** Thick cloth napkins, weighty silverware, and fresh flowers give the bakery the refinement of an old-fashioned tearoom. Southern mainstays, such as pimento cheese, share the menu with grilled panini, and there are plenty of fresh salads, inventive sandwiches, soups, and quiches to choose from. Be sure to take a peek at the desserts on your way in so you will know just what to save room for. As it is open only for lunch, you'll either have to get lucky or plan a trip around eating at Shelley's.

The **Clear Springs Café** has several locations in Texas, including a bustling one in Nacogdoches. One reason people keep coming back is the fish, especially the fried catfish, which is consistently cited as outstanding. The popular pan-seared tilapia with Dijon peppercorn crawfish sauce is usually served with a scoop of garlic mashed potatoes and steamed vegetables. The "small" Texas onion rings are enormous, as are the portions of just about everything else. Clear Springs Café sits next to a rail yard in what was once a refrigerated warehouse, the history of which is displayed on the walls inside. The turn onto Old Tyler Road is just west of the TX 21 and US 59 intersection. Also located here, and under the same own-

Cutting pie at Shelley's in Nacogdoches

ership, is **Auntie Pasta's,** where generous portions of familiar Italian dishes are served up every night. Locals pile in for lasagna, homemade meatballs, and huge plates of pasta.

For some local history, follow TX 21 from Nacogdoches west to Grapeland and the **Mission Tejas State Historical Park.** Though built in the 1930s, the structure is meant to resemble the Mission San Francisco de los Tejas, the very first Spanish mission in Texas, which was established in 1690, and once stood on these very grounds. When the Spanish first began missions in Texas, they started here to remind the French, building just over the border in Louisiana, of their presence in Texas. The peaceful Indians who lived in the area were friendly to the missionaries. As the story goes, the tribe's word for welcome, *tejas,* became the region's name, Texas.

After hopeful beginnings, however, the missionaries were blamed for the sickness and death that befell the tribe after their arrival; they had little choice but to burn the mission and return to Spain. In the early 1700s, a second attempt was made to establish a mission here, but the project was eventually relocated to San Antonio, where it began a new life as Mission San Francisco de la Espada.

Also nestled in the park is the **Rice Family Log Home,** which is thought to have been built in the early 1800s. A fine example of an early Texas dwelling, the home was a well-used way station for travelers along El Camino Real (see p. 177).

Farther along TX 21, you will come to the **Caddoan Mounds State Historic Site,** located about 6 miles southwest of Alto. Archaeologists estimate that the Caddoan people started living in the region in approximately A.D. 800 and stayed for 500 years. Though the term is now used in a general sense, prior to the mid-1800s, Caddo referred to only one of 25 separate groups living in sections of Texas, Louisiana, Arkansas, and Oklahoma. The site has three large mounds of earth, one of which served as a burial site, and several re-created structures, with a distinctive beehive shape. The site is an interpretive experience; there are some archaeological artifacts on display, along with artists' renderings of what life might have been like for the Caddoans and plenty of natural scenery, which remains relatively unchanged.

Continuing along toward Crockett, you'll pass through the **Davy Crockett National Forest.** While the thick, primarily pine forest is scenic to drive through, hiking is another popular way to explore the area; many people enjoy the **Four**

Davy Crockett National Forest

C National Recreation Trail, which stretches 20 miles from **Ratcliff Lake Recreation Area to Neches Bluff Overlook.** The trail follows old roads once used by the lumber companies that logged the virgin forests, taking the freshly harvested trees to a sawmill on Ratcliff Lake. As you walk the trail, look around; many of the trees you see were planted after the company stopped logging in the 1920s. The trail passes through **Big Slough Wilderness Area,** a parcel of primitive land untouched by modernity, and ends at an overlook atop the Neches River. Since there are hardwoods in the forest, spring and fall are particularly pretty times of year to hike. Outdoor enthusiasts may want to explore the two other national forests in the region, Sabine National Forest, just east of San Augustine, and Angelina National Forest, south of Nacogdoches and east of Lufkin; the Davy Crockett National Forest Web site will provide the details.

Just west of the Davy Crockett National Forest on TX 21 is the little town of **Crockett. Tchoupitoulas** (pronounced chop-uh-TOO-luss), aka T-Chops, serves great steaks in a historic hotel dining room that looks like it hasn't changed in decades. Built in 1920, the restaurant has high ceilings, exposed brick walls, a stunning bar, and a lovely outdoor patio, giving it an atmospheric charm that has locals lining up for lunch and dinner. In case you're wondering, the story is that the name is the Choctaw Indian term for River People.

Monday is fried chicken day at **The Moosehead Café**, and once it's gone, it's gone. Console yourself with your choice of any number of meringue-topped pies or perhaps a slice of warm apple pie with a scoop of Blue Bell. With red checkered tablecloths, counter seating, and ridiculously low prices, The Moosehead keeps it simple, and delicious.

The **Camp Street Café and Store** keeps feet tapping in Crockett with live concerts in its rustic 1930s-era tin storefront. Though the building has been many things over the years, it's now one of the best live-music venues in East Texas, with everything from blues to western to bluegrass on the lineup. There are two ways to catch a concert. One is to stop in Saturday evenings at 8 PM (sometimes Fridays) for a live show. The other is to tune in to the Camp Street Café and Store Music Hour Saturday mornings at 8 AM on the radio. Try 1290 AM or 92.7 FM.

Stay the night in Crockett at the comfortable **Warfield House** and you'll wake up feeling refreshed. This is an old-fashioned bed & breakfast, right down to the quilts, many of which were made by the very talented owner. Cozy beds, hearty breakfasts, and a backyard pool make the Warfield House a terrific base from which to explore the Davy Crockett Forest, or just hole up for the weekend.

From Crockett it is a 35-mile drive north to **Palestine** on TX 19/US 287 or a 46-mile drive northeast on TX 21/US 69 to **Rusk,** where you can hitch a ride on the **Texas State Railroad** and enjoy a view of the East Texas countryside from a moving steam train. The railroad has been around since the turn of the 20th century, when the line was built to provide freight and passenger service. In 1921, when it was no longer economically feasible to operate the line, it was sold to a company that used it to transport lumber. In 1972, the railroad was brought under the auspices of the Texas Parks and Wildlife Department, which refurbished the trains, built Victorian-style train depots at either end of the line, and kept the operation on track. The railroad changed hands again in September 2007, when the American Heritage Railroad Company took over operations.

Apple Pie at the Moosehead Café in Crockett

Today the railroad really shines. Seasonal theme rides, such as A Day with Thomas or The Polar Express, keep things fresh, yet the thrill of the whistle and the first lurch of the train as it gathers steam on the track just never grow old.

The railroad runs several steam and diesel engines, built between 1901 and 1956, along the 50-mile round-trip route between Palestine and Rust. You can get on in either town. The trip takes approximately four hours, one and a half hours each way with a layover in the middle. Time flies as you watch the East Texas scenery slip by, the flowering dogwoods in late March and early April and the red and gold leaves of autumn in November. From Palestine, it's a 112-mile drive back to Dallas and 130 miles from Rusk. A short way to drive for a trip back in time.

IN THE AREA

Auntie Pasta's, 211 Old Tyler Road, Nacogdoches, 75964. Call 936-569-2171. Sun. through Thurs. 11–9, Fri. and Sat. 11–10. Web site: www.auntie pastas.com.

The Bakery, 201 W. Austin Street, Jefferson, 75657. Call 903-665-2253. Mon. through Fri. 7–4, Sat. and Sun. 7–5. Web site: www.thebakery restaurant.net.

Caddoan Mounds State Historic Site, 1649 TX 21, Alto, 75925. Call 936-858-3218. Web site: www.visit caddomounds.com.

Caddo Lake State Park, 245 Park Road 2, Karnack, 75661. Call 903-679-3351. Fee. Web site: www.tpwd.state .tx.us.

Camp Street Café and Store, 215 S. Third Street, Crockett, 75835. Call 1-877-544-8656 or 936-544-8656. Web site: www.campstreetcafe.com.

Carriage House B&B, 401 N. Polk Street, Jefferson, TX 75657. Call 903-665-9511. Web site: www.carriage housejefferson.com.

Claiborne House, 312 South Alley, Jefferson, 75657. Call 1-877-385-9236 or 903-665-8800. Web site: www .claibornehousebnb.com.

Clear Springs Café, 211 Old Tyler Road, Nacogdoches, 75964. Call 936-569-0489. Sun. through Thurs. 11–9, Fri. and Sat. 11–10. Web site: www .clearspringscafe.com.

Crockett Chamber of Commerce, 1100 Edmiston Drive, Crockett, 75835. Call 936-544-2359. Web site: www .crockettareachamber.org.

Davy Crockett National Forest, 18551 TX 7 E., Kennard, 75847. Call 936-655-2299. Fee. Web site: www.fs .usda.gov.

Delta Street Inn, 206 E. Delta Street, Jefferson, TX 75657. Call 903-665-2929. Web site: www.deltastreet inn.com.

Excelsior House, 211 W. Austin, Jefferson, 75657. Call 1-800-490-7270 or 903-665-2513. Web site: www.the excelsiorhouse.com.

Graceful Ghost Steamboat. Call 903-789-3978. Fee. Web site: www.graceful ghost.com.

Hamburger Store, 101 N. Market Street, Jefferson, 75657. Call 903-665-3251. Daily 10:30–8.

Hotel Fredonia and Convention Center, 200 N. Fredonia Street, Nacogdoches, 75961. Call 936-564-1234. Web site: www.hotelfredonia .com.

Jefferson General Store, 113 E. Austin St., Jefferson, 75657. Call 903-665-8481. Sun. through Thurs. 9–6, Fri. and Sat. 9–10. Web site: www .jeffersongeneralstore.com.

Jefferson Historical Society Museum, 223 W. Austin Street, Jefferson, 75657. Call 903-665-2775. Daily 9:30–4:30. Web site: www.thegrove -jefferson.com.

The Pineywoods of East Texas

UNCERTAIN

Not sure where to start exploring Caddo Lake? Try Uncertain. This little town, with a population of around 150, welcomes Caddo Lake visitors with a laid-back nonchalance that characterizes the area. Just how the town got its name is…uncertain. Sometimes called Uncertain Landing, the town may have been named this due to the difficulty steamboat captains had mooring their boats along its irregular shoreline. Another popular explanation is that residents, unable to discern if they were part of the United States or the Republic of Texas, simply resigned themselves to the confusion. Nearby, and beside Caddo Lake Park, is the hamlet of Karnack, birthplace of Lady Bird Johnson (see p. 38), though it is not open to the public. The town was once anchored by an army ammunitions plant, but that has since been transformed into the much more peaceful Caddo Lake National Wildlife Refuge. Visit www.city ofuncertain.com for details.

Jefferson Hotel, 124 W. Austin St., Jefferson, 75657. Call 903-665-2631. Web site: www.historicjeffersonhotel .com.

Lamache's Italian Restaurant, 124 W. Austin Street, Jefferson, 75657. Call 903-665-6177. Wed. and Thurs. 5–9, Fri. and Sat. 5–9, Sun. 11–3. Web site: www.historicjeffersonhotel.com.

Marion County Chamber of Commerce, 101 N. Polk Street, Jefferson, 75657. Call 903-665-2672. Web site: www.jefferson-texas.com.

Marshall Pottery, 4901 Elysian Fields, Marshall, 75672. Call 903-938-9201. Mon. through Sat. 9–5. Web site: www.marshallpotterystore.com.

Mary Kay's Country Diner, 806 Highway 96 North, San Augustine, 75972. Call 936-275-0121. Sun. through Wed. 11–3, Thurs. through Sat. 11–9.

Mission Dolores Visitor Center, 701 S. Broadway, San Augustine, 75972. Call 936-275-3815. Free, but donations appreciated. Web site: www.san augustinetx.com.

Mission Tejas State Historical Park, 105 Park Road 44, Grapeland, 75844. Call 936-687-2394. Fee. Web site: www.tpwd.state.tx.us.

The Moosehead Café, 412 E. Houston Avenue, Crockett, 75835. Call 936-544-5278. Mon. through Thurs. 8–4, Fri. 8–8, Sat. 9–4. Web site: www.the mooseheadcafe.com.

Nacogdoches County Chamber of Commerce, 2516 N. Street, Nacogdoches, 75961. Call 936-560-5533. Web site: www.nacogdoches.org.

Old Mulberry Inn Bed & Breakfast, 209 Jefferson Street, Jefferson, 75657. Call 903-665-1945. Web site: www.oldmulberryinn.com.

Palestine Texas Convention and Visitor Bureau, 825 Spring Street, Palestine, 75801. Call 1-800-659-3484 or 903-723-3014. Web site: www.visitpalestine.com.

Rusk Chamber of Commerce, 415 N. Main Street, Rusk, 75785. Call 1-800-933-2381 or 903-683-4242. Web site: www.rusktexascoc.org.

San Augustine Drug Company, 104 E. Columbia Street, San Augustine, 75972. Call 936-275-3401.

Shelley's Bakery Café, 112 N. Church Street, Nacogdoches, 75961. Call 936-564-4100. Tues. through Sat. 10–3. Web site: www.shelleysbakerycafe.com.

Stillwater Inn, 203 E. Broadway, Jefferson, 75657. Call 903-665-8415.

Dinner only, Mon. through Sat. 5:30–close. Web site: www.stillwaterinn.com.

Tchoupitoulas, 208 E. Goliad Avenue, Crockett, 75835. Call 936-545-2467. Lunch Tues. through Fri and Sun. 11–2; Dinner Wed. through Sat. 5–9. Web site: www.tchops.net.

T. C. Lindsey & Co., 2293 FM 134 Waskom, 75692. Call 903-687-3382.

Texas Country Music Hall of Fame and the Tex Ritter Museum, 310 W. Panola, Carthage, 75633. Call 903-694-9561. Mon. through Sat. 10–4. Web site: www.carthagetexas.com.

Texas State Railroad Palestine Depot, Park Road 70 US 84, Palestine, 75801. Call 1-888-987-2461. Fee. Reservations by phone or online. Web site: www.texasstaterr.com.

Uncertain, 199 Cypress Drive, Uncertain, 75661. Call 903-789-3443. Web site: www.cityofuncertain.com.

Warfield House Bed & Breakfast, 712 Houston Avenue (Highway 21), Crockett, 75835. Call 936-544-4037. Web site: www.warfieldhouse.net.

Palo Duro Canyon State Park

9 The Panhandle Plains and Canyons

Getting there: Amarillo is the largest city in the Panhandle Plains, located at the intersection of I-40 and US 87. It is approximately 365 miles northwest of Dallas via US 287 or directly 240 miles north of Midland and 120 miles north of Lubbock on US 87.

This route uses the small town of Canyon as a center point. From Canyon it is a 10-mile drive along TX 217 to Palo Duro Canyon; to return, simply retrace your steps. It is an 18-mile drive along I-27 from Canyon to the intersection of I-40 in Amarillo, and from that point you'll need to travel 50 miles west on I-40 to reach Adrian. Again, retrace your steps to return. To reach Turkey and Caprock Canyons, take I-27 south from Canyon for 30 miles, then TX 86 east 54 miles to Turkey, passing signs to Caprock Canyons along the way, and retrace your steps to return.

Highlights: A long way from the triangle of traffic created by Dallas, Houston, and San Antonio, the laid-back **Panhandle Plains** are one of the best-kept secrets in the state. The region features miles and miles of classic western tableaux, punctuated by deep canyons and lovely backroads. The story of the Texas Panhandle very much revolves around the relationship between Native Americans, pioneers, ranchers, and the railroad, and this history is beautifully told at the **Panhandle-Plains Historical Museum** in **Canyon.** You can get a kick or two—or at least a burger and a piece of pie—on historic **Route 66,** spray-paint a half-buried car at **Cadillac Ranch,** and test the limits of your digestive tract with the 72-ounce steak challenge offered by the **Big Texan Steak Ranch** in **Amarillo.** Stunning views, native plants, cowboy cooking, and the musical **Texas** are all part of the **Palo Duro Canyon** experience. If you really want to get off the beaten path, con-

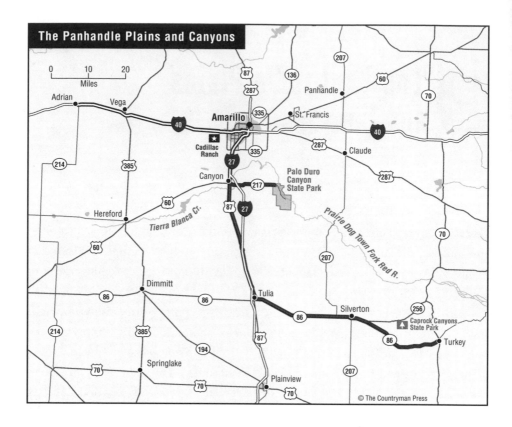

sider exploring **Caprock Canyon** and the nearby tiny town of **Turkey,** birthplace of music legend Bob Wills.

Total distance: From Canyon, most attractions are within 60 miles.

The northern section of the Panhandle, the high plains of Texas, is divided from the southern section, the rolling plains, by a dramatic escarpment known as the Caprock, which you will see if you approach the region from I-20 and US 84. The region has several natural resources, the largest of which are the Ogallala Aquifer located beneath the high plains, the grasses that have supported herds of buffalo and cattle, and the canyons that sheltered humans for millennia.

The herds of buffalo that roamed the area attracted Native Americans from several tribes. The Apache rose to dominance here in the 1700s; the Comanche, on horseback, overtook them by the 1800s. Though the peoples of the region traded, communicated, and interacted with other groups throughout what we now consider the Southwest, political events conspired to shift the region's focus from westward to eastward toward the growing United States.

The Mexican War of Independence in 1821 led to new trade relations throughout the region, thus altering trade routes. Soon after, Pacific Railroad surveyors and United States Army officers started exploring the Panhandle, and the various groups of the Plains Indians started to chafe at so many intruders in the land they had enjoyed with little disruption for centuries. Then the Civil War began and distracted all interested parties. It wasn't until the early 1870s, when professional buffalo hunters encroached on the Panhandle, violating the Medicine Lodge Treaties of 1867, which guaranteed exclusive hunting rights to the Native Americans, that tensions finally boiled over and the battle over the West began.

Native Americans, led by the legendary Quanah Parker and Isa-'Tai, mounted an attack on the intruders, an attack that would spark the Red River War of 1874–1875, a US military campaign to drive the Native Americans from the region. Many skirmishes, battles, and deaths later, in September of 1874, the Fourth United States Cavalry, led by Col. Mackenzie, encircled the Native Americans camped in the Palo Duro Canyon and took their horses to nearby Caprock Canyon for slaughter. Unable to defend themselves, hunt, or leave of their own will without their horses, the Native Americans were taken to reservations. Over the course of these years of conflict, the buffalo were hunted to near extinction, and with the Native Americans gone, the Panhandle lay empty.

In 1876, Charles Goodnight moved his cattle from Colorado into the Palo Duro Canyon, eventually partnering with James Adair to create the JA Ranch. Suddenly ranches were organizing, towns and businesses springing

The Old West is alive on the Texas plains.

ROUTE 66

One of the country's first highways, Route 66 was built to link Chicago and Los Angeles. Unlike many routes that cut a straight shot across the landscape between cities, Route 66 zigzagged its way along, linking the main streets of big cities and small towns. By the late 1920s, the route connected urban and rural America, allowing for the produce of the heartland to make its way to the densely populated cities.

In the midst of the Great Depression, tens of thousands of desperate people traveled Route 66 as they made their way from the Dust Bowl to the promise of California. In *The Grapes of Wrath,* John Steinbeck details this migration, christening Route 66 "the Mother Route."

Thousands of otherwise unemployed men paved the road between 1933 and 1938, and the military used it extensively during WWII. The thriving postwar economy made cars more accessible to the general public, and Americans itching to test their new wheels set out to see the country. Tourism mushroomed on the flat, practical, and efficient roadway, and drivers sustained the many mom-and-pop hotels, gas stations, and restaurants en route.

In 1956, President Eisenhower signed the Interstate Highway Act, designed to bring the Autobahn-style roads so popular in Europe to the United States. Since then, interstate highways have become ubiquitous and the more personal Route 66 a fading legend. Get a taste of what the journey was like in its heyday by visiting the precious few remaining institutions along this historic route.

For further reading, pick up a copy of *Route 66: The Mother Road,* 75th Anniversary Edition, by Michael Wallis.

up around them. The ranches themselves may have started as small enterprises with a hundred cattle or so, but soon corporations moved in, creating huge ranches and financing the large-scale projects that brought barbed wire, deep-drilled wells, and windmills. Some of this progress added worth, efficiency, and value, while some inflated the market, spawning poor management and many a personal disaster. A century later, however, modern ranching survives as an essential component of the Panhandle's economy and culture.

Everything changed again in 1888, when the railroad rolled into town. In its efforts to bypass the steep, rocky caprock between the high plains and the rolling plains, the Fort Worth and Denver line ran straight through Amarillo, ensuring the town's future as a regional cultural, social, and commercial center. Similarly, the path the railroad took determined where towns sprang up across the region; bearing testament to this fact are the tiny ghost towns scattered along the back-roads whose fate was sealed when the trains stopped coming.

When the ensuing world wars sent agricultural prices swinging, one group of risk-takers decided to strike out in a new industry. In 1921, local speculators com-pleted their geological research, crossed their fingers, and drilled on ranchland, striking pay dirt when they hit oil and natural gas. Amarillo became the com-mercial center for this new industry. The Panhandle as a whole became so wild with greed that martial law was required to restore the peace. Cars and cheap fuel are conditions ripe for traveling, and the 1920s saw the construction of Route 66 (see opposite page) as well as many of the farm-to-market roads that criss-cross the rural Panhandle, roads that served to link the economies of Texas, Okla-homa, and New Mexico.

While this newfound oil tempered the effects of the Great Depression for some, those still growing crops were devastated by the environmental conditions in the Panhandle, which were so severe they practically defined the Dust Bowl. Roosevelt's New Deal programs brought some relief, especially the Rural Elec-trification Project (see p. 43), which radically altered life positively and perma-nently when, in 1937, the lights came on in the Panhandle. These days, the economy remains a mix of agriculture and tourism.

The history of the Panhandle is fascinating, and the region has two remark-able vehicles for conveying it to visitors, both of which I highly recommend as essential elements of your visit: the Panhandle-Plains Historical Museum and the musical *Texas* (see p. 200).

Start the route with a visit to the **Panhandle-Plains Historical Museum** in **Canyon**. This superb regional museum, located on the campus of the West Texas A&M University in an art deco building made of Texas limestone, is the state's largest history museum. It began as the pet project of a young visionary, Hattie Anderson, who moved to Canyon in 1920 to teach history and then set out to record the changing world around her. The historical society she founded col-lected stories, objects, artifacts, and art that represented the area's natural and

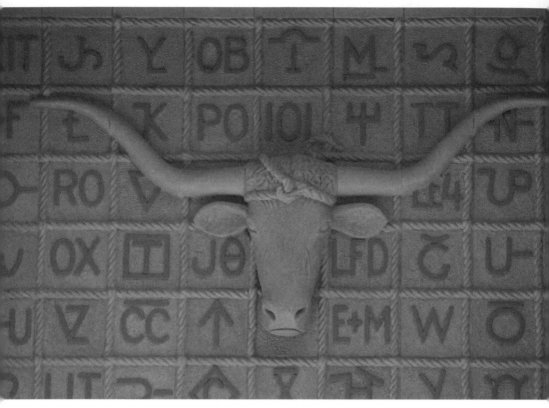

Panhandle-Plains Historical Museum in Canyon

cultural history and, by 1933, had completed the impressive task of building and opening a museum. Thoughtful and well-presented exhibits cover a remarkable range of topics, including Texas art, dinosaur remains, fascinating photographs, weapons, furniture, and skillfully made Native American baskets. The museum is appropriate and engaging for both children and adults. You'll leave with a better understanding of the region, seeing it through different eyes as you proceed with your journey.

Canyon is a wonderful home base for exploring the region. The small town, really more of a suburb of Amarillo, is quiet, peaceful, and well located to several attractions on your itinerary. While lodging is limited, thankfully there is the **Hudspeth House Bed & Breakfast**. Built in 1910, the home was ordered as a kit from a Sears, Roebuck & Co. catalog; it boasts 8,000 square feet of living space, including 10 bedrooms and 10 bathrooms. The guest rooms have been refreshed with paint, trim, towels, and fixtures and are spotlessly clean. A restrained use of embellishments and antiques keeps the rooms open, airy, and extremely pleasant. Owned at one time by a Miss Hudspeth, a teacher at the university, the home is now under the stewardship of delightful owners John and Connie, who welcome guests with genuine hospitality and thoughtfulness.

Other options in the region include camping or cabins in Palo Duro Canyon (see p. 200), a 10-minute drive from the town of Canyon, or booking a room in one of the many chain hotels that have sprouted up in the building boom along

Room at the Hudspeth House in Canyon

I-40 in Amarillo. Check a Web site such as www.tripadvisor.com for current guest comments. Also in Amarillo, the **Adaberry Inn,** located just west of town, is a newer home, built specifically as a bed & breakfast for business travelers and other adults looking to get away from the chaos that sometimes reigns in larger hotels. The inn is new, charming, and spotlessly clean with plenty of space for working or relaxing. Each room has a theme ranging from classic western to Key West. As a bonus, the inn backs onto Lost Canyon, a wildlife refuge and park, making sunset views even more stunning. From I-40 West, take the Coulter exit, north past the hospitals, right on Ninth Street, left on Quail Creek, and left on Plum Creek Drive. On 14th Street in Amarillo, the **Parkview House Bed and Breakfast** is on the National Register of Historic Places and is filled with antiques. Homemade muffins, high-quality coffee, a little koi pond amid lovely gardens, and the owners' hospitality make the Parkview House both pleasant and personable.

Cabins in the Palo Duro Canyon

CATTLE CALL

his is the part of Texas that cowboy legends are made of, and you'll still see plenty of cowboys around town. They're just riding their Ford pickup trucks instead of steeds, with cell phones at the ready instead of ropes. This is the heart of cattle-handling Texas, filled with blue jeans and muddy boots and all the other iconic images you'd expect.

Learn more about the ranching industry by visiting the Amarillo Livestock Auction, held every Monday throughout the year, and enjoy an old-fashioned breakfast and lunch at the onsite Stockyard Café. The Panhandle is also a great place to take in a rodeo. The World Championship Chuckwagon Roundup is held in June, the Cal Farley's Boys Ranch Rodeo happens in September, and the World Championship Ranch Rodeo, in November, rounds out the year.

Sometimes small towns have an interesting mix of eateries, and that's certainly the case in Canyon. It's slim pickin's here, but you can have your steak and eggs at the utilitarian Ranch House Café, a delicious spicy chicken curry at Sayakomarn's Thai & Lao Cuisine, referred to locally as "Soccer Mom's," and a malt at the Rock n' Roll Soda Shoppe, where you can sit at the old-timey counter. Though the shop is fairly new, it's festooned with 1950s-era memorabilia and has a fun vintage feel. The owner, Connie, and her college-aged employees have a wealth of information about the area. Be sure to say hi to them later at the *Texas* performance in Palo Duro Canyon; they are the folks selling ice cream at intermission.

A great lunch or dinner can be had at Feldman's Wrong Way Diner on Fifth Avenue at 17th Street. While the place may feel like any number of national franchises, the difference is it is local-owned and packed with people enjoying business lunches, family dinners, and birthday celebrations. The large menu includes the sorts of food you'd expect in this part of the state: huge and hearty stick-to-your-ribs steaks, fried chicken, and burgers, served with sides that are meals unto themselves elsewhere. Lighter eaters will enjoy the large salads and items from the Soup Menu, such as beans-n-cornbread, a bowl of slow-cooked pintos over cornbread. Friendly service and a casual, lighthearted dining room means you really can't go wrong with Feldman's.

Canyon is the perfect jumping-off point into the captivating **Palo Duro Canyon,** just a 10-minute drive east along Fourth Avenue then TX 217. The second-largest canyon in the United States after the Grand Canyon in Arizona, Palo Duro was created by the movement of the Prairie Dog Town Fork of the Red River over the course of 240 million years. The river cut its way through the flat caprock of the Panhandle, eventually carving a canyon 120 miles long and between 6 and 12 miles wide. Water and wind erosion exposed the mesa walls, with their bands of red, orange, and brown rock, caves, and "hoodoos"—or spindly totem pole–like spires created by the wearing away of the edge of a plateau. The Spanish christened the canyon Palo Duro, or "hardwood," for the trees and shrubs growing at its base along with prickly pear cactus, yucca, and plenty of wildflowers.

The land here in the Panhandle is flat. So very, very flat that the discovery of the canyon and its lazy river must have struck Native Americans as nothing short of miraculous. Vegetation, game in the form of bison and mammoths, shelter, and, of course, water drew Native Americans to the canyon approximately 10,000 to 15,000 years ago. In more recent history, first the Apache, then the mounted Comanche and Kiowa, lived in the canyon, trading with groups in New Mexico. The first Europeans came to the region in 1541 as part of the Coronado expedition searching for Quivira, the fabled Native American settlement thought to possess large holdings of gold and silver. While they didn't find any treasure, they did stumble upon the Apaches, whose culture and livelihood revolved around the abundant buffalo grazing throughout the region. The US military arrived in 1852, searching for the headwaters of the Red River; within two decades they had put an end to the Native American presence in the Panhandle.

In 1876, after the government completed a full-scale survey of the area, Charles Goodnight drove his cattle into the canyon. In 1933, the state of Texas was able to purchase a portion of the canyon to develop into a park. The Civilian Conservation Corps built the road to the canyon floor and several cabins, and made other improvements that made the park accessible and enjoyable. As you explore the park, bear in mind that the vast majority of the southern part of the canyon remains private ranchland, unseen by many, a staggeringly large, remaining piece of cowboy country.

One of the best ways to learn more about local history, and experience the beauty of the Palo Duro Canyon is to see the "Official Play of the State of Texas," *Texas.* People come from all over to experience the performance, a must-see event in the region. The show is staged in the Pioneer Amphitheater, the outdoor venue built at the bottom of the canyon, performed by college students from all areas of the state, acting, singing, and dancing the history of the region. From the pioneers to the railroads and relations with the Native Americans, this high-energy musical hits all the highlights, disappointments, elation, and despair that were part and parcel of settling the West. The canyon itself plays a part. For instance, when the script calls for someone to ride in on horseback, you will hear the galloping hooves in the distance, then see dust and bobbing hats, as the mounted riders approach the stage.

No need to rush through dinner to get to the play on time; the **Big Texan** (see p. 203) hosts a BBQ beside the amphitheater each night the play is performed. Folks gather for dinner around 6 PM. The buffet tables are loaded down with fresh fruit, homemade potato au gratin, green salad, and steak, served with sweet tea and cobbler for dessert. (Buffet tickets are $14, less for children under 12, and

The musical *Texas* in the Palo Duro Canyon

are available at the amphitheater or online at www.paloducanyon.com). There is usually live music and dancing before the show starts at around 8:30. The most wonderful thing about the whole experience is the simple passage of time spent in this inspiring setting. You arrive in the canyon in broad daylight, dance at dusk, watch the last bits of sun shimmering a burnt umber on the canyon wall, and gaze up at the stars as the show wraps up with an impressive fireworks display. The play and the BBQ are seasonal, running Tuesday through Saturday June through August, so please plan accordingly.

Whether you see *Texas* or not, count on spending another day just enjoying this spectacular natural area. There are plenty of ways to tour the canyon. Some folks drive in, taking in the sites from the comfort of their air-conditioned car, and others park and hike. Some enjoy the view from the saddle—both **Old West Stables** and **Palo Duro Stables** are happy to rent you a horse—and still more make reservations with **Elkins Ranch** for a guided tour. The folks at Elkins will take you into the canyon at daybreak and cook you breakfast cowboy-style. They'll cart you around in a jeep and explain the various natural wonders, historical facts, and cultural histories of the area. Heck, they'll arrange for Cookie, the camp cook, to whip up a chuck wagon dinner and treat you to some cowboy poetry, harmonica playing, and more Old West entertainment. Another option is to head out with a team of knowledgeable guides to trace the footsteps of the Native Americans who once called Palo Duro home. Basically, if you want to eat under the stars over an open fire and learn something new, the folks at Elkins Ranch have a tour for you. Call or visit; the ranch is located beside the entrance to **Palo Duro Canyon State Park**.

There are several **camping** options within the canyon, with designated areas for backpack and primitive camping, as well as spaces with elec-

QUITAQUE

Clearly, part of Caprock Canyon State Park's appeal is its remoteness; those who seek it out tend to be well prepared. Whatever your recreational plans, please be sure to pack plenty of fresh water and snacks, and wear clothing and shoes appropriate for the season of your visit. Stop in Quitaque (pronounced KITTY-quay or KIT-uh-kway), the tiny hamlet on TX 86 near Caprock Canyons, for supplies.

trical access. Even equestrian camping is offered for people who want to bring their horse along for the fun. If you like the outdoors but prefer some amount of creature comforts, consider renting one of the **cabins** built by the Civilian Conservation Corps in the 1930s. These stone structures are rustic, but have heat, air conditioning, and bathrooms inside and picnic tables and a charcoal grill outside. Those in the "Cow Camp" also have little refrigerators. Outstanding panoramic views and starry nights come standard with all cabins.

There isn't anywhere for a substantial meal in Palo Duro Canyon; if you've already eaten in Canyon, then the next stop on this trip is the **Big Texan Steak Ranch**, which, as they are quick to remind you, "ain't no chain or franchise." This Amarillo institution on I-40 really is one of a kind, as unique as the lanky cowboy sign out front. Founded by R. J. "Bob" Lee in 1960, the Big Texan Steak Ranch was

The Big Texan Steak Ranch in Amarillo

originally located along the old Route 66 in east Amarillo. As the new interstate was set to cut through the city, Bob had a hunch that the businesses on little Route 66 would suffer, so he moved his operation to its current location, bringing along the iconic cowboy sign by helicopter. And, true to its name, there's nothing small about the Big Texan. Whether it's breakfast, lunch, dinner, drinks, or desserts, the portions are huge, but the biggest of all is the 72-ounce steak, the "Texas King." If you can eat it along with all the side dishes in an hour, then it's yours for free. If you can't, the experience will set you back $72 and you'll have plenty of steak to take home for lunch tomorrow. The restaurant is a cavernous room with wood floors; deer heads on the wall complete the frontier theme. Part theme park, part

Pie at the Midpoint Café in Adrian

movie set, and part old-time fun, the Big Texan is the place to come for a slice of imaginative, old-time Texas. They'll even pick you up in a limo; call the restaurant to make arrangements. In another nod to the Texas of pop culture, the onsite **Big Texan Motel** has been made to look like an old western town. This low-riding cinderblock motel is friendly, clean, and well worn. With a Texas-shaped pool, old televisions, no Internet, and Texas decor in every room, the motel is not designed for business travelers or romantic honeymooners as much as for families with happy-go-lucky children, young couples who enjoy vintage touches, and anyone who just likes that worn-in feel of a family-run place. For horse owners, there's even the Horse Hotel, where you can let your four-legged friends out of their trailers for fresh air, space, water, and horse-sitting. Now that's service!

While the thoroughfare is no longer marked on modern maps, portions of Route 66 live on, such as a historic section of Sixth Avenue in Amarillo. Knick-knack shops and biker bars stand shoulder to shoulder for several blocks in this historic district, of which the keystone is the **Golden Light Café**. The consummate greasy spoon, the Golden Light flips some of the best burgers in the area, served in red plastic mesh baskets along with a mound of fries. You just have to appreciate the unassuming attitude of this joint. The dining counter is shoved right up against the grill, the ceilings feel like they are barely 7 feet tall, and no one bats an eye at cold beers at midday. The chili for the Frito pie bubbles in a huge vat on the stove, and the burgers and buns seem to fly off the grill as orders are filled lickety-split. This place is such a classic, it's on the National Register of Historic Places.

While you may or may not get any kicks on Route 66, you can definitely get one of the best pieces of pie you've ever sunk a fork into. From Amarillo, head west on I-40, where you will, 49 miles later, find yourself approaching **Adrian**. Exit 23A will put you right on Old Route 66, slightly north of the interstate, where you can't miss the **Midpoint Café** (and if you do, you will soon find yourself in New Mexico). While it may feel like the middle of nowhere, it is precisely the geomathematical mid-point of Route 66. Drive 1,139 miles east and you'll be in Chicago; 1,139 miles west and you'll be in Los Angeles. The Midpoint Café is pretty noticeable; it's practically the only thing in town. The retro chrome and Formica tables are dented and worn, and the vinyl seats have needed thoughtful packing-tape repair, but the place doesn't feel worn out; it just feels well loved. While the burgers are worth a mention, the pie is worth the drive. The Ugly Crust Pie hearkens back to a time before anyone counted calories or cholesterol and all that mattered was taste. The crust is marvelously crisp, a feat achieved by the use of pure butter. One forkful and the molten chocolate center oozes out, mixing with the ice cream, hot fudge sauce, and whipped cream. There's nothing halfway

Cadillac Ranch on I-40

Sculpture outside the American Quarter Horse Hall of Fame and Museum

about this pie; it hits its mark squarely on center. The sweetness carries over to the friendly service and the great feeling you get here, of being just one of many who've stopped in for some sugar.

Returning to Amarillo from Adrian is the perfect time to stop in and check out the bumper crop at **Cadillac Ranch.** Meant to represent the golden age of American automobiles, these ten caddies seem to have hit a bit of a rough spot in the road. Half-buried in the dirt and mud of a desolate wheat field alongside I-40, the cars have drawn a crowd since they were first planted. The collection was originally installed in 1974 several miles to the east by millionaire Stanley Marsh III with the help of some folks from the Ant Farm, a San Francisco art group. When growth around Amarillo threatened the desolation of the location, the whole shebang was moved to its current spot. The directions may sound somewhat imprecise, but you'll find it, just like thousands do every year. Cadillac Ranch is located along I-40, between exits 60 and 62. Take the frontage road on the south side of I-40, park your car alongside the road, and enter the field through the hole in the fence. Visitors are encouraged, at least by each other, to spray-paint the cars, and if you didn't bring paint, folks are usually happy to share. Wacky, free, fun, and as iconic as they come.

Back in Amarillo, there are two niche museums that may be of interest, the **Kwahadi Kiva Indian Museum** and the **American Quarter Horse Hall of Fame and Museum,** both located along I-40. The Kwahadi Kivi Indian Museum represents one man's personal collection of artifacts and art relating to the cultures of the Native Americans of the region. The modest museum comes alive during performances of traditional Native American dances, performed by the Kwahadis, a talented group of local Boy Scouts who have danced in venues all over the world; contact the museum for performance dates. The American Quarter Horse Hall of Fame and Museum, on the other hand, is sleek and modern, with plenty of information on America's most popular horse. Amarillo is paradise for horse lovers traveling with their four-legged companions, and as you drive through town, you'll see lots of horse trailers, some headed to area equine shows and rodeos, others just for a jaunt on the miles of riding trails in the canyon.

An hour-and-40-minute drive south of Canyon, **Turkey** is about as small and peaceful as towns come out here. What puts Turkey on the map is its most famous native son, Bob Wills. Diehard Wills fans—you know who you are—and the

A Turkey, Texas, welcome

merely curious will enjoy a trip to this windswept Panhandle Plains town that Wills called home.

James Robert (Bob) Wills was born in Texas in 1905, and, after several moves, his family settled into a little community between the Little Red River and the Prairie Dog Town Fork of the Red River. There he learned to play the violin from his father, grandfather, and laborers in the cotton fields, and went on to play at local dances. In 1929, Wills moved to Fort Worth, playing for radio shows and organizing a band, the Light Crust Doughboys, so named for their sponsor, Light Crust Flour. In 1934, he moved to Tulsa, Oklahoma, expanding his radio audience and starting the band for which he would become famous, the Texas Playboys.

Along the way, Wills pioneered an entirely new form of music, one deeply rooted in his home state of Texas: western swing. A synthesis of the depth of blues, the swing of jazz, and the expansive sound of big band, it was a style all its own, and Wills's compositions, most notably "San Antonio Rose," drew national attention. Wills, known as the King of Western Swing, won several awards and plenty of fame and recognition during his lifetime, and his unique contribution to American music has stood the test of time. Artists such as Asleep at the Wheel, George Strait, and countless others have covered many of Wills's originals to the delight of listeners. *For the Last Time: Bob Wills and His Texas Playboys,* recorded just before his death, is his best-selling album, a deserved Grammy winner, a classic for fans and a great introduction for newcomers. The **Bob Wills Museum** tells the story of his life, and the annual **Bob Wills Reunion** held in Turkey on the last Sunday in April is so popular that over 10,000 devotees routinely turn out.

For the rest of the year, however, Turkey may be just the ticket for those who like to get away from it all. Built in 1927, the **Hotel Turkey Bed and Breakfast** is unified by its interior's warm wood trim and doors, and decorated in themes ranging from Old West to pioneer days. Knickknacks, floral prints, quilts, lace, wallpaper borders, and longhorn skulls abound, and the B&B has that comfortable, lived-in, small-town feeling. Rocking chairs on the glassed-in porch are a great place to doze with an unopened book in your lap. A hot, family-style breakfast greets lodgers in the morning. Worn out to some and worn in to others, the establishment bills itself "as friendly and cozy as a trip to Granny's house."

If you've fallen in love with the land here and want to see more, consider visiting **Caprock Canyons State Park.** Less developed and even more remote than Palo Duro, the canyon sits out on the pristine plains, rewarding visitors with its views of the sunset, flowers, wildlife, and the wide open sky. Like Palo Duro, Caprock Canyons was home to various communities of Native Americans for thousands of years, some of whom traded regularly with traders (*comancheros*) and buffalo hunters (*ciboleros*) from New Mexico. Artifacts found nearby are strong evidence of a *cibolero* camp in the area and detail the area's fascinating past. Today Caprock Canyons is home to the state's official bison herd, brought back from near extinction in the region, and the rarely seen golden eagle.

The park has campsites, picnic areas, a lake for swimming and fishing, horseback riding, and 90 miles of trails. While there are trails suitable for hikers of all levels, some are only appropriate for skilled outdoors people. Please be sure to assess your skills accurately, and check your plans with a park ranger. An audio tour of the park, available for a refundable $5 deposit, is particularly enjoyable for visitors who might like to view the park by car. Equestrians can make arrangements for guided or unsupervised horse rentals through **Quitaque Riding Stables.**

The two canyons of the Panhandle Plains have also become a mecca for mountain bikers, folks who want the physical challenge of a good ride and the thrill of wide-open wild spaces. In 1992, the park was gifted a 64.25-mile stretch of former railroad right-of-way, which has vastly increased the possibilities for recreation in the area. The **Trailway,** as the rail-to-trail conversion is known, crosses over 46 bridges and goes through one tunnel (Clarity Tunnel, home to a colony of Mexican free-tail bats) as it makes its way between the towns of South Plains and Estelline. Trail maps are available online at www.tpwd.state.tx.us and at the park itself. You can reach Caprock Canyons State Park from Turkey by taking TX 86 west to CR 30, which becomes CR 29, and following signs to the park.

IN THE AREA

Adaberry Inn, 6818 Plum Creek Drive, Amarillo, 79124. Call 806-352-0022. Web site: www.adaberryinn.com.

Amarillo Convention and Visitor Council, the Bivins Mansion, 1000 S. Polk Street, Amarillo, 79101. Call 1-800-692-1338. Web site: www.visit amarillotx.com.

Amarillo Livestock Auction, 100 S. Manhattan Street, Amarillo, 79120. Call 806-373-7464. Daily 9–5. Web site: www.amarillolivestockauction .com.

American Quarter Horse Hall of Fame and Museum, 1600 Quarter

Saddle Up

Horse Drive, Amarillo, 79104. Call Call 806-376-4811. Fee. Web site: www.aqha.com.

Big Texan Steak Ranch, 7701 E. I-40, Amarillo, 79118. Call 1-800-657-7177. Daily 7–10:30. Web site: www .bigtexan.com.

Bob Wills Museum, PO Box 306, Turkey, 79261. Call 806-423-1253. Mon. through Fri. 9–11:30 and 1–5. Web site: www.bobwills.com.

Cadillac Ranch, located in a pasture on the south side of eastbound I-40, between exits 60 and 62. Free.

Canyon Chamber of Commerce, 1518 Fifth Avenue, Canyon, 79015. Call 806-655-7815. Web site: www .canyonchamber.org.

Caprock Canyons State Park and Trailway, PO Box 204, Quitaque, 79255. Call 806-455-1492. Gate hours Sun. through Thurs. 8–noon and 1–5, Fri. and Sat. 8–6. Fee. Web site: www .tpwd.state.tx.us.

Elkins Ranch, RR 2, Box 289, Canyon, 79015. Call 806-488-2100. Web site: www.theelkinsranch.com.

Feldman's Wrong Way Diner, 2100 N. Second Avenue, Canyon, 79015. Call 806-655-2700. Sun. through Thurs. 11–9, Fri. and Sat. 11–10. Web site: www.feldmansdiner.com.

Golden Light Café, 2906 W. Sixth Avenue, Amarillo, 79106. Call 806-374-9237. Mon. through Sat. 11–10, bar open until 2. Web site: www.goldenlightcafe.com.

Hotel Turkey Bed and Breakfast, Third and Alexander Streets. Call 1-800-657-7110 or 806-423-1151. Find them on Facebook.

Hudspeth House Bed & Breakfast, 1905 Fourth Avenue, Canyon, 79015. Call 806-655-9800. Web site: www.hudspethinn.com.

Kwahadi Kiva Indian Museum, 9151 I-40, Amarillo, 79120. Call 806-335-3175. Winter Sat. and Sun 1–5. Summer Wed. through Sun. 1–5. Open until 10 on show nights. Fee. Web site: www.kwahadi.com.

Midpoint Café, Historic Route 66, Adrian, 79001. Call 806-538-6379. Daily 8–4, closed Jan. and Feb. Web site: www.midpoint66cafe.com.

Old West Stables, 11450 Park Road 5, Canyon, 79015 Call 806-488-2180. Web site: www.oldweststables.com.

Palo Duro Canyon State Park, 11450 Park Road 5, Canyon, 79015. Call 806-488-2227. Sun. through Thurs. 8–8, Fri. and Sat. 8–10. Fee. Web site: www.palodurocanyon.com.

Palo Duro Stables, TX 217, just outside Palo Duro Canyon State Park, Canyon, 79015. Call 806-488-2799. Mon. through Fri. 10–6, Sun. 1–6.

Panhandle-Plains Historical Museum, 2503 Fourth Avenue, Canyon, 79015. Call 806-651-2244. Summer Mon. through Sat. 9–6. Winter Tues. through Sat. 9–5. Fee. Web site: www.panhandleplains.org.

Parkview House Bed and Breakfast, 1311 S. Jefferson Street, Amarillo, 79101. Call 806-373-9464. Web site: www.parkviewhousebb.com.

Quitaque Chamber of Commerce, PO Box 48777, Quitaque, 79255. Call 806-455-1456. Web site: www.quitaque.org.

Quitaque Riding Stables, FM 1065 beside the Trailway. Call 806-269-1209 or 806-455-1208. Web site: www.quitaqueridingstables.com.

Ranch House Café, 810 23rd Street, Canyon, 79015. Call 806-655-8785. Mon. through Fri. 7–9, Sat. and Sun. 7–3. Web site: www.theranchhousecafe.com.

Rock N' Roll Soda Shoppe, 404 15th Street, Canyon, 79015. Call 806-655-3381. Mon. through Fri. 10–6:30, Sat. 10–5. Web site: www.rocknrollsodashoppe.com.

Sayakomarn's Thai and Lao Cuisine, 419 16th Street, Canyon, 79015. Call 806-655-2698. Mon. through Sat. 11–9, Sun. noon–3. Web site: www.sayakomarns.com.

Texas: Musical Drama in Palo Duro Canyon, 1514 Fifth Avenue, Canyon, 79015. Call 806-655-2181. June through August, Tues. through Sat. nights. Fee. Web site: www.paloduro canyon.com.

Cattle grazing in Big Bend country

10 The Big Bend

Getting there: From San Antonio, take the 405-mile trip west to Marfa, via I-10, or from Austin, take TX 71 through Johnson City (see p. 41) and Fredericksburg (see p. 45) to the intersection of I-10 for a total of 430 miles to Marfa. Once on I-10 take exit 248 and follow FM 1776/US 67 56 miles south to Alpine and an additional 26 miles west to Marfa. From Dallas/Fort Worth, take I-20 approximately 500 miles west to exit 22, where you'll pick up FM 2903. Follow FM 2903 south to TX 17, which will take you through Fort Davis and straight on to Marfa. Marfa is located 194 miles east of El Paso, by way of I-10 and US 290.

If you start your route in Marfa, you'll take US 67 60 miles south to Presidio, FM 170 62 miles to Terlingua, passing Lajitas en route. From Terlingua, head east to the intersection between FM 170 and TX 118, where you can either turn north on TX 118 to Alpine (83.5 miles) or east on TX 118/Maverick Drive to the Big Bend Visitors Center (30 miles). Should you press on into the park, US 385 will take you to Marathon (87 miles).

US 67/US 90 runs between Marfa, Alpine, and Marathon. Marfa to Alpine is 50 miles and Alpine to Marathon is 30. You can reach Fort Davis from either Marfa (TX 17, 21 miles) or Alpine (TX 118, 24 miles), and from there it is a direct route 37 miles to Balmorhea on TX 17. Balmorhea is just south of I-10, making it a convenient ending point to the route.

Highlights: Start your trip in **Marfa,** the funky modern-art outpost; from there plan on visiting **Marathon,** with lovely lodging of its own, and **Alpine.** Use any of these three old railroad towns as a jumping-off point into **Big Bend National Park,** passing quirky **Terlingua** and historic **Fort Leaton,** while traveling **El Camino del Rio,** the River Road, along the Rio Grande. Head north through **Fort**

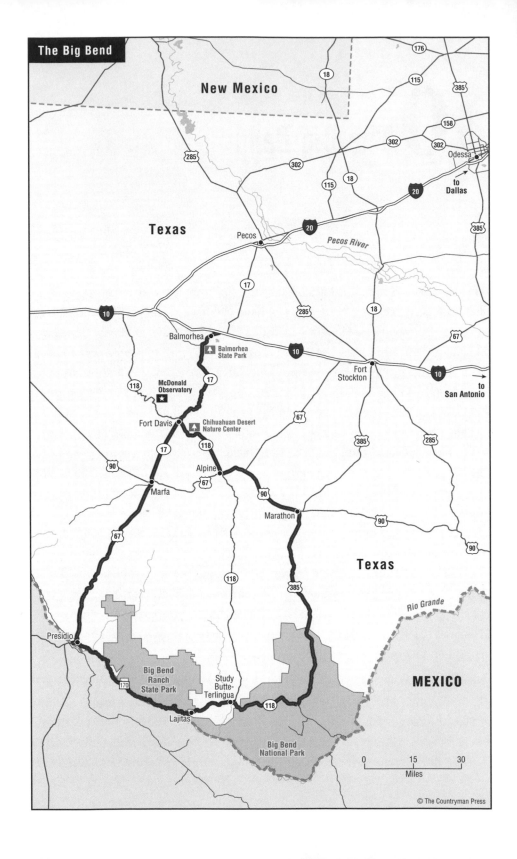

Davis, stopping to explore the town and **Fort Davis State Park,** before pressing on to **Balmorhea Springs State Park** and its enormous and refreshing natural-spring-fed pool. Spend some time in a **ghost town,** keep your eyes out for the **Marfa Lights,** and watch the huge sun rise and set over this wondrous western landscape.

Total distance: 200–300 miles

To drive west in Texas is to drive straight to freedom. As you leave the congestion of the cities of Central Texas, super highways funnel into four-lane highways, which, by the time you reach the Big Bend region of West Texas, have become abbreviated two-lane country roads stretching out between huge swatches of fenced-in openness. When you look around it would be easy to feel lonely or vulnerable, with only a gas station or two for company, but the stunning views of the magnificent mountains ahead are fortifying. And while many people joke about the nothingness out here, a closer look at this part of the state quickly reveals both a vibrant ecosystem in the desert and lively culture in the towns within it.

There are several ways to approach the area; I suggest choosing a home base and fanning out to the various sites on day trips. There are two reasons for this. First, this region can get very remote, very quickly, and having a home base means easy access to any necessities you may need. Second, the weather can be unpredictable, and staying in one place will allow you to custom-tailor your day trips around the whims of Mother Nature.

While the adventurous might enjoy staying in Big Bend National Park or one of the more far-flung lodging options outlined below, when it comes to amenities, it's hard to beat Marfa, though Alpine, Marathon, and Fort Davis are also very comfortable. For the purpose of outlining the route, let's start in Marfa.

Marfa is perched high on the Marfa Plateau, at an altitude of 4,830 feet; during a hot Texas summer, it's one of the coolest places in the state. But Marfa is cool altogether. With interesting architecture, lodging, gourmet food, and plenty of desert scenery, Marfa defines middle-of-nowhere chic.

Marfa, established in the 1880s as a stop on the railroad, has always been an outpost of sorts. Modest at the start, the original settlement was composed of three shelters: a one-room train station, a shack for gambling, and a tent with a restaurant inside. First known as Tank Town, Marfa was renamed at the sugges-

---

MARFA BOOK COMPANY

Modern design reigns supreme in Marfa, and this citywide aesthetic is beautifully captured at the Marfa Book Company. Founded in 1999, this pleasant bookstore is, in many ways, the town's meeting place. On the shelves, titles are very carefully chosen, and the selection, from fiction to travel, art to children's books, is admirable. From classics to the obscure, the Book Company, like many things in Marfa, is an epicurean treat.

---

tion of the railroad engineer's wife, who had seen the name in *The Brothers Karamazov*.

In 1911, the town became a station for the United States cavalry during the volatile Mexican Revolution. During Prohibition, "mounted watchmen" from Marfa patrolled the region to help curb alcohol smuggling, and later the United States Border Patrol did the same with drugs. In the 1940s it was home to the Chemical Warfare Brigades, a prisoner-of-war camp, and an advanced flight-training base. The military installation in town was known by various names including Camp Albert, Camp Marfa, and Fort D. A. Russell. Deactivated in 1949, the base was put up for sale. In the 1970s, artist Donald Judd purchased the compound, sparking Marfa's transformation from a utilitarian West Texas town to an offbeat cultural outpost.

Marfa is a tiny town, with a customary Texas courthouse at its center and a railroad running through it. Most of the action is on San Antonio Avenue, otherwise known as US 67, and N. Highland Avenue, which runs north to the courthouse.

There are few places to spend the night in town; fortunately two of them exceed expectations. **The Hotel Paisano** was built in 1930 as a hotel for cattlemen, who would spend hours in the lobby wheeling and dealing. When Hollywood breezed into Marfa to film the movie *Giant* in 1955, Elizabeth Taylor, James Dean, and Rock Hudson were all given rooms at the Paisano and quickly made themselves right at home. It's no surprise that the most popular room in the hotel is still the one Dean slept in.

While the hotel hit on some hard times in the years in between, it is now a heartwarming example of local landmark renovation. The courtyard centers

West Texas flora

The Hotel Paisano

around a bubbling fountain, with tables and chairs and window boxes lending a homey touch to an otherwise majestic entrance. With vintage tile work, cozy rooms—some even have balconies or enclosed patios—and plenty of historic detail, the Paisano is sure to appeal to guests who appreciate the individuality and quirkiness of older hotels. Since each room is different, be sure to check the Web site before you book and call with any questions.

If you are coming to West Texas to sleep under the stars, check into **El Cosmico**. You can bring a tent to pitch in one of their designated campsites, or spend the night tucked into a funky vintage trailer or white canvas yurt. The fenced-in, pedestrian-only camp includes outdoor showers, an open-air communal kitchen, and hammocks strung in a grove of trees. The brainchild of Liz Lambert, the Texas hotelier responsible for some of the coolest places to stay in Austin and San Antonio, El Cosmico is free-spirited and down to earth, a good balance for folks who like to go rustic without roughing it too much. Sure, you'll have to walk to the bathrooms in the middle of the night, but you'll do so by the light of the moon. Theme weekend getaways—cooking classes and music festivals—keep El Cosmico fresh and fun. If you'd rather have a roof over your head and want to feel a bit more like a local, consider **Stay Marfa**. This collection of studios and one- and two-bedroom apartments is hidden behind candy-colored doors across the street from **The Get Go**, Marfa's pricey gourmet food depot, and a short stroll from the center of town. The apartments are efficient, relaxing, and fairly sparsely decorated, with white walls, pops of color and artwork here and there, simple IKEA furniture, and full kitchens.

Marfa is a foodie's delight. There aren't many places to chose from, but the caliber belies the town's size, appealing to an urbanite's epicurean palate—and wallet. You'd almost have to make a spreadsheet to figure out what is open, when,

---

THE MYSTERY OF THE MARFA LIGHTS

One of the more confounding and fascinating phenomena in West Texas is the **Marfa Lights**, sometimes called the Marfa Mystery Lights or Ghost Lights. According to the lore, people have spoken of seeing the lights as early as the 1880s, but the first confirmed report dates only to 1957. Regardless of the decade or transmittance, the stories bear similarities. The lights are generally described as glowing orbs about the size of a soccer ball. They tend to appear only at night, organized in pairs or groups, and are said to be white, yellow, orange, red, and sometimes blue or green.

There seems to be no rhyme or reason for their appearance; they are seen with unpredictable infrequency throughout the seasons. The myriad explanations—temperature gradients, thermal expansion and contraction of quartz, headlights on nearby TX 67—add to the allure of this mystery. While no one knows what they are, folks agree that the lights do exist. The best place to have a look is at the Marfa Lights viewing platform on the south side of I-90, just east of town.

Every Labor Day, the town celebrates their local oddity with the **Marfa Lights Festival**, a long weekend of food, parades, music, and street dancing.

and those who aren't paying attention to operating hours may find themselves going hungry.

Frama @ Tumbleweed Laundry is one of the precious few places in Marfa open every day for most of the day. They don't serve much—just coffee and ice cream—but their little shop is a good place to sit, meet some folks, and chat for a spell while your clothes spin in the massive machines of the attached Laundromat.

Lunch is a bit easier. **Food Shark** works some Mediterranean-inspired magic inside their food truck. Order a Marfalafel and you'll get falafel wrapped with lettuce, tomato, cucumber, onions, tahini, yogurt, and a spicy harissa sauce in a flour tortilla. Falafel, hummus, and salads dominate the menu, and an eclectic mix of daily specials adds variety. They've served everything from carne guisada tacos and a warm maple-glazed ham sandwich on rye to *bahn mi* sandwiches— Vietnamese-spiced chicken or tofu on a baguette dressed with hoisin mayo and pickled vegetables—a hearty beef curry with rice, and a cucumber peanut salad. The desserts are always fresh and homemade. Order at the truck and find a seat at the super-sized outdoor picnic tables beside a railroad track. Good food and friendly folks make this place tick, though it can be tricky to get here in time to enjoy a meal. Only open for lunch Tuesday through Friday (though they may

Food Shark in Marfa

THE CHINATI AND JUDD FOUNDATIONS

Minimalist sculptor Donald Judd and several artist friends purchased the old military compound in Marfa in the 1970s knowing it would make a perfect venue for their enormous permanent art installations. Coming from cramped New York, they found the unrestricted space in which to create liberating; Judd quickly filled the town with his art. Since his death in 1994, the caretaker of Judd's artwork and vision has been the Marfa-based Chinati Foundation/La Fundación Chinati. The foundation has an expansive collection of large-scale installations produced by various artists, each set against the stunning backdrop of West Texas. The rub is that visits are by guided tour only, so you'll need to plan ahead. The second Judd-related institution in Marfa is the Judd Foundation, which is dedicated to preserving the artist's studio and living spaces in Marfa and New York, totaling 15 in all. A quick walk around town and you're sure to spot many of them. The two foundations pair up each October for the annual Open House, which offers visitors a weekend-long concentration of art in the form of concerts, readings, and exhibits. The Chinati Foundation regularly draws crowds of national and international art lovers, who happily cross Texas just to partake.

serve food on Saturday if the mood strikes), so plan accordingly or hope to get lucky. Squeeze Marfa is a delightful little café shoehorned into a building across from the courthouse with a tiny shaded patio tacked onto the side. The homemade yogurt, granola, and berry bowl is a wonderful breakfast, and the lunchtime panini sandwiches, made with fresh bread and various meats, vegetables, and spreads, are served hot from the grill.

Now that you've enjoyed breakfast and lunch, it's time to consider dinner. With so few places to eat in Marfa, consider waiting in line an inevitability. If waits don't bother you—after all, once you are in Marfa, you really don't have anywhere else to go, do you?—then just enjoy an evening spent on "Marfa Time." However, if you have your heart set on dinner at a particular place at a particular time, especially on a Friday or Saturday, make reservations to avoid disappointment.

You'll find The Miniature Rooster on the outskirts of town. The two small dining rooms are light and airy, sophisticated without feeling stuffy. The menu is

Shafter views

a mix of southern staples such as chicken and waffles, and international flavors like the tamarind chickpea curry dish served with whole-wheat fry bread. Sides and small plates offer options to customize your meal. Can't decide between the stone-ground grits with cheddar or the lentil fritter with coconut chutney? Try both for under $10. Rich, homemade desserts and a small wine list complete the fare.

One of the least complicated places to eat is the **Pizza Foundation,** a fun and funky pizzeria housed in an old gas station. Pizza Foundation pizza doesn't suffer from any of the usual pizza complaints—too much cheese, soggy toppings, or an overly thick and chewy crust. The pizza here is crispy, yeasty, zesty, and tangy, the making of great pizza. Generous salads and fruity frozen limeades round out the offerings at this inexpensive and very casual spot.

Another good bet in the evenings is the town's "family-friendly" bar, **Padre's.** Simple bar food—burgers, chips and queso, chili, and the like—make it a good place for a bite, and the foosball, pool, and air hockey tables out back are fun for all ages. The kids tend to clear out by bedtime and Padre's becomes an adult hangout into the night.

At the other end of the price scale is **Maiya's,** that little slice of gourmet heaven in Marfa. The focus here is on fresh and familiar Italian dishes such as a melon and prosciutto appetizer made special with locally grown Pecos melons and Prosciutto di Parma. Desserts are a revelation, and the wine list seems to stretch on forever.

Cochineal, sparse and modern without seeming cold, serves a limited seasonal menu of essentially up-market comfort foods. Pretty pricey, but with dishes like "twice-risen gorgonzola cheese soufflé with a bubbling parmesan sauce and crisped sage," one expects to pay a little extra. The meats are top notch, the desserts divine, and the summer garden salad is made with baby greens picked from the onsite garden. Cochineal feels like any tasty, big-city bistro, just in the desert of West Texas.

From Marfa, it's an easy 60-mile drive south along TX 67 to Presidio, and along the way, you'll pass through the tiny, former silver-mining town of **Shafter**—nearly empty save the precious few homes and single white church huddled beside the mountains. In the 1890s, silver was discovered in northern Mexico, and cinnabar, of which mercury is a by-product, was found in Big Bend. A mining boom hit the region, with mining towns popping up around the countryside. Then, after a quick 20 years, it was all over; ghostly old towns like Shafter remain, stark and picturesque.

Nineteen miles later, the road brings you straight into **Presidio,** a little border town on the Rio Grande. Inhabited for centuries, this area is in fact the oldest continuously cultivated area in the United States, with archaeological evidence of farming dating back to 1500 B.C. The Spanish encountered Native Americans living here in organized communities in the 1500s; Anglo settlers did not arrive until 1848. Today Presidio is a modest town, and most notably for this book, is the starting point of **El Camino del Rio (The River Road),** the scenic 66-mile drive along FM 170 that hugs the Rio Grande and offers stunning views of the landscape shared by the United States and neighboring Mexico.

Leaving Presidio and turning eastward on scenic TX 170, in 3 miles you will come upon **Fort Leaton,** the private fort built in 1848 by Indian bounty hunter Benjamin Leaton, which he used as a lucrative trading post with the Apache and Comanche Indians. It is now preserved as a state park. Upon entering, coming from the relentless heat outside, visitors are immediately struck by the cool air and thick walls of the fort and can easily imagine its promise of safety. Take a look inside, where a particularly informative display of the region's history and a helpful park ranger await.

The fort is at the western entrance to **Big Bend Ranch State Park,** 300,000 acres of very remote and rugged land that includes deep canyons, waterfalls, and even an ancient extinct volcano. There are two main routes into the state park. One takes you northward along FM 169/Casa Piedra Road, and then east to a string of hiking trails, campsites, and scenic overlooks. The second, FM 170, also includes opportunities for camping and hiking, and ends at the **Barton Warnock Education Center.**

Nature lovers and the naturally curious will appreciate the center's interpretative, detailed displays of the five biological landscapes represented in this part of the Chihuahuan Desert. A stroll through its 2-acre botanical garden is also nice. The presentation "Una Tierra—One Land," a collaborative effort between the state and national parks in Big Bend and the Mexican states of Coahuila and Chihuahua just over the border, illustrates the two nations' shared ecological heritage. If you're camping or hiking, Big Bend Ranch requires a permit, which you can pick up here or at Fort Leaton along with maps and information.

Return to Presidio to continue the route. The distance between Presidio and

El Camino del Rio—The River Road

AN OUNCE OF PREVENTION...

Big Bend National Park is simply stunning. Hundreds of thousands of visitors come to the park each year, drawn to its remote location, quiet stillness, and wildness. You can stay overnight in the park or leave Marfa, Alpine, or Marathon in the cool of the early morning, take a scenic drive, and still be back by dinner.

First, a word of caution. Despite stories of exotic poisonous snakes and spiders, the leading cause of injury in Big Bend is much more commonplace: automobile accidents. Be extremely cautious of weather conditions, sharp curves, and unexpected wildlife in the roadway. Note that the speed limits within the park are low, and federal seat-belt laws are always in effect. Before you go, be sure your automobile is in good working order, with properly inflated tires and a full tank of gas.

The second most common problem is dehydration, a condition that can prove fatal. Avoid strenuous exercise in the heat of the day and use the more mild mornings instead for hiking or outdoor activity. You should plan on drinking at least a gallon of water per day to stay properly hydrated, so stock up before beginning your journey and remember that alcohol and soft drinks, while refreshing, are dehydrating.

In Big Bend, the summer is very hot and the winter very cold. Coupled with a propensity for storms and flash flooding, this makes the weather in Big Bend a force to respect. Bring along sunscreen and insect repellent, a blanket, a simple first aid kit, and snacks. Regardless of the season for the hike, wear long pants, a long-sleeve shirt, hat, and proper footwear for a hike. Before setting out on a trip into the park, let someone know where you are headed and your estimated time of return. You most likely will not be able to rely on your cell phone for communication.

These warnings are not meant to deter you, just advise you of the dangers so that you can best plan your trip. The National Park Service is the final word when it comes to conditions and safety within the park. Checking with its extremely informative Web site (www.nps.gov), rangers, and staff before you head out could, quite literally, save your life. Assess your skills realistically, take the time to become informed, and prepare properly.

the next stop is only about 50 miles, but you should plan on leaving at least an hour and a half for travel. Now is also a good time to purchase some water and snacks (see box on opposite page), and fill your gas tank before starting your journey, since you won't have the chance to do so again for quite some time.

On the road again, enjoy this gorgeous stretch of El Camino del Rio (TX 170), which follows the Rio Grande eastward as best it can, dipping and rising with the hills, and widening for scenic overlooks, all the way to **Lajitas.** Formerly a trading post for miners, ranchers, and smugglers, Lajitas was transformed in the 1970s into a luxury resort. Located just yards from the Mexican border, parts of the resort have the look and feel of a frontier town, but the overall tone is of a country club in the desert, complete with a golf course, upscale restaurant, and private airstrip.

Mosey on down the road a stretch and you'll find yourself in the old mining town of **Terlingua.** Those who really like to get away from it all fall in love with Terlingua at first sight. At one time, 40 percent of the quicksilver mined in the United States originated in Terlingua. As with most other mining towns, the heyday of production was relatively short-lived. By 1942 the mine had closed and the population scattered, leaving the abandoned town to its solitude in the hot Texas desert. Fate smiled on the little ghost town when, in the 1960s and 1970s, a steady stream of tourists rolled through, stopping to marvel at its charms. A spicy annual chili cook-off earned it the nickname Chili Capital of the World. If you're around in November, be sure to try a bowlful; all the details are online at www.abowlof red.com.

When it comes to dining, **India's** definitely takes the cake. This little coffee shop—comfortable as eating at a friend's house—serves huge, steaming-hot breakfast burritos and a very good cup of coffee. The lunchtime hamburgers are fresh and hand-formed, and all the baked goods are homemade. India and William are lovely hosts, and the good feeling you get eating here stays with you all day. The friendly folks at **High Sierra** serve burgers, steaks, salads, and Mexican standbys, but it's the frozen mugs of ice-cold beer and a chance to shoot the breeze with other customers in this ultra casual hangout that have them coming back. The **Starlight Theatre** was built in 1931 to bring a little culture to the hardscrabble town. The old-timey place is now a restaurant and bar, with dinner daily and live music on its three stages most nights of the week. The food ranges from stick-to-your-ribs chili and homemade tacos to a grilled filet mignon with garlic and mushrooms—their signature dish. Who says there's nothing to eat in the desert?

If you can't get enough of the scenery, the history, or the charm of Big Bend, then stop in at the **Terlingua Trading Company.** The store, at one time the largest general store in West Texas, now houses hundreds of regional specialty books and loads of memorabilia, making it the perfect spot to find a piece of Terlingua to take home with you.

Want to tour Big Bend, but nervous about being a novice? With all of Big Bend laid out in front of you, you might want to get outfitted for hiking, biking, or boating. Check in with the knowledgeable folks at **Angell Expeditions, Big Bend River Tours, Desert Sports,** or **Far Flung Adventure Center**—they'll help you assess your skills, offer suggestions, rent equipment, or accompany you as guides. They'll have you safely hiking, biking, off-roading, or rafting in a jiffy.

By now you've noticed that there certainly aren't many options when it comes to lodging; fortunately there is **La Posada Milagro,** which lets four lovely rooms, each decorated with sophisticated simplicity. Stucco, stone, straw, and splashes of color are tempered by crisp white linens and bright sunshine. Perched on a hill, the little historic inn enjoys its vantage point over the old town and stunning views of the Chisos Mountains.

DESERT HOT SPRINGS

As hard as it may be to imagine a hot spring in the desert, there is one here. Folks have come for generations to take a dip in the curative 109-degree waters. The Chinati Hot Springs resort has expanded the springs' natural popularity by formalizing the experience. The resort takes a communal approach to desert hospitality, with the large kitchen available to all guests, and shared baths and hot tubs. Cabins are clean, cheerful, and creatively decorated, and camping is also an option. To reach the resort from Marfa, take US 67 to Presidio; then it's 36 miles to Ruidosa, where you will see signs. Alternatively, while TX 2810 to Pinto Canyon Road looks like a straight shot on the map, the road, while gorgeous, is rugged, only partially paved, and recommended only for vehicles with high clearance.

A mural in Alpine

From Terlingua it is just a few miles east until TX 170 dead-ends into TX 118 at the settlement of **Study Butte**. Here you can either head north, following TX 118 83 miles to **Alpine**, or widen the route by taking TX 118 east to US 385 to Panther Junction, the headquarters of Big Bend National Park. The sojourn outlined thus far, from Marfa to Presidio, through Terlingua and back to Alpine, is a leisurely day trip totaling approximately 200 miles, taking you past stunning scenery and imparting a taste of the region's history. The route is easily navigated, and while you may enjoy times alone on the road, it is traveled enough that you are unlikely to find yourself isolated. Those heading on into **Big Bend National Park** should be sure to take the necessary precautions (see box "An ounce of prevention," p. 226). While the park's enormous size, remoteness, and rugged beauty give it an air of intrigue that has drawn visitors to the region for decades (see box "The Big Bend," p. 230), these same factors mean that it is essential to plan your

THE BIG BEND

The Big Bend region is just over one million acres of vast West Texas wilderness, cradling a wide bend of the Rio Grande. Archaeological finds date back almost 9,000 years. Communities of Native Americans have lived in the region, crisscrossing its peaks, valleys, and riverbeds as they hunted and gathered.

The Spanish arrived in the 1500s and, despite ruling the region for centuries thereafter, left the mountainous area unsettled. When Mexico gained independence from Spain, Mexicans, too, largely avoided the region. Both the Spanish and the Mexicans referred to what we now know as Big Bend as *El Despoblado,* or "the uninhabited land." Not only did the rugged terrain resist settlement, the Mescalero Apache and the Comanche thoroughly controlled the hills, keeping intruders at bay for centuries.

After the end of the Mexican-American War in 1848, forts built to suppress Native Americans at the country's expanding boundaries and defend pioneers gained a foothold in the region. By the 1880s, sprawling ranches spread like patchwork across Texas. Both Big Bend National Park (see p. 229) and Big Bend Ranch State Park (see p. 224) are made up of former privately owned parcels of ranchland.

In the 1890s, silver and cinnabar were discovered in northern Mexico and Big Bend. A mining boom hit the region, then ended, leaving the deserted towns of Shafter (see p. 223) and Terlingua (see p. 227) in its wake.

By 1910, the Mexican Revolution had filled the Big Bend region with revolutionaries and bandits, including the legendary Pancho Villa. Things had qui-

trip wisely and in advance. While you can visit the park as a day trip from Marfa or Alpine, many find Marathon (see p. 232) to be a handy base for exploration, as US 385 will take you directly to the park's visitors center in Panther Junction.

Big Bend offers various sites for primitive camping as well as an RV park, but you'll find only one place to stay within its borders that has a traditional roof. The

eted down by 1944, when Big Bend National Park was dedicated. Remote and rustic, the new park had no paved roads and was surrounded by far-flung ranches, a ghost town or two, but few people. In the 1960s, tourists started to get more adventurous, and Big Bend's reputation as a great place to hike, raft, bird-watch, and camp grew. The traits that attracted people for centuries—swift rivers, native plants, wildlife, and breathtaking sunsets—are the very things that attract visitors to the park today.

Big Bend is part of the enormous Chihuahuan Desert, which also takes in parts of central Mexico and southern New Mexico. The region includes desert, river, and mountain ecosystems, and displays an astounding amount of diversity. For example, with 65 species of cacti, Big Bend National Park has the most of any in the park system, some of them unique to the Chihuahuan Desert. Of course, this fascinating ecology, foliage, and wildlife extend into Mexico.

South of the Rio Grande, or Rio Bravo del Norte as it is called in Mexico, the Mexican states of Chihuahua and Coahuila have declared the hundreds of thousands of acres known as Maderas del Carmen and the Cañon de Santa Elena as protected natural areas. While the idea of an international park with areas on both sides of the border has been circulating since the 1930s, the reality is two adjoining national parks, each country administering the land within its own boundaries; the net gain is the same—a piece of protected Chihuahuan Desert, unified as nature intended. You cannot visit the Mexican Park—border crossings within Big Bend are illegal—but it is nice to know that the land has been set aside for conservation.

For more details and suggestions, visit www.nps.gov and www.visitbig bend.com online.

Chisos Mountains Lodge complex isn't fancy, but it's just right for a good night's sleep after you've spent the day hiking, horseback riding, or rafting. The rooms are reasonably priced; some, such as the Roosevelt Stone Cottages, are equipped with three double beds, perfect for large families or friends traveling together. The restaurant serves solid meals, and there is a store for provisions and a visi-

The Gage Hotel celebrates its ranching roots in decorative touches.

tors center for those in need of maps and guidance.

Marathon is located just 30 miles southeast of Alpine on US 90, and when you drive in, it seems the entire place is lined up enjoying the view, since most of the small town is built along the north side of the highway, and the mountains to the south are an unobstructed vista. Another 20th-century railroad town, Marathon was a shipping point for cattle from surrounding ranches, silver and mercury from nearby mines, and a natural rubber made from a native desert plant called guayule. When Big Bend National Park opened in 1947, Marathon was declared the Gateway to the Big Bend, a designation it still carries with pride.

Marathon offers very pleasant, diverse lodging options. **The Mara-thon Motel & RV Park** is one of those family-friendly spots where memories are made. Located on 10 acres along an unhurried section of I-90 a half mile west of Marathon, the facility dates back to the 1940s and has the look and feel of historic Americana. Over the years, the motel fell into disrepair, and it might well have been condemned were it not for the imagination and vision of two retirees, John and Mary Hoover, who saw the hotel's charm beneath its many needed repairs. By 1999, the Hoovers had transformed the hotel into a place so charming that when Daniel Self from Austin saw a "For Sale" sign out front, he jumped at the chance. Since taking over, Self has added an adobe courtyard, complete with a fountain and fireplace, from which guests can enjoy the stunning view.

Down the street, the grand **Gage Hotel** has been sheltering weary travelers in style for decades. Built by a former cattleman as a hub of activity for ranchers and miners, the hotel opened in 1927. A fortunate and familiar tale by now, the neglected hotel was given a much-needed renovation by a Houston couple who saw a special something in the old building. The hotel is solidly built, with an impressive entrance, stately living room, handsome library, and well-appointed rooms. Some rooms in this historic hotel have shared baths, with separate ones for men and women. All maintain their old-fashioned charm. The hotel was expanded in the 1990s; the hacienda-style rooms in the Los Portales addition are filled with old-time details, artfully and individually arranged, and each room overlooks the lush courtyard. The hotel restaurant, **12 Gage**, has steaks, game, and seafood on the menu, a fireplace for atmosphere, and a fantastic courtyard for romantic evening dining. The desserts, all made in-house, are certainly worth saving room for. To complete the decadence,

The Gage Hotel in Marathon

consider scheduling a session of seaweed body wrap, hot stone massage, or other pampering at the hotel's spa.

Pick up provisions at the **French Company Grocer**, a store that has been serving Marathon since 1900. Given Marathon's fairly remote location, it's no surprise that the Grocer is still a general store of sorts, with a little bit of everything and maybe just the thing you're looking for. Walk in on any given morning and you'll find anything from fresh banana bread to warm breakfast tacos on offer.

Hop back on US 90 and travel 30 miles west to **Alpine**. While Alpine isn't

THE BORDER

The stunning scenery that defines the 118-mile border between Texas and Mexico is shared by both countries. In fact, many of the sweeping vistas you'll enjoy on the US side are of distant mountains on the Mexican side. When you witness the Rio Grande slicing through this natural wonder, the fact that it is an international border can seem an afterthought. While the border is ever the subject of contentious debate and the brunt of social, political, and environmental stressors, it has been fairly permeable for a large portion of its history. As you travel near the border, please be aware that the National Park Service warns visitors of the possible presence of drug smugglers and illegal immigrants, the latter of whom may be in need of medical care due to exhaustion and dehydration. In all cases, the Park Service asks that you alert a ranger or dial 911.

blessed with quite the same views that Marathon enjoys, it is still a great place, full of West Texas character. Larger than either Marfa or Marathon, Alpine has services and shops that can be useful to travelers.

For years, Spanish, Mexican, and American traders passed through this area, camping near Burgess Springs (now called Kokernot Springs) for its steady supply of reliable water. In 1882, the railroad came, and since steam engines required water, Alpine became an important stop. A town took root, with restaurants, hotels, saloons, and shops springing up along both sides of the track. Now, surrounded by huge ranches, some in excess of 200,000 acres, and a jumping-off point into spectacular Big Bend, Alpine is a little town in the vastness of West Texas where folks just keep bumping into each other.

The heart and soul of Alpine may be the Holland Hotel, a sprawling building that takes up a solid city block right in the middle of town. The hotel was built in 1912, and more than one heroic owner has had a hand in the wonderful restoration you'll see when you arrive. The hotel has two dozen rooms, each well decorated and individualized along the same hip, rustic, romantic, historic theme. All are well maintained and quite comfortable, and some have balconies. The downstairs common areas and sitting rooms are dramatic, with tile floors, wooden ceiling beams, and huge leather couches. The Holland Hotel has definitely captured and preserved the celebrated spirit of the Big Bend region. Looking to house a group or family? Try the **Alpine Guest Lofts.** The lofts are large and spacious, with kitchenettes and plenty of light, and are perfect for longer stays in the area. Nearby, the **Bread and Breakfast Café** serves breakfast and lunch, with freshly baked cookies, pastries, and breads. This friendly, cozy place is a good spot for a midmorning snack. For an indulgent steak dinner, head straight to **Reata;** the Alpine outpost of this Fort Worth restaurant is the real deal. From the fried alligator with Creole aioli appetizer to the steaks and pork tenderloin plus warm pecan pie for dessert, Reata is gourmet cowboy cooking at its best. Despite its decadence, the menu includes nods to vegetarians and the health-conscious. Cap off an evening with live music and a drink at **Railroad Blues,** a funky West Texas original.

You'll see the distant hills grow steadily closer as you drive an easy 24 miles along TX 118 from Alpine (21 miles from Marfa on TX 71) to the town of **Fort Davis.** Forts were common in Texas, with many dotting the landscape from San Antonio to El Paso, and they played an essential part in the state's history. Fort Davis, the fort, was built in 1854 in a little community beside Limpia Creek known as Painted Comanche Camp. It provided both protection and a reliable water source for the thousands of migrants, wagon trains, pioneers, goods, and mail making their way west across Texas. The fort was used, abandoned, and pressed back into service several times, sustaining repeated attacks from raiders and Native American groups before finally being retired in 1891. In 1946, a Houston lawyer bought the old fort with hopes of restoring it. Unfortunately, he died in 1951 and the project lay dormant. In 1961, however, the fort was given national historic site status and the **Fort Davis National Historic Site** was opened to the public five years later. The historic site showcases five buildings with period decor and furnishings from the 1880s, but almost two dozen other structures and 100 ruins are found here in the protective shadow of the mountains. On holidays, spring break, and summer vacation, staff and volunteers don period dress to further the feel of the times. Spend the 15 minutes to watch the short film in the visitors center; it will give you the background needed to appreciate the site fully.

Four miles of hiking trails connect the Fort Davis National Historic Site to

Davis Mountains State Park. To reach the park by car, leave Fort Davis, travel 1 mile north on TX 17 and 3 miles west on TX 118 to Park Road 3.

The Davis Mountains are one of the most extensive mountain ranges in Texas and are unusual for the large amount of rainfall they receive in comparison with the rest of West Texas. As a result, the mountains are home to a far greater variety of vegetation than the desert surrounding them. The higher you climb, the greener it gets, with Texas oak, black cherry, and yellow pine trees rising up to fill in the landscape.

The parkland was given to the state by a local family. In the 1930s, the Civilian Conservation Corps (CCC) arrived and built the jewel of the park, **Indian Lodge.** The lodge is reminiscent of the southwestern Indian pueblos, with 18-inch-thick walls that keep the interior cool throughout the summer. There are campgrounds and trails for visitors who like to commune with nature, and modern amenities such as a full-service restaurant and swimming pool for those who just like to watch. Your cell phone may or may not work, and don't count on accessing the Internet; then again, no one comes here to catch up on email or phone calls. The reason most people come is for what *is* here—the mountain views, the warm, dry days and cool mornings and evenings, not to mention the awesome starry nights.

For a closer look at the sky, consider taking a drive to the **McDonald Observatory.** Built on Mount Locke in 1932, the observatory is part of the University of Texas and home to the Hobby-Eberly Telescope, one of the largest in the world. While there is plenty to do and see at the observatory during the daytime hours, the evening Star Party is really special; there is just nothing like the night sky out in rural West Texas. From Fort Davis, climb TX 118, 6,800 feet up, to enjoy a stellar view of both the heavens and the countryside.

Back in town, you can't miss the **Hotel Limpia** on Main Street. Built in 1912, the hotel has a decidedly Old World feel. In fact, staying at the **Hotel Limpia** feels a lot like staying at Grandma's house—in the best way possible. The carpets are a little worn from constant use and the linens are a tad faded from plenty of laundering, but the overall effect is of lovability. The lights are soft, the armchair cushions are concave from plenty of relaxing, and the wooden rockers and wicker patio sets practically beg guests to have a seat and put their feet up. The attached, newly renovated **Blue Mountain Bistro** is a good bet for coffee and pastries in the morning and more formal dining in the evening. The menu includes close to a dozen tapas to choose from; larger entrées include grilled shrimp with prosciutto and cream sauce, mocha-crusted pork tenderloin, and filet mignon.

Also in town, but on a quiet side street near the old fort, is the **Old Schoolhouse Bed & Breakfast**, in a grove of pecan trees. This former schoolhouse was built in 1904, and its thick adobe construction has stood the test of time. The rooms are simple and charming, with colorful quilts, uncluttered antiques, and beadboard ceilings. The hearty, hot, and delicious breakfasts are a treat to wake up to.

Stone Village Tourist Camp offers a range of options in its old-school motor court. Unassuming and unfussy, the rooms are basic, yet quintessentially West Texas, and the entire "camp" has a communal, folksy feel. Exposed stone walls, campy lampshades, a modest pool, and wooden lounge chairs help guests loosen up a little. A stone's throw from the Davis Mountains, Stone Village is a good bet for easygoing guests who appreciate the charms of this Depression-era gem. Stop in **Stone Village Market** for snacks, supplies, or staples. This health-food convenience store is a good place to pick up sandwiches, since they make them to

THE CHIHUAHUAN DESERT UP CLOSE

While it might seem a bit counterintuitive to come to the great outdoors only to spend time indoors, there are two educational centers in the Alpine area that are worth a quick visit. The **Museum of the Big Bend**, on the Sul Ross University campus in Alpine, has a large collection of artifacts that tell the stories of the Native Americans, Spanish, Mexicans, and Anglo-Americans who have lived in the region. While the museum will interest most, the onsite Discovery Center is geared specifically toward children. The Chihuahuan Desert Cactus Garden on the grounds gives a great visual overview of native cacti.

In addition, a visit to the **Chihuahuan Desert Nature Center & Botanical Gardens**, between Alpine and Fort Davis along TX 118, is a wonderful way to acquaint yourself with the flora and fauna of the desert. Botanical gardens and a greenhouse allow a close-up look, and several miles of nature trails provide a safe and easy way to explore the regional terrain.

Balmorhea State Park

order as fresh as can be. **Fort Davis Drug Store** is a reliable stop for burgers and Blue Bell shakes. With its creaky floors, tall ceilings, and old-fashioned soda fountain, the Drug Store anchors State Street. From Fort Davis, it's another 37 miles north on winding TX 17 to **Balmorhea,** notable as the home of the San Solomon Springs and **Balmorhea State Park,** which is an oasis in the Texas desert.

In this arid region, water means life; not surprisingly, the San Solomon Springs have drawn people for centuries. In the mid-19th century, the marshy springs were known as Mescalero Springs, named after the Mescalero Apache, who frequently brought their horses here for water. Mexican farmers channeled the springs' waters into irrigation ditches for their crops.

These days, however, the centerpiece of the springs is an enormous, almost 2-acre swimming pool constructed by the Civilian Conservation Corps in the 1930s. It's filled each day with 22 to 28 million gallons of pure artesian water fresh from the San Solomon Springs. A constant 74 degrees, the water takes a minute to get used to, but almost everyone who starts with a toe in ends up floating around with the fish. Yes, fish; consider bringing a pair of goggles for an underwater view.

The park is popular with locals, and it's a frequent site of picnics and family reunions. Many of the people who come to take a dip also come to spend the night. The park has two types of accommodations: campsites and the hotel.

San Solomon Courts is a Spanish colonial-style motel with white adobe walls and red clay tile roof. Also built by CCC workers, the hotel is modern enough, with heat, air-conditioning, and cable TV, but details such as exposed wood beams impart an air of nostalgia. The hotel is popular with families; picnic tables and grills outside each room ensure that evenings are spent eating, talking, and relaxing. All rooms have double beds and some have kitchenettes. People come here to slow down and just enjoy a summer day as it slips away behind the mountains.

The route ends here, conveniently close to I-10 for your return to the more populated parts of the state. As you drive and the mountains recede behind you, pause to consider that having made this trip, you've been let in on the secret of West Texas: precisely what everyone thinks of as just miles and miles of emptiness is actually miles and miles of the most living, breathing, precious land in the state.

IN THE AREA

Alpine Chamber of Commerce, 106 N. Third Street, Alpine, 79830. Call 1-800-561-3712 or 432-837-2326. Web site: www.alpinetexas.com.

Alpine Guest Lofts, 117 N. 6th Street, Alpine, 79830. Call 432-837-1818. Web site: www.alpineguestlofts.com

Angell Expeditions. Call 432-229-3713 or 305-336-2787. Web site: www.angellexpeditions.com.

Balmorhea State Park, TX 17, Toyahvale, 79786. Call 432-375-2370. Fee. Web site: www.tpwd.state.tx.us.

Barton Warnock Education Center, HC 70, Box 375, Terlingua TX 79852. Call 432-424-3327. Daily 8–5. Web site: www.tpwd.state.tx.us.

Big Bend National Park, Panther Junction, 79834. Call 432-477-1107. Web site: www.nps.gov.

Big Bend Ranch State Park, Box 2319, Presidio, 79835. Call 432-358-4444. Web site: www.tpwd.state.tx.us.

Big Bend River Tours. Call 432-371-3033. Web site: www.bigbendrivertours.com.

Blue Mountain Bistro, 100 Main Street, Fort Davis, 79734. Call 432-426-3244. Web site: www.blue-mountain-bistro.com.

Bread and Breakfast Café, 113 W. Holland Avenue, Alpine, 79830. Call 432-837-9424. Tues. through Sat. 7–2, Sun. 8–noon.

TRAIN WHISTLE

While this region may seem wide open except for some cattle and a few cars, every once in a while a train will come speeding in from one horizon, bringing traffic to a halt, whistles blaring and wheels grinding, before disappearing into the other. Stay in just about any hotel in the area and chances are you'll hear numerous trains; it's just that the ones you'll remember will be the ones that woke you at night.

Chinati Foundation, PO Box 1135, 1 Cavalry Row, Marfa, 79843. Call 432-729-4362. Guided tour only Wed. through Sun. Check web site for schedule. Web site: www.chinati.org.

Chinati Hot Springs, Box 67 Candelaria Route, Marfa, 79843 (located near Ruidosa, TX). Call 432-229-4165. Web site: www.chinatihotsprings.com.

Chihuahuan Desert Nature Center & Botanical Gardens, PO Box 905, Fort Davis, 79734 (4 miles south of Fort Davis on TX 118). Call 432-364-2499. Mon. through Sat. 9–5. Web site: www.cdri.org.

Chisos Mountains Lodge, Big Bend National Park, Basin Rural Station—Big Bend National Park, 79834. Call:

432-477-2292. Web site: www.chisos mountainslodge.com.

Cochineal, 107 W San Antonio Street, Marfa, 79843. Call 432-729-3300. Web site: www.cochinealmarfa .com.

Davis Mountain Indian Lodge, PO Box 1707, Fort Davis, 79734. Call 432-426-3254. Web site: www.tpwd.state .tx.us.

Davis Mountains State Park, PO Box 1707, Fort Davis, 79734. Call 432-426-3337. Web site: www.tpwd.state .tx.us.

Desert Sports, PO Box 448, Terlingua, 79852. Call 1-888-989-6900 or 432-371-2727. Web site: www.desert sportstx.com.

El Cosmico, 802 S. Highland Avenue, Marfa, 79843. Call 432-729-1950. Web site: www.elcosmico.com.

Far Flung Adventure Center, Call 1-800-839-7238. Web site: www.big-bendfarflung.com.

Food Shark, 105 S. Highland Avenue, Marfa, 79843. Call 432-386-6540. Tues. through Fri. 11:30–3. Web site: www.foodsharkmarfa.com.

Fort Davis Chamber of Commerce, PO Box 378, Fort Davis, 79734 or 4 Memorial Square. Call 1-800-524-3015 or 432-426-3015. Web site: www .fortdavis.com.

Fort Davis Drug Store, 113 TX17, Fort Davis, 79734. Call 432-426-3939. Web site: www.fortdavisdrugstore.net.

Fort Davis National Historic Site, PO Box 1379, Fort Davis, 79734. Call 432-426-3224, ext. 20. Web site: www .nps.gov/foda.

Fort Leaton State Historic Site, PO Box 2319, Presidio, 79845. Call 432-229-3613. Fee. Web site: www.tpwd .state.tx.us.

Frama @ Tumbleweed Laundry, 120 N. Austin Street, Marfa, 79843. Call 432-729-4033. Daily 8–9. Web site: www.tumbleweedlaundry.com.

French Company Grocer, 206 N. Avenue D, Box 477, Marathon, 79842. Call 432-386-4522. Mon. through Fri. 7:30–9, Sat. 8–9, Sun. 9–9. Web site: www.frenchcogrocer.com.

Gage Hotel, 101 I-90 W., Marathon, 79842. Call 1-800-884-GAGE or 432-386-4205. Web site: www.gagehotel .com.

The Get Go, 208 S. Dean Street, Marfa, 79843. Call 432-729-3335. Daily 9–8. Web site: www.thegetgo marfa.com.

High Sierra, 100 Ghost Town Road, Terlingua, 79852. Call 432-371-3282. Daily noon–10; bar open until midnight. Web site: www.highsierra .homestead.com.

Holland Hotel, 209 W. Holland Avenue, Alpine, 79830. Call 1-800-535-8040 or 432-837-2800. Web site: www.thehollandhoteltexas.com.

Hotel Limpia, PO Box 1838 (on the Town Square), Fort Davis, 79734. Call

432-426-3237 or 1-800-662-5517. Web site: www.hotellimpia.com.

Hotel Limpia Restaurant, PO Box 1838, Fort Davis, 79734. Call 432-426-3241. Tues. through Sun. 5:30–9, and also Sun. 11–2. Web site: www.hotel limpia.com.

The Hotel Paisano, 207 N. Highland Avenue, Marfa, 79843. Call 1-866-729-3669 or 432-729-3669. Web site: www.hotelpaisano.com.

India's, Bee Mountain Plaza, Hwy 118, Study Butte-Terlingua, TX 79852. Call 432-371-2888. Thurs. through Mon. 6–4. Web site: www .indias.homestead.com.

Indian Lodge State Park, PO Box 1458, Fort Davis, 79734. Call 915-426-3254. Web site: www.tpwd.state.tx.us.

La Posada Milagro, 100 La Posada Lane, Terlingua, 79852. Call 432-371-3044. Web site: www.laposadamilagro .net.

Maiya's, 103 N. Highland Street, Marfa 79843. Call 432-729-4410. Wed. through Sat. 5–10. Web site: www .maiyasrestaurant.com. Reservations recommended.

Marathon Chamber of Commerce, 105 US 90, Marathon, 79842. Call 432-386 4516. Web site: www.marathon texas.com.

Marathon Motel and RV Park, I-90, PO Box 141, Marathon, 79842. Call 1-866-386-4241 or 432-386-4241. Web site: www.marathonmotel.com.

Marfa Book Company, 105 S. Highland Street, Marfa, 79843. Call 432-729-3906. Wed. through Sun. 10–7. Web site: www.marfabookco.com.

Marfa Chamber of Commerce, Hotel Paisano, 207 N. Highland Avenue, Marfa, 79843. Call 432-729-4942. Web site: www.marfacc.com. Also, www.marfatx.com.

McDonald Observatory, Fort Davis, 78734. Call 432-426-3640. Web site: www.mcdonaldobservatory.org.

The Miniature Rooster, 1300 W. San Antonio Street, Marfa, 79843. Call 432-729-3030. Tues. through Thurs. 5:30–10, Fri. and Sat. 5:30–11. Web site: www.miniaturerooster.com.

Museum of the Big Bend, TX 90, Alpine, 79830. Call 432-837-8143. Tues. through Sat. 9–5, Sun. 1–5. Free. Web site: www.sulross.edu.

Old Schoolhouse Bed & Breakfast, 401 N. Front Street, Fort Davis, 79734. Call 432-426-2050. Web site: www .schoolhousebnb.com.

Padre's, 209 W. El Paso Street, Marfa, 79843. Call 432-729-4425. Mon. and Tues. 5–10, Wed. through Sat. 11:30–10; Bar open until midnight, 1 AM on Sat. Web site: www.padresmarfa.com.

Pizza Foundation, 100 E. San Antonio Street, Marfa, 79843. Call 432-729-3377. Thurs.–Mon. 11 until the pizza's gone. Web site: www.pizza foundation.com.

Railroad Blues, 504 W. Holland Avenue, Alpine, 79830. 432-837-3103.

Mon. through Sat. 4–2. Web site: www.railroadblues.com.

Reata, 203 N. Fifth Street, Alpine, 79830. Call 432-837-9232. Tues. through Sat. 11:30–2 and 5–10. Web site: www.reata.net.

San Solomon Spring Courts at Balmorhea State Park, TX 17, Toyahvale, 79786. Call 432-375-2370. Web site: www.tpwd.state.tx.us.

Squeeze Marfa, 215 N. Highland Avenue, Marfa, 79843. Call 1-800-655-0327 or 432-729-4500. Tues. through Sat. 10–5. Web site: www.squeeze marfa.com.

Starlight Theatre Restaurant & Bar, Terlingua Ghost Town, 100 Ivey Street, Terlingua, 79852. Call 432-371-2326. Dinner daily 5–10. Web site: www.starlighttheatre.com.

Stay Marfa, Dean and San Antonio Streets, Marfa, 79843. Call 888-627-3246. Web site: www.staymarfa.com.

Stone Village Tourist Camp and Market, 509 N. State Street, Fort Davis, 79734. Call 432-426-3941. Web site: www.stonevillagetouristcamp .com.

Terlingua Trading Company, 100 Ivey Street, Terlingua, 79852. Call 432-371-2234. Daily 10–9. Web site: www.ghosttowntexas.com.

12 Gage, 102 I-90 W., Marathon, 79842. Call 1-800-884-GAGE. Sun. through Thurs. 6–9, Fri. and Sat. 6–10. Web site: www.gagehotel.com.

INDEX